PRAISE FOR *ALL OF A PIECE*

"This grittily realistic and sharply observant account of a life, moving as it does through experience on six continents, is equally attuned to the personal, the political, and the intellectual. It will be a treasure-trove for future historians of the conditions of academic life, moral and otherwise, in the second half of the twentieth century and the first quarter of the twenty-first—and not without value to students of the pontificate of Francis I."

—**AIDAN NICHOLS OP**, author of *The Thought of Pope Benedict XVI* and *The Shape of Catholic Theology*

"In an age of fractured identities and moral disorientation, *All of a Piece* dares to ask whether a life can be—not seamless—but meaningfully whole. Rich in historical witness, philosophical insight, and cultural critique, this remarkable memoir offers a compelling portrait of a lifelong pursuit of truth and integrity. For readers familiar with John Rist's scholarly work, *All of a Piece* reveals the personal journey behind the ideas; for newcomers, it serves as a friendly invitation to reconsider what it means to live a thoughtful, examined, and fully human life."

—**FR. ANTONIO MALO**, professor of Philosophical Anthropology at the Pontifical Università della Santa Croce (Rome)

"An absorbing academic memoir from an acclaimed academic 'totally unsuited,' in the estimation of a venerable mentor, to an academic life. In a series of vivid sketches, Rist recalls a childhood in blitz-battered London, the decidedly mixed blessings of life at a 'minor' British public school, national service duty in Iraq as an electronic snoop, running the gauntlet set by post-war Cambridge classicists, a lightning climb up the rungs of the academic ladder in Toronto, and subsequent academic appointments in Aberdeen, Jerusalem, Rome, and Washington, not to mention an induction as a tribal chieftain in Nigeria and dozens of other such adventures around the globe. *All of a Piece* is animated throughout by the author's disdain for humbug, his fierce independence of mind, an unflagging interest in the truth, a keen appreciation for the many memorable souls he has encountered over the years, and wonderment at the strange or rather providential interplay of disparate factors that have shaped his years on earth. It is also by turns funny, intriguing, insightful, and—should you be paying close attention—even occasionally tender-hearted."

—**JOHN C. MCCARTHY**, associate professor and dean emeritus at Catholic University of America, Department of Philosophy

"This fascinating book is a free-wheeling journey from a humble background, through a Cambridge scholarship, to a major academic career in Classics, both at home and abroad, notably Canada, the U.S., and Rome. The author exemplifies those who have fought unceasingly against the present malaise in academe, which he identifies as 'an ideological denial of truth.' His own development can be traced primarily through two classical figures, Plato and Plotinus, and their witness to the solidity of moral judgment. This led him on from a non-religious humanism to the transcendent in its personal form, and thereby to the Catholic Church. From this perspective he has taken on many unpopular subjects in the secular and religious worlds. The book gives witness to years of research into the ancient and modern; and also contains much humor, including something rare in memoirs—the use of limericks to emphasize certain important points! This is a book to be very highly recommended."

—**JOHN BEAUMONT**, author of *The House With a Hundred Gates: Catholic Converts Through the Ages*

ALL OF A PIECE

All of a Piece

THE AUTOBIOGRAPHY OF AN ESSEX MAN AND WANDERING PHILOSOPHER

JOHN M. RIST
assisted by Anna Rist

Angelico Press

First published in the USA
by Angelico Press 2025
Copyright © John M. Rist 2025

All rights reserved:
No part of this book may be reproduced or transmitted,
in any form or by any means, without permission

For information, address:
Angelico Press, Ltd.
169 Monitor St.
Brooklyn, NY 11222
www.angelicopress.com

Ppr 979-8-89280-131-7
Cloth 979-8-89280-132-4

Book and cover design
by Michael Schrauzer

For Anna

"With all due respect, Mrs. Rist."
—A builder employed by us
shortly before he was imprisoned

TABLE OF CONTENTS

INTRODUCTION   xi

1. Schicklgruber and I   1
2. Snobs, Sods, and Skeptical "Humanism" with Sir Anthony Browne   11
3. At the Fag-end of Empire   36
4. The Fenland Don Reserve in the Later Fifties   55
5. The Long Sixties: Academia and Catholicism in a Branch-plant State   99
6. A Scottish Principal Fails to Get a Knighthood   161
7. Augustine and the Enigma of Israel   170
8. Across the Tiber and Along the Potomac   203
9. On Chance and Providence   240

INDEX OF CONTEMPORARIES   263

INTRODUCTION

> If only that pesky John Rist
> would suddenly cease to exist.
> But now's no time to lose heart:
> he'll soon depart.
> —Unwritten antistrophe

> *Quidquid agunt homines, votum, timor, ira, voluptas,*
> *Gaudia, discursus, nostri farrago libelli est.*
> —Juvenal, *Satires* 1, 85–86

> Know yourself.
> —The Oracle at Delphi

This book is intended as autobiography in a philosophical frame, for were it merely autobiography, it might seem of some interest only to my friends and family. Yet that my life has spanned nearly ninety years of more rapid change than in any other period in history might allow it wider significance. Already few can remember all of the following: the Second World War, the defeat of the competing ideologies of Hitler and Stalin (and the arrival of the latter's successor in the yet more murderous tyranny of Chairman Mao), the Sexual Revolution of the 1960s, the near disappearance of Christianity in Western Europe, the collapse of marriage with its resulting millions of single women struggling to bring up their children, the apparent apogee followed by the inevitable fall of the British Empire, the coming of space exploration, as of the Internet and social media with their potential for vile anonymous mischief-making, and the growing threat to freedom of speech in academia, the world of art and culture, and beyond. To have lived through these varied events is to have the ability to bear first-hand witness to features of a world in which pressures on increasingly homogenized Western individuals have driven them into moral, intellectual, and spiritual confusion without historic parallel. Against this background autobiography can serve as a source of social history.

But this autobiography also calls for a philosophical frame, for the extraordinary period of history through which I have lived offers an ideal opportunity for the conducting of a philosophical and psychological thought-experiment whereby to examine in a single case — my own — a psyche evolving amid the endless novelties of the age, and thereby benefitting from an unparalleled opportunity for an increase in self-knowledge coupled with a growing understanding of our information-sodden but increasingly value-free society. Profiting from that opportunity I here present my seemingly random experiences in chronological sequence from conception and on toward what I still trust will be a natural death.

Construction of this chronological frame enables me not only to record my life in an intelligible sequence but to highlight my differing judgments at varying points in time and hence explain the inaccuracy of many of my naïve opinions: a procedure to be recommended to anyone scrutinizing his life. Thus when I write of my time in Iraq as an "airman," in Cambridge as an undergraduate, and as an academic at the Universities of Toronto and Aberdeen, I can show how I then thought and acted with insufficient understanding of the rapidly changing contemporary world to be able to behave entirely rationally or coherently or with much awareness of where I was going. Nor was I always accurate in assessing my beliefs — let alone able to identify them as stages in what would eventually come to look like a well-marked path.

For history (as the great ancient historians Thucydides and Tacitus were well aware) is made up not only of what happens but of the often-erroneous beliefs of contemporaries about what is happening around them, which erroneous beliefs become springs of action and impediments to the continuing formation of reliable character. Autobiography offers the opportunity to recognize in one's own life the effects of gradually correcting one's beliefs over time. Thus, and for example, I was obliged to correct my belief about what would follow upon the demise of Western colonialism, my assumption — and that of many contemporaries — being that "native" peoples were free from what Christians denote "Original Sin." Indeed, having recently returned from lecturing in Cape Town, I can report that under the post-apartheid régime I heard repeatedly that "for any substantial business transaction 'backhanders' are essential" and that to relate effectively with the government "you need at least a master's degree in Corruption."

By being elsewhere, whether in time or space, one is helped to see where one *is*. Hence, when I narrate my family life and various

Introduction xiii

travels, I can recognize how I learned to relate my experiences of people, places, and events to my later more comprehensive grasp of their context, thus allowing a more complete understanding of what I saw and heard and felt—as (again) of the intelligibility of my earlier judgments about my experiences. In looking back on my past, both public and more personal, I realize that my lack of awareness of the wider world, or at least of specific aspects of it, allowed me a but limited understanding of the significance of the changing scene even when I vaguely intuited something of its impact on my character. Thus when I first realized that there was something amiss in current beliefs about the papacy and noted the confusing effect these beliefs had on the individuals who held them, I still could not yet see that what was happening was not simply the result of the idiosyncrasies of a particular pope, but of a distorted mentality with regard to the papacy which had been building up in the Catholic Church for at least two hundred years.

There is also the matter of the unexpected and unpredictable. In his *Decline and Fall of the Roman Empire* Edward Gibbon observed that had the Emperor Theodosius not died falling off his horse, the history of Europe (and by extension of the world) would have been radically different. On March 13, 1943, Fabian von Schlabrendorff put a bomb concealed among a few bottles of whisky on a plane carrying Hitler from Smolensk back to his headquarters in Rastenburg. The plane landed without incident and Schlabrendorff immediately took another plane following the same route, retrieved and dismantled the bomb and complained to his confederates Hans Oster and Hans von Dohnányi about the inadequacy of their detonator. Had things turned out otherwise (as there was every reason for the conspirators to hope), the destiny of Europe might have turned out very differently—and perhaps even my own. I have come to wonder whether such "chance" events might prove a hidden source of the ongoing formation of my own character. If so, does "formation" imply a "Former"?

The unpredictability of both natural events and human behavior compels us to recognize a something more than the effects of "free" will and its often unexpected consequences. It compels us to recognize the impossibility of constructing a strictly logical version of our individual or collective human story. "Stuff happens": stuff like death and disease. Machiavelli noted that

Cesare Borgia was ruined because he foresaw everything except his serious illness at the time of his papal father's death. Erratic behavior (due perhaps to alcohol, greed, fear, or lust) may derail any interpretation of our own past or the past of others if based on an assumption that men always behave rationally. Counterfactual historical speculation, though otherwise absurd, serves to remind us of erratic (or at least unpredictable) events in the cosmos, as of those individual circumstances which may, even without being observed, influence our decision-making. Some of my most significant decisions could so easily have been otherwise, their consequences being unforeseeable at decision time, recognizable only in hindsight.

Thus this book should be seen as an examination of the truth in an individual case—my own—of John Henry Newman's remark that "Ten years later I found myself in another place; the whole man moves; paper logic is but the record of it." But who is this mysterious "I" and what is its relationship to the variable circumstances in which the individual lives? David Hume thought that we are serial selves, our character—our loves and hates—varying radically enough over time to suggest that we are different people from those we once were: a convenient theory for those wishing to evade responsibility. If I am not the same person as I was when I fathered my children, I have no responsibility to provide for them: thus Rousseau, at one point Hume's friend, seems to have thought, whereas the now demonstrated persistence of our unique DNA from conception to death (and beyond) will encourage us to reject such a theory and seek to explain the seeming discontinuity of our self otherwise. If I find myself, in Newman's phrase, "ten years later in another place," it is the same "I" who does the finding; otherwise no "finding" would be possible. And Freud was surely right that even those experiences of my early childhood—and perhaps even prior to that—which I cannot recall affect what is *my* future and continuing "self."

In the course of my narrative I shall try to account for the various lives that I seem to have lived by assuming that they are all to be subsumed under one—individual and by hindsight explicable—life and that my earliest memories (even if not accurately recalled) are indeed *my* memories. And if there is this single life transcending all my "local" experiences of it, I must recognize the possibility that my life might be moving as a whole in some direction perhaps recognizable by hindsight and perhaps to be viewed in terms of following (or refusing to follow) a guide — in which case the effects of apparently simple, even casual, decisions may reveal something of the character of that guide.

The attentive reader of this autobiography will notice that I have recorded how my growing awareness of the complexity of the world in which I have lived often shows up as a sense of being outside the authoritatively-structured conventions surrounding me. I do not think this was a mere rejection of authority, but rather a sense that all authorities, whether of Church or State, risk becoming an authoritarian sum of old tribal conventions or of psychological pressures to conform in new and perhaps less honest ways.

Over the years this sense of the inadequacy of things has led me at times to feel alienated, first from my family background and, as I matured, from the passing Nazi, fascist, Marxist or so-called liberal democratic ideologies (or their spin-offs), and thus to seem persistently counter-cultural, and certainly unwilling to kowtow to those wielders of mere power whose motto is "Live in fear; you're easier to control" (a variant on Caligula's "Let them hate so long as they fear": *oderint dum metuant*). To be counter-cultural is not necessarily to be anarchic or libertarian, but to recognize that many powerful cultures demand a mindless servility to official "goods," whether these take the form of "My country right or wrong" or that truth is only perspectival, or that popes must always be heeded. In light of all such mindlessness — and recognizing it as easily transforming society into a fear-driven tribalism — to accept the dictum of Socrates that "the unexamined life is subhuman" will subject even the mildly honest person to condemnation if he resists the conventional — even brutal — practices of the day (or the day before). In our own day abortion is a conspicuous example of brutal practice.

The recognized need for constant self-correction in my thinking about individuals, individual places, and individual situations can be summed up as my growing realization that throughout my life I was coming across, and often ignoring, "Catholic" phenomena, thus failing to realize that not only do they hang together but that they point to truths both positive and negative. For I came to believe not only that Catholicism was a path to which much of my previous experience pointed but also that it enabled some kind of understanding of why I had the "right" to dislike what I disliked: tyrannical governments, lying politicians, and brutal practices such as torture and abortion. It gave me permission, as well, to deplore the unwillingness both of myself and those around me to recognize what is blindingly obvious if viewed in a wider context: that is, that Catholicism not only represented a coherent account of what I found inspiring and intelligibly desirable but also an account of what I found intellectually repellent though curiously attractive: a *nostalgie de la boue* pointing to a nihilism which can ultimately only be incomprehensible. Far from appearing in triumphalist terms, such a realization rather invited further location of what I had come to recognize as the right path. Not that I thought I had reached the end of the road but rather that I had been granted an intuition as to where—and how—the road had brought me thus far. A lengthening life, as I shall try to explain, would confirm that intuition.

Socrates himself—not to speak of Jesus—ran into trouble for being a "gadfly" in ancient Athens. Yet he struck a correct balance between an acceptance of the demands (including the patriotic demands) of the state, or of any other legitimate authority (to include the "gods")—and rejecting the pressures of an amoral radicalism or servile conventionalism, thus retaining and displaying his integrity. In following the Aristotelian mean (which is really a high point) between extremes, he has always seemed to me a worthy model.

Parts of the following narrative concern my "love affair"—now sadly all but concluded—with Italy and with rural Tuscany in particular. Details of this can be found in Anna Rist's *We Etruscans*;[1] the tale provides further evidence of how, when one starts an "affair," one knows neither its context nor its outcome. My first impressions of Tuscany were of its soon-to-be-threatened old-fashioned charm; my later impressions were overshadowed by my recognition that hiding under the quaint exterior were examples of what Italians call *disgrazia*: as that the Resistance in Italy was all too largely a myth whereby politicians and opinion-formers would present themselves as heroes in a past often more murderous than appealing, a myth which—as Giampaolo Pansa

---

[1] Anna Rist, *We Etruscans: Old and New in a Forgotten Landscape* (Cambridge: Lutterworth Press, 2006). This book can be obtained directly from Anna or from me.

in particular has explored in several books—has corrupted Italian politics and Italian society even down to the present day.

In my final chapter I draw whatever conclusions present themselves about my continuity in diversity as well as about my awareness that—like everyone else bar One—I still fail to be an entirely coherent and continuous "I": this because of our seemingly inevitable attempts to avoid embarrassment and maintain a *bella figura* by compartmentalizing our beliefs and experiences. Such compartmentalization, I shall assume, is one of the outcomes of "Original Sin": otherwise as owed to a "surd factor" in human nature.

Details of the reaction in what I call "branch-plant Canada" to Catholic abortion-pushers and complicit clergy can be read in *Catholics against the Church* (University of Toronto Press):[2] a work I was later asked to review by the *New Oxford Review*—which then refused to publish said critique because I was unwilling to remove my observation that "It was fascinating to watch Cardinal Carter struggling to be honest." Well, at least he was struggling, though at the time of writing I was hardly aware of the adulation of a significantly corrupt clergy which underlay the magazine's response; only later would I observe the need here, too, to understand and so to evaluate and assimilate the wider truth accurately into oneself rather than encourage that self further to disintegrate into separate compartments.

Small portions of my wider narrative may be found in an earlier—though occasionally inaccurate—version titled "Where Else?" in *Philosophers who Believe*,[3] as also and more circumspectly in "On the Trail of *Animal Academicum* (1956–2013)" in *Passionate Mind: Essays in Honor of John M. Rist*.[4] The inaccuracies may derive from that same inability I have more generally highlighted to set immediate experiences into their wider cultural contexts. On details of what happened in the distant past, where I have been unable to corroborate what I relate, I have tried to indicate where lapses of memory cannot be ruled out, though I have always

---

[2] Michael W. Cuneo, *Catholics Against the Church: Anti-Abortion Protest in Toronto, 1969–1985* (Toronto: University of Toronto Press, 1989).
[3] Kelly James Clark, ed., *Philosophers Who Believe: The Spiritual Journeys of 11 Leading Thinkers* (Downers Grove, IL: Intervarsity Press, 1994), 83–103.
[4] Barry David, ed., *Passionate Mind: Essays in Honor of John M. Rist* (Baden Baden: Academia Verlag, 2019), 71–89.

attempted to verify my memories by the memories of others.

Sometimes contemporary jokes and populist rhymes convey the reality of a life as it is lived better than facts and mere statistics, so I have sprinkled a few of these on the mix; some that are bawdy I have included not in the hope of attracting sales, but rather to enable me to tell it as it was, or at least as it seemed to be. I had originally titled my first chapter "Adolf and I" but changed it in deference to Anna who remembered that when she had asked her Jewish father what his father's name was, he had replied, "It was Adolf—but don't tell anyone!" Despite the epigraph at the head of this Introduction, I must conclude it by thanking all those, and especially Anna—prime cause of this memoir, improver of its style and contents and to whom it is dedicated—who, often to my surprise, have been prepared to put up with me.

CHAPTER I

Schicklgruber and I

(1936) REICHSMARSCHALL HERMANN GOERING:
I apologize for my lateness, Ambassador, I have been out shooting.

BRITISH AMBASSADOR HENDERSON: Animals, I hope.

> Kindly pardon my correction.
> This stuff is there for your protection.
> —Warning during the blitz not to
> interfere with shatter precautions
> on the London Underground

> The Germans were above God. Unlike the Italians and our own mob, they could use any means to get the job done. Without wincing! With no fear! No passion!... You had to see them with your own eyes... They were magnificent.
> —A Greek recruited by the pan-European SS[1]

I was born on July 6, 1936 (about the time of Goering's shooting expedition above), so the specter of Schicklgruber haunted my early childhood: Schicklgruber being the name, uttered with a quiet mixture of contempt and foreboding, by which my father correctly named "Hitler," the upstart Austrian corporal and failed painter who by then was hailed by his largely gratified *Volk* as Führer of the Thousand-Year Reich. Not that to me the Nazi dictator and his thugs always seemed frightening, but rather an inevitable part of the scenery—though at some point, when my teddy-bear had been packed off to relations in South Africa (I being judged too old for it), I got the idea that it had been arrested by the Gestapo. My parents and relatives saw things differently, so when war broke out in 1939 my mother (so I heard later) formed the idea that I too

---

[1] Yanis Varoufakis, *And the Weak Suffer What They Must?* (London: The Bodley Head, 2016), 203.

should be sent for safety to that country, where she had been born and where two of her brothers were still living. It seems that my father vetoed that, and instead I was dispatched to a fashionable kindergarten in Cirencester. There the much-lauded female commandant had my mouth taped up on the charge that I had bitten one of my fellow inmates. Evidently my objections to the place were effective as I was released shortly afterward and allowed to rely on a Morrison-shelter bed at home for my safety.

I used to think that my earliest recollections were of watching the Battle of Britain being fought overhead each evening, but dredging my memory I dimly recall not only my earlier "adventures" at the kindergarten in Cirencester but also the deep anxiety apparent at Dad's mother Josephine's house in Brentwood—then a quiet Protestant town far from the swinging vulgarity it was later to achieve in the days of the reality show *TOWIE* (*The Only Way Is Essex*)—when the news of Dunkirk came over the airwaves. Fear of invasion was palpable, though as yet I had little idea of what that might mean, and it morphed into a deep parental hostility and contempt for the French who, most people strongly believed, had typically sold "our boys" down the river: the hostility compounded at home by the fact that there were family connections with Leigh-on-Sea, where fishing boats were plying the Channel to help rescue the stranded Brits. One such, owned by a member of the Osborne clan, made a dozen such rescues and on the thirteenth was sunk by a Stuka.

On both sides of the family, at least during the war, all were very patriotic, and Dad's brother George fought in the Eighth Army as a sapper in North Africa and Italy until, at Monte Cassino, he lost an eye—and as a result also his fiancée. One of "Brentwood Nan" Josephine's sisters had been a nurse in the First World War and her politics were decidedly of the Right, as were all the rest of the Rist clan, with the exception of her sister Eva who was a Stalinist and in later years would be recalled by the shop-steward in *I'm All Right Jack* who evokes the Soviet Union as "All them cornfields and ballet in the evenings." Eva and her sister Rose, not to speak of my grandmother Josephine, had one thing in common, apart from their patriotism: on Boxing Days when we would gather in Brentwood, they would brighten up what were for me these boring occasions by complaining about the dispositions of some family-member's will.

My post-Dunkirk memories are much clearer, especially of the evening scanning of the sky. Romford, of which our Gidea Park was the posher bit, was not an immediate German target, but both the nearby Dagenham car plant and the railway linking London and Harwich—constantly used by troop trains—were. By morning the battle had usually passed and we boys were able to wander about and pick up bits of shrapnel. Our street never took a direct hit, as the next one did several times, though once on returning from a visit to my mother's mother—Littlebury Nan—we were unable to get home since the road was cordoned off, there being an unexploded landmine that had to be defused in the garden opposite ours.

Normally, however, we could hope that we would not be hit, and I would fall asleep in the stout Morrison Shelter—so named for the Home Secretary—which on top provided a dining room table and underneath a sleeping place for me. My safety was judged, it seems, a higher priority than that of my parents whose last act at night would be to fill the bath with water in case of attack by incendiaries. The "Anderson" shelter in the garden was never used, and in common with other such would half-fill with water each time it rained. As for the house, it survived, though ceilings were partly brought down on three occasions—providing an opportunity for "spivs" to make botched repairs paid for by the Council at exorbitant cost.

I spent most of the war years in Romford, with a few extended periods at the primitive but welcoming house of Littlebury Nan (and Granddad) who had built it, assisted by their children who included my mother. It was located in a still very rural part of Essex where many of the inhabitants had not journeyed more than three or four miles from the village unless, like Granddad's friend Charlie Ryder (not to speak of Granddad himself), they had served in the First World War or in some other military operation. After which Charlie seemed content to spend the remaining years of his life scything the grass on the sides of the village roads.

Littlebury was two and a half miles from the nearest railway station at Audley End, a distance I traversed on foot after I had reached the age of seven or so—on one occasion, as it turned out, while suffering from pleurisy. There was no water or electricity in the house. There was an outside privy into which children had to be warned not to fall. There was also Paddy, a large Airedale which let me ride on his back.

Granddad was a veteran soldier and mercenary in wars in Africa and elsewhere: present at the siege of Mafeking and the disaster at Spion Kop, later surviving a gas attack near Ypres. Now long retired to his extensive garden and orchard, he liked in the evenings under paraffin lighting to play me at draughts — I never won — and would at times chant bits of a song sung to the tune of "Onward Christian Soldiers," which I only came to recognize many years later after reading Niall Ferguson's *Empire*:[2]

> Onward chartered soldiers, into heathen lands
> Prayer books in your pockets, rifles in your hands.
> Spread the joyful tidings, where trade can be done.
> Spread the peaceful gospel, with the Maxim gun.
>
> Tell the wretched natives, wicked are their hearts;
> Turn their heathen temples, into spirit marts,
> And if to your preaching, they will not succumb,
> Give them another sermon, with the Maxim gun.
>
> When the Ten Commandments, they quite understand,
> Then their chiefs you hocus, and annex their land,
> And if they, misguided, call you to account,
> Give them another sermon, with a Maxim from the Mount.

Nan, daughter of the Fighting Cocks pub, near Audley End Station, where as a girl she had been a barmaid, while also earning a little more as a servant at Audley End Mansion, was five feet, two inches tall, quite fearless, and astonishingly able to control all kinds of animals (and she could skin a rabbit in seconds). She was generally tough, as she needed to be when travelling on a troopship to South Africa, where my mother was born. Jehovah Witnesses brought out her particular contempt, since they refused to do any kind of war-related work; if they ever appeared at her door, they were warned to get off the property in thirty seconds or she would set the dog on them. The dog, I should add, regularly bit postmen.

Nan and her — by now — rotund husband Robert might be seen of an evening sharing gin out of a bottle outside their front door

---

[2] Niall Ferguson, *Empire: How Britain Made the Modern World* (London: Penguin Books, Ltd., 2018).

or frequenting their favorite public bar in the village. Nan never thought of limiting herself to the Saloon Bar, then designated for "Women and Escorts." Though nominal Anglicans, they had never to my knowledge been seen in a Church and regarded Vicars as posh, like local "squires," though with less excuse. Granddad's religion seemed limited to insisting that at death he would require a headstone lest his spirit walk. Needless to say, they too were patriotic, so voted conservative and in that spirit retained respect for Lady Braybrooke, last survivor of the ancient family once owners of the Mansion at Audley End. Lady Braybrooke's only son had been killed in the First World War; his memorial was in the village churchyard, as was his family vault.

From time to time in Littlebury I went to the one-room village school where I learned nothing except undercurrents of wartime rural life. At the bottom of "our" road was an old-fashioned family farm, and on the other side of the village a second farm now belonged to an incomer; he and the situation he generated would later seem to reflect the arrival of Mr Farfrae in Hardy's *The Mayor of Casterbridge*, for our new farmer too was a Scot, Mr McLaren, and his farm sported all the latest mechanical equipment, especially the combine-harvester which would soon put the old reapers-and-binders out of business. Some of McLaren's work was done by Italian prisoners of war who seemed happy to be far from the front-line, and at school I would be asked by boys who suspected I might be an "evacuee" whether I would like to work for him myself, and if I hesitated, I would be told, in unfamiliar but informative terminology, that if I did I would have to "lick his arse." But in general I had little trouble with the locals. Once I reported to Granddad that in a fight a boy had pulled a knife on me, slightly cutting my hand—whereupon he proceeded to accompany me to the home of the offender and when the father opened the door, he was told that if it happened again he would kill him. It didn't happen again, though I was to have trouble with knife-wielders on three later occasions.

Wandering around Littlebury with my mother—Dad could rarely get away from his work in London—with its fields and woods and gleaning and avenues of chestnut trees, was an occasional idyll, even if Mum's over-concern about my drinking enough water was a regular irritation: "Have some more water" she would say. "Lions drink it, John." To which (when I had acquired the relevant vocabulary) I would mutter to myself, "I'm not a bloody lion." Still, it really was idyllic, though our talks to a paratrooper, one Captain Webb, then billeted with my grandparents, kept us in touch with the brutal and ever-changing military scene.

Romford was much more aware of the war, as was I when I was there. In addition to trying to spoon out the Russian frontline in my porridge, I managed to get hold of a map of Russia and would mark out on a regular basis the various maneuvers of von Bock and Guderian, Zhukov and Rokossovsky. I listened joyfully one morning to the news of El Alamein and on another occasion a little later when my father came down to get ready for work and turned on the radio there came the voice of the announcer informing all and sundry that Von Paulus's Sixth Army had surrendered at Stalingrad: "Ah," exclaimed my father, "we have won the war!" If that were true, as I assumed it to be, I wondered whether there would be any newspapers when there was nothing left to report.

Entertainment, religion, and the local Gidea Park College — in reality a more up-market primary school which I began to attend when I was about seven — were the other significant parts of my life in those gradually more peaceful days as, despite V1s and V2s, the war drew to a close. Entertainment, however, might be problematic: Tommy Handley and ITMA ("It's That Man [scil. Hitler] Again"), were seen as part of the war effort, but when I developed a taste for the often vulgar "Workers' Playtime," it was made clear that vulgarity was not our "bag." Since, however, it certainly was the "bag" of my friend Clive's family down the road, I found objections to it odd and irritating. Of course, Clive was himself rather unacceptable, and even more his elder sister who worked for the Entertainments National Service Association (ENSA) entertaining the troops: that is, according to more exacting tribal Christians like my father, "just finding an excuse to show off all she's got." The anti-vulgarity campaign was to reach its zenith some years later when I listened to an unusually (for that time) vulgar closing radio line by Max Miller (the "cheeky chappie"):

> When roses are red and ready for plucking,
> Young girls of sixteen are ready for... Goodnight, ladies
> and gentlemen.

Had this not caused a commotion, my father designating the comedian a "filthy tripe-hound," I would hardly have noticed it.

Nor was the cinema judged much better. I was not allowed to go to the Romford "fleapit" which on Saturday mornings in the school holidays offered low-grade Westerns in which (of course) the cowboys were the good guys and "the only good Indian is a dead Indian." By what my parents came to think of as a mistake, however, I was taken before the end of the war to see *The Road to Morocco* (Bing Crosby, Bob Hope, and Dorothy Lamour) which in my parents' opinion had too much sex (i.e., kissing) in it and should not have passed the eye of the censor, being unfit for minors. And there was a rumor that Hope was a Roman Catholic, which presumably made things worse, if perhaps explicable. (He did in fact join the Church, but not until 1996.)

Which brings us to religion. At my mother's parents' home, as I have said, it was non-existent: except that Granddad said that when younger he would join those villagers who guarded the churchyard against others who hoped to steal the bodies of the recently dead to sell to Addenbrookes' hospital in Cambridge; the first time I had heard of the university located there. But my own parents were quite different—not least in their fear of alcohol which was permitted minimally and only at Christmas—as at this time they both attended the Church of England's liturgies and would drag me, unwilling as I soon became, along with them.

Apart from the sheer boredom of such occasions and what I was already beginning to recognize as the sentimentality of many of the hymns, my particular *bête noire* was the presiding Reverend Elvin. Dad was no fan of his either, claiming that he indulged in dodgy dealings on the Stock Market. Mind you, Dad's view of what was "dodgy" was probably unusual; when he died one of his business associates told me that "your father could have been a millionaire if he had been willing to make use of the information he sometimes acquired" (as, I can suppose, the Reverend Elvin had tried to do).

My father's objections to Elvin were not limited to matters of finance; he seemed to dislike almost as much as I did the clergyman's obsession with the iniquities of young children who needed to be licked into shape: presumably a heritage of the Calvinist wing of the Church of England. In fact, my father had only joined (or rather "moved into") that Church when he married, being one of the last of a long line of Congregationalists: successors, that is, of the Cromwellian Independents, some of whom were happy to tolerate all varieties of Christianity apart from the Catholic. Not that Dad (who never mentioned his own father in my hearing) knew much about his ancestors—except that some were buried in East Bergholt—nor did his religion include much theology. I was never clear exactly what were the grounds for his apparent respect for Jesus, since his Christianity was entirely of the moral sort: decent people did not steal, murder, rape, or disparage the virtues of the British Empire and its "White Man's burden." Nor did they drink alcohol, except on the rare occasion.

Mum's religion, or eventually non-religion, was different: always a member of the Church of England even when apparently disbelieving its widely variable doctrines, she disliked the term "Anglican" as pointing to Rome and would not worship (if that's the right word) in a church where the vicar called himself a priest or where there was any trace of "smells and bells." After leaving home and dreaming of becoming a Labour-loving sophisticate in her twenties, (though English country-dancing was her nearest approach to the Marxism she came across at trendy places like Thaxted where the parson flew a red flag from the church tower), she settled for the Established Church—from which she always wanted to escape without knowing where else to go.

At some stage I was persuaded to accompany her of a Sunday evening to various conventicles where the worship was even more tedious than at the Reverend Elvin's Saint Michael's (and often enacted in studiously ugly buildings), but none of these godly performances interested her any more than they did me. The best that could be said of some of them, as she would note, was their offering the communion wine in separate glasses, that being more hygienic. So since Mum certainly objected to the sexual libertinism which normally accompanied the socialism of her day, she had to stay with the Church of England, which was at least respectable. I believe she once risked hearing a Catholic Mass, though I was not invited on that occasion to accompany her. Nor do I think she indulged in any further experience of such "hocus-pocus."

At that stage the only Catholic I had met was our Romford neighbor, Mrs. O'Brien, who—apart from being Irish which hardly commended her to my parents, being hardly if at all better than French or even German—unjustly accused Clive and myself of breaking her manhole cover in the alleyway between our house and hers. (Clive told me later that he "mooned" her as payment for this injustice—not that the word "mooning" was yet widely current.) In any case Mrs. O'Brien was soon to give up her superstitions after being publicly reprimanded by her parish priest for not covering her head at Mass.

Gidea Park College was certainly not religious either, though it may have claimed to be Church of England. Nor, even if it had the capacity (which I doubt), did it manage to teach us very much, since we spent large portions of each day in underground shelters while the rockets passed overhead—and occasionally the odd German bomber, inspiring a new version of "Ten Green Bottles": "Ten German bombers flying through the air...." And we might do even better. American soldiers were now very visible ("over-fed, over-sexed, over 'ere") and we could belt out "Colonel Bogey," beloved of Allied troops on the march, in all its full-blown "military" vulgarity—despite parental opinion that we were imbibing too much vulgarity already.

> Hitler, has only got one ball;
> Goering, has two but very small;
> Himmler, has something similar,
> but poor old Goebbels has no balls at all.

All of course sung in a delightfully "German" accent.

Back at Littlebury the cheering villagers would assemble in the main street to look up at a sky darkened in the daytime by American Flying Fortresses and Liberators setting off from the local airfields for their "Thousand-bomber" raids. At night British planes took over. It was too dark to give them the same enthusiastic send-off expressing our hatred of the Boche whom we hoped they would now blast off the face of the earth.

As the war drew to a close, bananas arrived for the first time in years, provoking riots by those anxious to get hold of more than the assigned one or two. Also peaches needed to be protected in London by notices reading "Don't squeeze me till I'm yours" and an extra ration of sweets was no longer to be secured only "under the counter." Schicklgruber and his cronies might soon be forgotten—though I would come to realize that should not happen, at least among students of human behavior. For by then I had recognized among the Canadian undergraduates I was teaching a difference between those who remembered or learned from their parents something of the Second World War and those who did not: the latter being more likely to indulge "progressive" fantasies, perhaps flavored with the excitement of a left-liberal violence to be directed at "fascists."

CHAPTER 2

Snobs, Sods, and Skeptical "Humanism" with Sir Anthony Browne

> Pay no heed to the alien preacher
> and his Church without reason or faith,
> for the foundation stone of his temple
> is the bollocks of Henry the Eighth.
> —Children's song in early
> twentieth-century rural Ireland

> My wife wanted a more aristocratic name for our son, something with "horse" in it.
> —Strepsiades in Aristophanes' *Clouds*

Sir Anthony Browne, a sincere and courageous Roman Catholic courtier with a somewhat buccaneering past, founded Brentwood School in 1557 while a member of Queen Mary's Privy Council (and soon to be created by her Viscount Montagu)—apparently as an act of reparation for his role as Justice of the Peace in the death of William Hunter, a seventeen year old boy burnt at the stake for handing out Protestant bibles. Hunter's memorial "tree" still stood outside the school when I arrived at its preparatory section in 1944. But that was not quite the story I then learned. Whether unintended falsehood or deliberate lie, the story then was that Browne, a bitter foe of the sadistic papists, had founded the school to honor Hunter, his heroic co-religionist. At the time I was neither informed enough nor smart enough to realize that such overtly Protestant behavior was highly implausible in 1557 with Catholic Mary still on the throne. Indeed even when in 1993 I wrote an essay for *Philosophers who Believe* and touched on Sir Anthony Browne's School, I still followed the main lines of the "Protestant" distortion of the story.

The implications of the mythical version were developed in various ways during the next ten years in which I studied at

Browne's aspiring institution. Thus on a table at the end of the school library, which doubled as the form room for the Classical Sixth of which I was eventually to become a member, lay Foxe's *Book of Martyrs*, open at an exciting scene of tortures inflicted by papists. Next to it was fixed a bust of Milton, that seventeenth-century crazed genius of Protestant millenarianism and revenge, whether human or divine. But I never thought of asking why he had been selected to accompany Foxe.

When I started my two-year stint in the Prep School in 1944, Jimmy Hough was still Headmaster. It is said that in his younger days he had been efficient and effective, and presumably my parents knew that, since my uncle George and my cousin Ted had both been at the school (if to very little academic effect in those balmy days), but by my time Hough had clearly lost his grip on an institution which I later would have compared with Macaulay's "unreformed Eton": "anarchy tempered by despotism." His successor, C. Ralph (pronounced "Rafe") Allison, was very different. He pronounced "Romford" differently too, as "Rumford"—as did the Reverend Elvin. He was not popular with the boys and knew few of their names. The older ones preferred Hazel, his glamorous Secretary, whose summer dresses were always so loose that there seemed a good chance of being able to look down them!

I remember little of my Prep School days—except that on April 30, 1945, Schicklgruber shot himself. The news spread fast and by the time I was ready to catch the train to school—located five or six miles from Gidea Park—I was happily aware of it. At almost the same time I had heard my father's roar of disgust at the further news that the Irish President, Eamon De Valera, had sent his country's condolences to the provisional German Government of Admiral Doenitz—hardly improving Dad's opinion of the Irish. For my part, I decided that action, however symbolic, was called for, so I would to go to school without the black tie which was part of the regular uniform. If I thought this would be a popular way of celebrating the Führer's demise, when I reached the school gate I was immediately disabused:

MASTER: Where's your tie, boy?

ME: Sorry, Sir, I didn't want to appear to be lamenting the death of Hitler.

MASTER (after brief hesitation): Detention!

It was well worth it, and I could dine out on the denouement in later years.

In 1946 I entered the Upper School, passed the eleven-plus (though suffering at the time, as transpired, from both mumps and chicken pox) and thus enabled my father to pay no further fees to what was by then a "Direct Grant School." I could continue my education at government expense: a lucky break for both father and son. Had matters been otherwise, I might have been condemned, like Clive, to the brutal rigors and academic mediocrity of the local Secondary Modern. With Hitler gone and austerity continuing—indeed in some ways becoming worse—my secondary education unfolded against a backdrop of Churchill's departure from Downing Street and the new Labour Government of Clement Attlee pledging to put an end to one of the regular sights of those years: poor men tramping the streets with few teeth, poor sight, and little likelihood of medical support.

But the deposition of Churchill still seemed strange to me, while to my father and his immediate family—Grandmother Josephine and her children George and Gwen—it was horrific. Churchill, I had assumed, was almost a god. Nor did the reputation of "Monty" (Field Marshal Bernard Montgomery)—still a hero in the opinion of much of the public—survive untarnished in the view of those who knew of his arrogant and self-serving behavior after D-Day. It was all rather puzzling, but that, it seemed, was how things were. The newspapers were going as strong as ever, with such changes worth reporting.

And some of what they reported was horrific. I was at Nan's at Littlebury with both my parents when I noticed them all poring over a newspaper—it was either the News Chronicle or the News of the World—where they had found pictures of Allied troops entering the concentration camp at Bergen-Belsen, with accompanying narrative derived from the BBC reporting of Richard Dimbleby, embedded in the Allied troops entering the camp. I saw only the pictures but heard the outraged and furious comments the text provoked, touching on such articles as lampshades made of human skin. It would be something which I (and many others) could never get out of our minds, nor indeed in a way did we want to. Decades later I read the comment of Martha Gellhorn, similarly embedded on a comparable occasion: "What we saw is unintelligible to the liberal imagination; only a long-abandoned theory of human mass depravity could begin to explain it."

Although what happened in the camps was known to high government officials during the war — indeed in the case of Dachau before the war, since the camp outside Munich was already a tourist attraction for Nazi visitors come to bait the political prisoners over the barbed wire perimeter — the general public were largely in ignorance of the appalling specifics of, in particular, Belsen. Of course, some of the soldiers had learned much more in the course of war duty, or at least had a rough idea: I would be told forty years later by a former Catholic chaplain with the Canadian Armed Forces that "The troops I was with shot all SS prisoners out of hand." He (and I) could, if regretfully, see the point. Sometime in 1945 General Eisenhower addressed a group of soldiers who had just liberated a "camp": "You may not know what you are fighting for, but you know now what you are fighting against."

In fact, back in 1945, at ten years of age, I was being unwittingly introduced to the Christian theory of Original Sin and I suppose that theory may also have had some remote connection, in its Calvinist manifestation, to the Reverend Elvin's discourses on the iniquity of children. Be that as it may, specifically German iniquities might take strange forms in youthful minds. At a time when children, with reason, feared the visit to the school dentist, our particular dentist — female and of Central European extraction — became the subject of an "urban myth" alleging that she had been trained in Dachau. If so, the training was poor; twenty years later a prominent Canadian dentist, viewing some of her work, was to roar "What clown did that?"

Urban myths apart, the reality of Nazi rule, backed as it was by the votes of thirteen million electors, has left me permanently unable entirely to separate the words "German" and "Nazi," and has forced me to think hard about why what seemed to many the most civilized and learned nation on earth should so easily have reverted to a worse-than-pagan barbarism. I still believe that a study of Nazism and Nazi history should be a prerequisite for anyone starting to think about human psychology and moral philosophy.

Yet it was Dachau, not Auschwitz, that provided the supposed formation for our school dentist. In the early days after the war we hardly recognized the difference between the "ordinary" concentration camps, famed only for murder and sadism, and the exterminating versions developed to their full diabolical size — primarily to eliminate European Jewry — after Reinhard Heydrich's Wannsee Conference in 1942; perhaps this ignorance was at least in part because most of these latter were liberated by the Red Army rather than by the British and Americans. Thus we knew about the sadism before we tried to comprehend the industrialized genocide, and we remained largely unaware of Hitler's further "eugenic" intention to exterminate, beside the Jews, the disabled, those with mental illnesses, gypsies, and homosexuals.

About the last, however, we got to learn more in my early days in the Upper School — or at least about such activity as might morph into a homosexual "orientation." Though buggery remained largely unknown, at least to me, and was apparently to be associated only with "queer" aristocrats like Lord Montagu of Beaulieu or with sailors — we had heard of Churchill's remark about the traditions of the British Navy being "Rum, sodomy, and the lash" — the onset of puberty generated a sexual curiosity about other males which was encouraged by some of the masters: thus a scout master was happy to urge his campers to smear black boot polish on the testicles of anyone who had infringed the Baden Powell code. That was not the only reason I disliked the Scouts — more up-market though they were than the determinedly Protestant Boys Brigade patronized by my father's family — and I endured them for only a single day.

The most immediate effect of the onset of puberty was recognition that the penis was no mere waterpipe but the source of pleasurable sensations. This had nothing to do with girls, perhaps not least because many of the boys were from one-child families, as was I. That could be due in part to opportunities to develop a more sexually varied family background being impeded by the war effort. Even less did interest in the pleasures to be obtained, whether autoerotically or homoerotically, arise from our new awareness that phallic action is required if the human race is to continue. Normally the boys learned the "facts of life" not from their parents (which might have sounded a moral note) but from their peer group, so the new gratifications available incurred no moral unease, though morality could seem more relevant when masters were involved: a fact which discouraged my interest in experimentation. It was widely assumed, however, that the more intelligent boys would be sexually backward and inhibited and — especially if they were late to develop their pubic hair — anxious not to be seen naked, an anxiety which I could not understand, and which encouraged a desire by the more sexually fascinated to humiliate them by stripping them without consent.

What mattered to many of the sexually advanced was that by showing off the size of their "cock" ("Tony Harrison has got a ten-incher") and their ability to reach orgasm, they would be respected by their less developed companions. Dayboys like me had less opportunity to indulge in such displays than those in the boarding houses, some of which were run by masters who tolerated and at times participated in homosexual entertainments. Sundays — when you could lie in — could be the occasion for younger boys to be "tossed off" by their older fellows in the dormitory.

Such behaviors, at least among the boys, seem to have attracted the notice of the three odd characters who, as ministers of the Church of England, were responsible for our religious instruction and spiritual development (except that of a few Catholics and Jews who, as recognized oddities — since surely all decent people would be members of the Church Established — could opt out of formalized Anglican practices such as being prepared for confirmation). In those tedious hours of instruction, the rest of us were encouraged to believe that the only sin that might come our way was masturbation. God got little mention and Jesus appeared to be a nice bloke provided you stayed on the right side of Him.

Such unbalanced introduction to adult Christianity will become more intelligible if we turn to the wider behaviors and reputation of the school clergy. Of one of them, an apparent nonentity, I remember nothing. Another, a victim of shellshock at Alamein, was so affected that if a boy mentioned a miracle in the New Testament he would get into an uncontrollable rage and hurl any object to hand (book, chalk, board-rubber, etc.) at the culprit; hence miracles would be raised in class whenever opportunity knocked. A third, who also taught Chemistry, gifted me with two special memories: that he always seemed to want to talk about Dagon the Tyrian Fish God and that he seemed unable to recognize that he was regularly baited in the "Alphabet Game," the aim of which was to induce the master to mention a word beginning with each sequential letter of the alphabet. One effect of this — some letters being rarer than others — was frequent discussions of missionaries in Québec and Zululand, even though to the best of my knowledge none of the boys had any interest in Christian missions — unless that some of the better informed knew that indiscreet missionary activity had been a major cause of the 1857 Indian Mutiny. In accordance with the assumed Imperial traditions of the School, the Raj was the highpoint of British generosity to the underprivileged natives of the world, Robert Clive being the hero in India along with Wolfe in Canada and, for some, Rhodes in South Africa.

Rhodes was of special significance for me, for although I did not yet know that he claimed only to have gone to South Africa because he could not stomach any more cold mutton in England, my grandfather had fought for him as a "Chartered Soldier." And of course we all assumed that such people as Rhodes, Wolfe, and Clive were heroes in their day as well as ours. Only as an aging man did I learn of a contemporary clerihew about the hero of Plassey:

> The best thing about Clive
> is that he's no longer alive.
> There's a great deal to be said
> for being dead.

Clive, missionaries and other stalwarts apart, I took my confirmation seriously, regularly attending the C. of E. communion service early of a Sunday morning — which among more intended benefits relieved me of the Reverend Elvin's sermons. But such Erastian joy lasted only briefly. When Elvin had passed on to his heavenly recompense, my mother began to realize that my Church of England enthusiasms were waning, so she summoned the new vicar at Saint Michael's, a young and pleasant man, to come and help me recover my faith.

The task was hopeless. I had spotted two problems about religion as I had met it thus far: the Church of England appeared to have been founded by Henry VIII who I realized had little personal connection with Jesus. The whole thing, I had come to believe, was a historical con-job or, as Norman Tebbit was later to put it, a piece of unnecessary and ideological nationalization which could be corrected if the Church were privatized. More basically, I had picked up from the miracle-hating schoolmaster that there were grave doubts about any version of Christianity. Jesus had written nothing; perhaps those who later set down what were supposed to be his teachings and the events of his life, being fraudsters or — more likely — hysterics, had invented the whole thing.

I also picked up the suggestion — then and still now deployed to make more sense out of an exaggerated concern with discrepancies in the Gospels — that two of our "Synoptics" (Matthew and Luke) were dependent on a varying combination of Mark, which has only a few ("perhaps interpolated") miracles, with a mysterious "sayings-source" called "Q" (from German — them again — *Quelle*). This too struck me as a self-serving fraud, perpetrated not this time by the founders of Christianity but by their latter-day and similarly deluded descendants, now pushed into fantasies by the well-aimed blows of their more enlightened agnostic critics. I suppose the invited vicar went away disappointed; I had no idea that many were more capable than he of facing the objections I posed — albeit not those to the Church of England.

School religion was not limited to the classroom. It was sprayed over us each morning at an assembly where, after we had drawled out some maudlin hymn (or if it was eugenic, perhaps "These things shall be, a loftier race than ere the world hath known shall rise"), and sometimes endured a reedy rendering of Admiral Vernon's March by the School Orchestra, the Headmaster or his deputy or one of the Housemasters would call for prayer. On one occasion, I recall, it was the deputy who elected to open not with "Let us pray" but with "Shall we pray" — to be immediately answered from the back of the hall by "Let's take a vote on it." The Headmaster was not pleased. This school, he always insisted, like other public schools, is religiously serious. Since ours was "minor" as public schools go, he might have added "We are climbing the social ladder and the Established Church is integral to that ladder. It is not therefore to be mocked."

⋄∞∞✴∞∞⋄

There were other rungs on the ladder too, but in a dim way most of us realized that religion in and of itself was not the basis of the intended edifice; the basis was snobbery. Not that we should have drawn the conclusion that this was an unwelcome truth in the eyes of the boys, and even less of their parents. Most of the pupils at Sir Anthony Browne's came from an upwardly-mobile class, keen not to eliminate snobbery but to enjoy its benefits. I was certainly aware from long before the time of Headmaster

Allison how greatly class differences mattered in Romford and environs. Even our own Woodfield Drive was divided, being at one end—where Clive's family and ours lived—decidedly down-market (my father, though securely employed, enjoyed at this stage no marked prosperity), while at the other end salaries and the consequent sense of superiority were markedly higher—not though as high as those of the lawyers, doctors, and other professionals who lived on the other side of "The Park" and "The Main Road" whose sons would normally pass through the doors of Sir Anthony Browne's foundation. But not always: there was a private school in Romford itself, the Royal Liberty, which had a reputation for teaching the rich but more or less unteachable, and in some cases the more violent.

Not that the Liberty was the only violent feature of Romford; there were areas where the police needed to patrol in pairs, liable as they were to be attacked by youths with "chivs" (razors) and needing to protect themselves when breaking up weaponized brawls among such youths for whom penalties were still quite savage, the birch rod serving to a degree as a deterrent until 1948, while some longed nostalgically for the days of the cat o' nine tails. Looking back I am still surprised how tolerant almost everyone (including my parents) was of such "cruel and degrading punishments," unless presumably the youths themselves or their parents.

Even then at times the "boys" might strike back. I later had a friend whose father was in charge of a Borstal—what would now be called a correctional institution for minors—whose career was cut short when, emerging from a man-hole, he was struck on the head with a mallet. At least he did not die. Romford's urban myths included that of the two boys spotted by their father awaiting Santa Claus on Christmas Eve. Standing by the chimney armed with hammers and screw-drivers, they could hope to grab the bloke and relieve him of more of his Christmas gifts than they would be entitled to.

At Brentwood, even among the "gangs" which schoolboys are inclined to form in all-male educational establishments, the class division was clear: by far the larger group in my cohort were called "Coullies"—after their leader David Coull, the sport-skilled son, I think, of a prominent lawyer; the smaller group revolved around a rather charismatic buccaneering individual named Robert Markham: smart but of more humble origins and thought of by the masters as "a bit cocky." For my part I disliked the Coullies and tended toward the Markhamites, though always reserving my own hand. Once I emerged from the crowd to run as the Labour candidate at the school's Mock Election — and managed to get a dozen or so votes out of the approximately 500 who voted. The Communist candidate did slightly better; perhaps he seemed to offer the more logical anti-snobbish alternative.

The snobbery was developed at school at two levels, one centered around the Headmaster, the other around the various heads of Houses into which we boys were divided. Mr Stone, in charge of my own West House, was the finest example of the snobbery-promoting type, being sports-obsessed with a tendency to anti-intellectualism. I enjoyed some sports myself, especially soccer and swimming, and was grateful for having been taught to swim by the bronzed and well-formed Miss Trott with whom the other gym teacher (ex-army PT instructor Mr Shortland, inevitably referred to as "Shorty") was widely and almost certainly wrongly held by the older boys to be having an affair. But in no sport was I particularly proficient, while already beginning to appear an intellectual; hence Mr Stone and I disliked each other almost from the start. As for Miss Trott, she was soon to leave the school to get married and (as I think I remember) to emigrate to Canada.

The wider promotion of snobbery was controlled by the Headmaster and, as we began to believe, by his wife Rita, a former actress. His aim, as I have noted, was to make the public school he ran less "minor" and in so doing, as the boys soon understood, to promote his own social standing. We assumed that he aimed for a knighthood and certainly he managed to get himself appointed to various educational quangos, the members of which did little to improve the now-imposed comprehensivisation of most of the country's educational establishments.

Part of Allison's policy at Brentwood was to develop new school traditions; we called them "instant traditions." Thus we started to make a yearly pilgrimage to South Weald Church where, three miles or so from the school, Sir Anthony Browne was to be commemorated at the family burial site. And we had to play rugby; the "better" public schools preferred it to the more proletarian football, though in view of the small enthusiasm for the more snobbish game among the boys, soccer had to stay too. Indeed it remained the primary sporting activity in the winter months.

In the summer, of course, it was cricket, which I found boring to play but exciting to watch when played at a higher level; one of the Essex County Grounds was opposite the School's playing fields and games took place there for a week each summer.

And there was the Combined Cadet Force (CCF); all proper public schools had one, and Brentwood's long predated Allison. From the second to the fifth form you spent part of one day a week in uniform, starting with an "army" section. Then, if you passed "Cert. A," you could become an air-force cadet: a route I chose not because I realized it would help me get into the RAF for National Service (though it may have done), but because if you went to camp (usually at Cranwell), a flight in an Anson was on offer, that being my first (very bumpy) ride in a plane. Though I was comparatively patriotic, I had no interest in a military career, as a few of the boys did; at that age I would have preferred to drive locomotives. At Cranwell I learned about various lunatic pilots, usually Poles, one of whom was famed for doing wingtip turns around the spire of Lincoln Cathedral, though in fact the Cathedral has no spire.

Another less pleasing "tradition" was a developed version of the long-established public-school practice of beating the boys, on pretexts better or worse. Almost all public schools favored this and it was widely approved by parents and indeed, if administered by a Head or Housemaster, by many of the boys. What they did not approve, however, was the instant tradition that senior prefects, particularly the chief prefect in each House, could on appropriate occasions be counted among the beaters. Only those who hoped to beat when the time came approved of this; most thought it outrageous, as did I, not least because I recognized that in contrast to most of the masters, the senior boys generally enjoyed a chance to thrash.

I do not know whether Allison approved the encouragement of sadism but he certainly gave that impression. My known objection to the whole system, certainly voiced when I was in the Sixth, was probably part of the reason why, almost alone in my cohort, I was only promoted to prefect the day before I left the school. People have told me that I should have refused the dubious honor, but there was a (less than edifying) reason for my accepting it which will be identified later in the story.

Such traditions having been thus clearly explained, I must admit that in Allison's version of the ideal public school, academic excellence had a limited but significant place. Good food, however, did not; the quality of the muck we were served for lunch meant that the wealthier pupils preferred to eat at their own expense at the Tuck Shop rather than gulp down the low-grade more or less cold stuff officially provided. One of the masters, when retired, would boast that he had cut up some fifteen miles of stodgy suet pudding (currants conveniently omitted, perhaps on grounds of expense), to be washed down with pallid drops of custard. He himself, after cutting it up, could resort to the pub for a meal.

On one occasion there was a contretemps about a stew in which I found a fair-sized stone—and was duly reprimanded for making a fuss about it. I took the stone home as a souvenir, but my parents showed little interest in it either, presuming it par for the course. I was already aware of a famously relevant limerick:

> A gentleman dining at Crewe
> discovered a mouse in his stew.
>   Said the waiter "Don't shout
>   and wave it about,
> or the rest will be wanting one too."

The suet-roll-cutting teacher was a new addition, and a lively one, to the English department, and it must be admitted that Allison managed to improve the quality of the academic staff quite substantially in a number of the humanities: Classics, History, and English in particular: this the growing number of Oxbridge admissions in these subjects would bear out. Modern languages, however, remained a bad joke, and not entirely because of the contemporary English contempt, shared by many of the boys, for "Johnny Foreigner." In French the department head seemed to imagine he was part of one of the more authoritarian schools in his native country and would hand out "zero out of twenty" for dictations with more than two mistakes. The comic opportunities in that became apparent when we were asked to read out the marks we had just received, and in a class of about thirty not more than two or three had achieved a numerical tally.

The artistic side of the school was even less well provided for, and I ran into trouble both with singing and with art: that is, drawing and painting. In the third form I was banned from singing altogether, which—although my parents never sang and Littlebury Nan was limited to snatches of *The Old Rugged Cross* which had she learned as a child—I rather resented. After making a forlorn attempt at *Sweet Lass of Richmond Hill*, I received a sharp rebuke from our "queer" though musically very competent master: "Shut up boy, you sound like a frog."

In art things were not much better. The male (and senior) teacher seemed to have little interest beyond selling expensive erasers which crumbled away when used inexpertly so that another had to be bought: we believed the master pocketed the extra cash. The second teacher, Miss Phyllis Hall (whose name will recur), found it impossible to understand why a boat I attempted to paint turned out to be so badly executed and hence wrongly judged my effort a deliberately subversive act, so that a detention for impudence followed.

That said, I must admit to being at that time rather given to impudence and rule-breaking. During the lunch period, if the weather was good, some of us took to racing about the "Common," that being contrary to school rules, perhaps for moral reasons, since it was impossible not to notice—with a mixture of disgust and fascination—the discarded "frenchies" in more out-of-the way spots. And when a master drew attention to Mallory's answering the question, "Why do you want to climb Mount Everest?" with "Because it is there," I could not resist inserting in an essay on "civics" a "related" question, "Why do you want to blow up the House of Commons?," and proposed the apparently similar answer, "Because it is there." That was not well received. Decades later (I think during the Thatcher years) an *aficionado* of political reality made a not unrelated suggestion by spray-painting a wall around the House of Commons with the text "Guy Fawkes, Thou shouldst be living at this hour/ England hath need of thee."

Less absurdly, again in better weather, some of us would walk into the town center and point to the nearest church steeple, shouting loudly, "Look at that, look at that." Gradually a crowd would join us in gazing up into the sky—and of course failing to see the nothing to which we were drawing attention. We could then slip out of the crowd and estimate the number of the deceived, it becoming a challenge each day to raise the tally higher—which eventually attracted the interest of the local police who drew it to the attention of the school. While I was delighted to find on that term's report, "He must not take the lead in disorder," my satisfaction was met by the conspicuous though short-lived fury of my parents. On the other hand, though I had only a fairly small number of close friends—the closest at this time being Bernard Dobson who would die prematurely after suffering for some years from schizophrenia—my "street-cred" certainly benefitted from the "Steeple affair."

At the beginning of my fourth form year, I had to take a decision which, without my then realizing it, would affect the rest of my life. On the train to school I remembered that I was required to choose between Greek and German. I was already enthusiastic about Latin and that, coupled with an ongoing antipathy to German-speakers, made the choice obvious. And the selection of Greek proved a huge success, completing my initiation into an ancient world where I seemed to live in an endlessly fascinating foreign country. Viewed from a larger perspective it turned out to be the second event, after the war, substantially to affect—even to form—my later character and concerns.

My parents seemed not to care what I studied at school provided I was good at whatever I decided on. This was partly, as I now began to realize, because their own education had reached only a low level. My mother had been a teacher of primary children in the industrial slums of Dagenham—where she found it hard to persuade a sizeable number of her male pupils that it was worth learning to read: after all, "my elder brother can't read and he makes a lot of money at the docks." She herself, however, seemed to have learned very little at school, though she later developed a certain interest in the romantic parts of the English literary canon and at least dabbled in the fashionable "Fabian" literature of the age: Shaw, Wells, Galsworthy, from whom I fear she picked up little beyond an unedifying attitude to eugenics.

My father's case was, it seemed, even odder; sent to a comparatively good London school he still appeared to have learned almost nothing: no literature, no languages, no history, no geography, no science; even, it seemed, no mathematics, though he eventually worked hard to become a chartered accountant. So I entered into no discussion with my parents about Greek versus

German; it was "all Greek" to them, and my choice marked a further stage in my intellectual isolation at home. This I regretted but accepted fatalistically, not yet realizing that I was becoming a would-be cosmopolitan: still less that a citizen of everywhere is a citizen of nowhere or that a love of "humanity" may preclude a love of individual humans.

The following five years, two in what should have been the O-level years[1] and three in the Classical Sixth, were probably the most academically rigorous time of my life (leaving me with the strong impression that if those years are intellectually wasted — as increasingly they are — the loss can rarely be entirely recovered). In my case, the demands of study were increased because of an absurd Government policy — soon, but too late for me, to be reversed — that no O-levels should be attempted until the pupil had reached the age of sixteen. As a result I had to forego the exams in most subjects I studied for O-level — all, that is, apart from English Language, Maths, and French which were necessary for university entrance. Thus no certification in English Literature, Biology, Geography, or History, for although I had studied the material in these subjects, I had no time for further examinations during my first Sixth Form year when I was already working toward my A-levels in Greek, Latin, and Ancient History.

Not that the unexamined courses were without value; in fact English Literature and especially History were generally well taught. "Spud" Barron was excellent on Chaucer and Shakespeare — his treatment of the bawdy being especially attractive to the boys — and we read *Julius Caesar*, *Macbeth*, *A Midsummer Night's Dream*, *Romeo and Juliet*, and *Henry IV part 1*, the last of these being the first Shakespeare I saw on the stage when my mother took me to Stratford. Barron had produced more than half of the plays for performance and it was his ambition to produce them all; I hope he pulled it off.

The only problem with English, which was neither the fault of Barron nor of my other instructor, Mr Chignell, was that parts of the official syllabus were much disliked by boys who had no time for *Silas Marner* and still less for Hardy's *The Woodlanders* or *Under the Greenwood Tree* ("All that stuff about the fuckin'

---

[1] Ordinary (O) Levels were sat in high-school at about age 16; Advanced (A) Levels were usually sat about age 18.

shepherds"), even if more sympathy with *The Mayor of Casterbridge*. Wordsworth was not popular either, Byron and — more surprisingly perhaps — Milton being much preferred, especially the latter's heroic presentation of Satan.

One of the oddities about the curriculum was that English history seemed to end with the death of Richard III at Bosworth Field and to restart with the accession of the Stuart James I and VI; presumably the Reformation was judged too hot a topic, risking, if accurately taught, some dilution of English myths about Merry England and Good Queen Bess. (Kingsley Amis's *Lucky Jim* had not yet appeared.) Yet in view of that omission the question posed by Mr Gibson at the beginning of the Stuart part of the program was particularly striking. On entering the dusty room in the Old School he started straight in with: "Who can give me any of five good reasons for the Tudor *despotism*?" That phrase "Tudor despotism" has remained lodged in my mind ever since as only too apt. Such stoking of intellectual curiosity apart, the History teachers as a group were, in the eyes of the boys, attractively brutal and consequently somewhat awesome, one claiming in dry tones that his grandfather — I think it was — had walked fifty miles in his bare feet to watch the last public hanging in England.

When I started on my A-levels (plus S-levels[2]) in the Classical Sixth, with much else left behind, I was happy enough. Our formroom was the library with its opened Foxe's book and its bust of Milton presiding. The latter's popularity, however, had now waned somewhat and it seemed appropriate soon after the start of the year to adorn him with a cloth cap and stick a cigarette to his lower lip. Naturally this was not officially appreciated and when the culprit could not be identified, we were told we would be kept in until he was. That did no good either, being greeted with an untraceable muttered, "What, without food?" Milton's popularity was substantially restored when someone found his denunciation of a "debauched king who in the public theatre could be seen fondling the bosoms of virgins and matrons as well as their more private parts," we little realizing that the description derived less from fact than from Milton's lurid imagination.

Once we settled down to work, however, we realized that we had two excellent teachers: (no more now of the "Old-school"

---

[2] S is for Scholarship level.

deputy-head and Orbilian professional "Hector" Higgs nor of the gentler Mr Cluer). Michael Benson and Riddiford—whose Christian name I never discovered—were both different from these and from one another, though they shared a knowledge of Greek and Latin which, in my estimation, would be the envy of many of those who now teach these subjects at even the more prestigious universities. Benson, though an ex-soldier and interpreter at the Japanese war crimes trials, was an evangelical from a clerical family and still unmarried, though as we soon discovered, with an erotic interest in the art-teacher Miss Phyllis Hall. On one memorable occasion that was to cause him a certain embarrassment. Asked to provide him with an example of multiple elisions in Latin verse, someone instantly came up with *"Phyllida amo ante alias"* ("I love Phyllis before other women"). But they never married, and Benson would try elsewhere with less than happy results.

Riddiford was temperamentally quite different. High spirited, a convert to Oxford linguistic philosophy and hence materialist and (at least in theory) anti-religious, he had as a boy been expelled by Allison when that man was in his former role as Headmaster of Dulwich College: when we learned this, even I had to award our Head a few "brownie" points for later employing him at Brentwood. He was married to a Venetian woman who taught me some Italian in the idyllic summer of 1954, the last months of my schooldays before military service; we read parts of Dante's *Inferno* and for a more contemporary version of that beautiful Italian language, the tales of Don Camillo, which introduced me to some of the more comic, but fascinating and endearing, features of twentieth-century Italy.

By now, the war being long over, summer holidays had returned. My mother loved the countryside—as to a degree did my father, especially if it gave him the chance to observe new varieties of birds and if a bit mountainous—so already in 1945 we had managed to go to Eskdale in the Lake District, to reach which took about fifteen hours on the train. I climbed Great Gable and was irritated at not being allowed to attempt Scafell Pike, the highest peak in England. Here in the Lake District I discovered a love of the mountains which has never left me, suggesting that the universe would be a divine creation were it not spoilt by men. In

Eskdale we also celebrated VJ Day, one of a group of New Zealand soldiers encamped nearby setting the tone with his accordion.

Next year, also with a group of walkers, mostly from the North of England, it was Surrey and the Devil's Punchbowl and the following year the Peak District with its limestone caves and stalagmites (though the higher points were still private lands and off-limits). The following year took us almost "abroad": to Scotland, where I managed Schiehallion and Ben Lawers, the latter my highest point so far, being dull and grassy with little rock though affording majestic views when we reached the summit.

The sun was blazing hot and when later in the day we reached a gleaming lochan, some of the party decided to swim. I was keen on that too and joined in, hardly noticing, until an intervention by my parents called it to my attention, that some of the women, being without costumes, entered the water in their underclothes, while those not wearing a suitable bra exchanged what they had for knotted headscarves which in several cases tended to come off in the water. When my parents realized the situation I was ordered out and told it was "too adult" for me, but not before I had taken note, though without much interest, that women's bodies were markedly different from men's. Of course I had no sisters and Clive's sister, despite my parents' suspicions, kept her clothes on, at least when I was around. Perhaps the following contemporary "nursery rhyme" is appropriate comment:

> Mary had a little lamb.
> She also had a bear.
> I've often seen her little lamb.
> I've never seen her bare.

Nor did I particularly want to.

Even in 1948, holidaying was still in places restricted. At Leigh-on-Sea—the posher part of Southend to which my parents moved when I entered the Classical Sixth and which entailed my seeing much less of them in term-time because the train journey from Southend to Brentwood was much longer than from Gidea Park, as well as rather slower—the beach was still out-of-bounds because of remaining undetonated mines and rusting stretches of barbed wire intended to deter the Krauts. But 1950 was to be a breakthrough; flying from London to Munich, where many of the buildings were still in ruins, we progressed by train to the

Berner Oberland whose peaks and glaciers delighted us. Of the inhabitants I retained no significant memories except that most of them spoke what I took to be German.

And by the time of my first Italian lessons with Signora Riddiford I had already visited Italy twice, though in very different circumstances: first to the Dolomites on another walking holiday, during which I climbed the nearly eleven-thousand-foot Monte Marmolada, the highest peak I have ever reached on foot. There I realized even more how distant my interests were from those of my parents: first the spaghetti, of which they were suspicious but which I immediately enjoyed, realizing how different was the real thing from the muck served out of a tin under the same name in the school tuck-shop. Olives also divided us, as did wine, which I was not allowed to taste.

Just before my second year in the Classical Sixth, there was a school trip to Venice and Rome which revealed—apart from the majestic art of Venice and the Classical ruins of Rome—some unexpected features of youthful life in Italy. Whether by accident or design our teacher guides kept us clear of most that was Christian (i.e., Catholic) in the Eternal City: apart, that is from Saint Peter's which on the inside reminded me of a large railway station and where I noticed that the "temple" (*fanum*) of Saint Paul in London was designated on the floor of the nave as rather small in comparison with the neo-classical replacement of Constantine's original construction.

Venice could only charm: among the wonders of its canal-circled palaces I was especially delighted with the bronze horses outside Saint Mark's Cathedral (stolen, I was glad to learn, from Constantinople by Crusaders) and with the swirling canvasses by Tintoretto in the Doges' Palace and the lordly Bellinis in the Academia. At the more human level there was a further opportunity to get an update on the habits of a smart Venetian high-school.

We were the guests of one of the more prestigious *Licei Classici* (in the halls of which we slept comparatively uncomfortably), and its students were supposed to look after us and initiate us into the Italian scene. Their principal attempt to accomplish this worthy aim was to invite us to join them of an evening at the local high-class brothel; for them such sportings constituted a *rite de passage* and they were surprised and somewhat contemptuous when we declined the invitation. The *rite*, indeed, has been common in Mediterranean countries since ancient times, and features in Longus's second-century AD novel *Daphnis and Chloe*, in which Daphnis learns from a whore-instructress the practices and techniques which as bridegroom he will later teach the "nice girl" (in modern Italian a *"ragazza perbene"*) he will marry. I do not know whether our masters were aware of the offer we received. I know that their attempts to pronounce Italian must have generated as much puzzlement among the locals as the varying local dialects produced among the boys.

Rome was different again, some of our group by then choosing to be drunk at night and hung-over in the morning, but others—and certainly myself—largely rejecting the wine in favor of intense rubber-necking in the city: I managed to get to the Forum, Palatine, Colosseum, Baths of Caracalla, and several museums, including that on the Capitoline Hill—guarded still by the "original" Marcus Aurelius on his horse—and that at the Vatican. In 1952 tourists were comparatively rare and not only was there no need for advance booking but it was not—as it was later to become—necessary, when visiting the Vatican Galleries, to race through the earlier parts of the structure and head straight for the Sistine Chapel if one wanted to see Michelangelo's masterpiece in a fast-diminishing peace. The trip, only ten days in all, offered merely a taste, though leaving with me a determination to return and additional motivation to pursue studies in Latin and Greek with a renewed vigor. To hell with modernity, I thought; the ancient world is where the real intellectual life lies. I believe that philosophically and culturally it still largely does.

⊸∞∞✺∞∞⊶

Even at O-level the syllabus in Greek for the fifth year (though I did not sit the exam but moved straight to A-level) was well chosen: Aristophanes' *Clouds* from a part-Greek part-English text whereby one could enjoy the plot without yet being able to read the choruses in a Greek complicated in meter, vocabulary, and syntax. The comic deconstruction of Socrates as an intellectual charlatan (which according to Plato did Socrates a lot of harm, contributing to his unpopularity among those who sought his death—yet apparently not affecting the friendship of Socrates himself with the deriding poet) introduced me to much about the ancient world at its best: the search for truth combined with a healthy contempt for pretentiousness and hypocrisy, whether on the part of philosophers, politicians, poets or indeed anybody.

The *Clouds* was partnered with a prose text, full of ideas of fundamental philosophical importance presented in the highly sophisticated literary form of the Platonic dialogue. That text was book one of Plato's *Republic*, a work which has probably affected me more than anything else I have read. For the *Republic* is Plato's crystalline introduction to the only logical (rather than fudged) alternative to a Socratic and transcendent metaphysics being nihilism and its cynical manipulation by "realists" of good-natured idiots who believe in objective value judgments. That alternative in all its challenging rawness is what Plato's Thrasymachus proposes and Socrates aims to unpick in book one. As I soon confirmed from reading the *Apology*, that contrast between nihilism and transcendence—in light of Socrates' claim that "the unexamined life is subhuman"—is what we all ought to ponder. I realized even then that it matters whether Socrates or Thrasymachus is right, and I recognize now that no one has set out the problem as clearly—if almost as brutally—as Plato in the *Republic*—all in that combination of seriousness and comic relief (in Greek *spoudaiogeloion*) which remains for me the most helpful mode of intellectual enquiry.

The A-level syllabus in Greek (Aeschylus's *Persians* and Herodotus book nine), if less exciting, was still full of interest, and the Latin was magnificent: Virgil's *Aeneid* book six and large parts of Cicero's *Second Philippic*: a no-holds-barred attempt to discredit Mark Antony, if not to knock some belated sense into him. And to the delight of an aspirant *aficionado* of politics, the texts to be studied in detail for Ancient History were the last and violent years of the Peloponnesian War and the First Triumvirate in Rome, which enabled me to think about revolutionary savagery and political deception as practiced by real professionals, propped up on the Roman side by first acquaintance with Syme's *Roman Revolution*. Especially memorable in that was chapter twelve on "Political Catchwords," which shows how successful orators (in Rome especially Cicero) could brazenly contradict themselves when different circumstances demanded—and get away with it.

But not, of course, always: at one point in his life Cicero, attempting to defend a certain Milo who had just murdered a political rival, was so intimidated by the armed thugs hanging about the courtroom that he messed up. Still, it being the practice among Roman orators to publish not what they had said in court but what they might have said, Cicero published his improved speech for Milo and sent it to him. Milo, now in exile in Marseille, was quick to write back to express his gratitude that this "real" speech had not been delivered; otherwise he would not have been able to enjoy Marseille's magnificent red mullets!

Nor even at this period of my life was my reading limited to ancient texts; I tried to widen it as much as I could, especially in accounts of "world" or "universal" history. Gibbon's *Decline and Fall* was a favorite, and I even attempted Ibn Khaldun, but I was also especially impressed by Arnold Toynbee's *A Study of History*, particularly by his ideas about how civilizations can be undermined, simultaneously or sequentially, by what he called an internal and an external proletariat, not to speak of his analysis of military history where he strikingly draws attention to the fact that David frequently beats Goliath: that is, that light-armed, fast moving fighters (in the past including archers) can often bring down over-encumbered warriors whether on horseback or conveyed by other means. Naturally when I first read of such things I thought (with Gibbon) about the fall of pagan Rome—and when eventually I became an academic, about the pagan-Christian "dialogue" in the late empire, which, for Toynbee, played a substantial part in that fall, involving, as it did, a changing "internal proletariat."

All that and much more, and I had no difficulty in working very hard indeed: the result being in an exam taken in one year rather than two that I achieved—out of 150—149 for Ancient History, 143 for Latin and 139 for Greek. Even now I feel astonished at managing that! All that remained was to spend a further four terms trying to get a scholarship at Cambridge. For although Riddiford was himself a graduate of the other place, Benson was a Cambridge man. I myself knew little of either institution, though more about Cambridge—including Granddad's attempts to circumvent the Addenbrookes body-snatchers—since it was located only some fifteen miles from Littlebury. Hence I was content to accept my instructors' advice: yet another decision with unforeseen consequences.

Nor at the time did I understand why (perhaps recklessly) Benson not only affirmed Cambridge but urged me (at the first attempt) only to put down Trinity College, highly regarded as it was for Classics—albeit for a kind of Classics which I did not really want; still it gave me much to think about along with a variety of technical skills. For although I knew nothing of this at the time, Oxford and Cambridge Classicists were trying to decide whether Classics implied a "humanist" emphasis on the editing of texts requiring a profound understanding of the minutiae of ancient languages or whether the emphasis should be less on Greek and Latin than on Greece and Rome (of which the languages and the corresponding linguistic skills were only a part, if a vital one).

So began a further period of hard work in which I managed to some extent to catch up with those from more major public schools who had started Latin and Greek earlier than had I. Luckily, as it turned out, I still had little interest in the heterosexuality now rampant among a fair part of my academic cohort. Gone were the homosexual fantasies which according to Freud accompany the immaturity of immediate puberty, testosterone-fueled lads now directing their attention toward females. Of these there were in Brentwood two possible sources of supply, the Ursuline Convent and the Girls' County High. With the posher Ursuline girls (some said to be minor European royals) there appeared little prospect of immediate success; it did not occur to me that this might be because they were largely Catholic. Girls from the County High were more amenable, being, in the current London language, "cheap and cheerful"—in fact an early version of the proverbial "Essex girl." Some at least seemed up for strip-poker and on occasion the boys won big, a pair of knickers once appearing at school as a trophy.

At least the real sex-game might seem more rewarding than the mechanical version you could try out at the Kursaal fairground and other tourist-amenities in Southend where you could play the more-you-grip-the-more-you-strip devices only if you had the strength of a Hercules. That said, other and less innocent features of sexual maturity came to our attention. Thus one day we realized that the Head Boy was no longer attending Brentwood School and it was said that he had been "done" for rape, the case being not mentioned in Assembly, except by implication in that a new Head Boy was announced.

I, largely uninterested in all this, stuck doggedly to an older world; that involved reading most of Homer along with Virgil's

Aeneid, many of Cicero's letters, two or three plays of each of the major Greek tragedians and comedians, and most of Juvenal's satires. Of these I admired most those lashing out at debauched aristocratic females, at place-seekers liable to die in the Baths if they entered the hot-room too soon after gulping down a whole peacock, and at various squalid homosexuals. And it paid off in that, over a series of foggy November days in Cambridge, and a set of fairly difficult papers — the general essay paper contained the simple injunction "Write an essay on the following: Nostalgia" — plus a perfunctory interview with a tutor (who asked me about Mozart's operas), I got a Minor Entrance Scholarship at Trinity, the best academic achievement of the school that year. Benson and Riddiford were of course delighted, but Housemaster Stone said nothing and Allison contented himself with reading out all the Oxbridge results at the School Assembly.

Indeed his attitude to me hardly changed. I had never been asked to become a member of what he and his wife Rita dubbed "The Candlesticks," a fortnightly evening meeting with those senior boys who were thought to be intellectually — or perhaps rather socially — on the "way up." Not that I was bothered by the absence of an invitation but certainly I rejoiced at a mishap in "Spud" Barron's Shakespeare play for the year, to be performed by the staff dramatic society. This was *Othello*, with Allison and Rita seemingly happy to play Othello and Desdemona. The auditorium was packed for the performance, and when Othello smothered Desdemona there was a roar of applause. Later I came to think of this as an oddity analogous to that of the Scottish "poet" William McGonagall playing Macbeth and refusing to die in the final duel with Macduff, to the delight of an audience who cheered him on.

After my Cambridge success, now being almost the only boy in the third year Sixth not appointed a prefect, I enjoyed myself in more leisurely fashion while awaiting the next stage of life: induction into military service. Reading still more widely beyond Greek and Latin and learning Italian was a humanist's dream and, for the first time at Sir Anthony Browne's establishment, I felt content. Benson even managed to persuade the Headmaster to allow me to give the Latin address at that year's Speech Day. This I did in an attempt at Catullan hendecasyllables (eleven-syllable lines) which oddly I found easier to compose than the hexameters and elegiac couplets I was normally expected to squeeze out.

And so it came to an end, though I kept up with Riddiford for several years and with Benson—after a lapse of several decades—until his death. Before finally leaving Sir Anthony Browne's School I had a last encounter with my Housemaster. He was not happy when I suggested that the School had served me well despite his best efforts to tarnish my progress. Nor was he appreciative when I observed that although I had accepted the offer of becoming a prefect the day before I left, I assumed that he was the explanation for the lateness of the promotion. On these bad terms we parted. Now on my own I looked forward to the next stage of my journey.

Though Trinity College had a policy of insisting that its incoming students should already have completed National Service, I had now become an "Old Boy" of Sir Anthony Browne's School and as such would eventually join, in what some of us were to call the "Fenland Don Reserve," a slightly older "Classical-sixth" contemporary who then seemed to be Allison's ideal upwardly-mobile student. In our time, however, there were rather few Old Brentwoods studying in Cambridge: none of my closer friends managed it, but in the following years the school sent an increasing number of its high achievers both there and elsewhere, the Cantabrigians including Jack Straw, Foreign Secretary under Blair, Nick Griffin, founder of the British National Party and David Irving who managed to be both a historian and a holocaust-denier.

CHAPTER 3

At the Fag End of Empire

> REPORTER: What do you think are the principal goods the British Empire has bestowed on the world?
>
> THE LAST GOVERNOR OF ADEN (reputedly): The game of Association Football and the phrase "Fuck off."

> *Così è, se vi pare.*
> —Pirandello

The first step toward National Service was a test designed to ascertain whether, having been in the School Cadet force and so considered a candidate for a preferred service, I was capable of reaching a higher intelligence standard than that required by the army. (I had not considered the navy.) Having passed that hurdle with fair ease, at the beginning of October 1954 I reported to RAF Cardington—the one-time airship center—for preliminary induction into the Royal Air Force—known in the service itself as "the mob." This consisted of being issued with a uniform, being able to prove on inspection that I was not suffering from a venereal disease and being allotted a service number; mine was 2591666. The so-called "last three"—which apart from our name and rank were all we were supposed to disclose if we were captured by an enemy—were useful as identification at Pay Parades where we recruits received our twenty-eight shillings a week.

For me that was enough, since all my immediate needs were provided for; for some who might smoke more than sixty fags a week, it made things tight, even though you could get fags cut-price at the Navy, Army, and Air Force Institutes (NAAFI). But I never smoked. Neither I nor my comrades knew at the time that my "last three," 666, was the Number of the Beast of the Apocalypse. Finally at Cardington came a talk on military discipline, of which all I can remember is that we were told it was contrary to King's Regulations for officers or NCOs to swear at "airmen." Were they to do so, they ran the risk of "being on a fuckin' charge."

Cardington was merely a way-station and after a couple of days we were bused to R.A.F. Hednesford which was to supply us with "Basic Training" for the next eight weeks. It consisted of a collection of Nissan huts ("billets") on the edge of Cannock Chase, a rather desolate piece of moorland surrounding Cannock, a dirty and seedy town where the main "industry" seemed to be prostitution. Not that I went there more than the once; in the next two months we hardly left the camp, though, as I recall, we would enjoy one forty-eight-hour leave after some five weeks had passed. Somewhat to my surprise (perhaps because I was "Essex Man" born and bred), I found my comrades quite congenial. Most were fairly anonymous though one or two had been nabbed for petty crime in London and tended to refer to those who did not support Millwall football club as "peasants," often accompanying this insult with oaths such as "Jesus wept." None of them were particularly patriotic, and many would claim not to know why they were there, National Service seeming a hangover from the past which no one as yet had thought of abolishing.

Each billet was the responsibility of a corporal called a Drill Instructor (DI). Some of these inclined to bullying, but ours was cheerful enough. The whole intake was under the nominal command of a young pilot-officer whom we saw soon after we arrived (when he told us that he was no "bull-maniac"[1] but that if he saw a speck of dust in the billet someone would be on a charge), after which he was invisible until our final Passing-out Parade. Something we never saw was an aircraft, and an odd fact that I had learned at school applied here too: that parents need to be careful about the names and initials they give to their offspring. At school one boy whose initials were G.G. had been regularly referred to by other boys (and at times by masters) as "Horse."[2] In our billet an "airman" named Anthony Black might be called for some duty with the barked question, "Is there a black in here?" No racism intended, merely some slight humiliation.

The routine was simple and repetitive: rise (Reveille) at 5:30 ("Hands off cocks, on socks," as the DI might urge), then breakfast (Compared with Sir Anthony Browne's the food was good), then drill, Physical training, weapons-training on rifles and Bren-guns.

---

[1] Someone obsessed with "spit and polish," etc.
[2] Gee-gee is child talk for horse.

The handling of these last always generated some sexual reference: thus of a kind of button underneath the gun and not easy to find quickly, we heard that "you'd find it quick enough on a Saturday night if it had hair round it"—thus echoing a Victorian ditty still to be heard in Littlebury and such rural parts: "Oi 'ad 'er, Oi 'ad 'er/ Oi upp'd and Oi 'ad 'er / Oi 'ad 'er on Saturday noight." Indeed almost everything was given sexual coloring: thus if we marched too limply we were told "Open your legs, you have nothing to lose," or if we lingered too long on a loo-break we were informed that "More than three flicks is a wank."

Occasionally while dwelling in this unexpected world I would wonder how it connected with my years of intensive study, and perhaps surprisingly I detected a similarity: not with "The Glory that was Greece" and "The Grandeur that was Rome" but with the more earthy side of the ancient world: the world of (at times) Archilochus and Aristophanes, Catullus and Martial. What did this parallel add up to? Was the Church of England being replaced "on the ground" by neopaganism, with the worship of a fertility goddess and her Priapic devotees? If so, was this a good thing? Was there any alternative? Could gladiatorial shows be back and what was there to prevent that happening? Was there a difference between paganism and neopaganism?

Near the end of our "basic training" we stumbled through a mild assault course and a few minutes in a chamber filled with what I assumed to be tear-gas, and that was about the lot! For me the high point had been reached during bayonet training when in front of us was a row of dummies and the sergeant shouted, "Them's the Boche," only to provoke the objection, "But, Sarge, I thought the Germans were our allies now!" It was a reminder—and surprisingly well received by Sarge—that the war was only a few years behind us and with perhaps the implication that if there were another, we would be fighting its predecessor.

Eight weeks completed, and the Passing-out Parade marched and photographed (I still have the photograph), another decision had to be made (not of course by me) about where I should be sent next. I cannot remember whether I applied to go on a Russian course or whether—as must be more likely—the authorities proposed this option. Either way, it seemed a splendid idea, and I was accepted for the Joint Services School for Linguists (JSSL) at Bodmin in Cornwall, where would-be intelligence people from the three services were assembled to learn Russian. (Later on Chinese would be offered—on the principle perhaps that "optimists learn Russian, pessimists Chinese.") The decision, however, implied that I had to wait some seven weeks before the next course began, and although a week or so was allowed as "leave," a further six remained. For that period I was posted to R.A.F. North Coates, on the Lincolnshire coast, which had been converted from an active airfield to serving as a unit to which unexploded ordnance from the Second World War, mostly dredged from various beaches, was brought to be detonated in comparative safety.

⋄∞∞✹∞∞⋄

But first the week's leave. I took the chance (illegally, I later suspected) to return by boat and train to Italy, this time to a Florence bearing more marks of the war past than either Rome or Venice. Not that there was much evidence of bombing or fighting, but the city seemed run-down, dejected, grubby and, it being December, with limited daylight and less limited rainfall. I found a cheap *pensione*, and the family who owned it seemed very pleased to welcome a paying visitor, and told me much about the recent misfortunes of their town and country. No-one had been a Fascist—as was more likely to have been true in Florence (and in Tuscany generally) than in more southerly parts of Italy. Nor did any of them admit to being Communists, though I had a strong impression that this was the case. Perhaps they were naïve enough to think that any threat from the Soviet Union had abated with the death of Stalin the previous year. I did not tell them that I was about to learn Russian.

Communism and bad weather notwithstanding, art was still available, and I raced about from the Cathedral and Baptistery to San Marco, the Uffizi and the Piazza della Signoria. Of all the marvels on show I think Ghiberti's doors on the Baptistry impressed me most. It was easy to move safely in the center of the city because there was very little traffic, the locals having resort to Vespas and other *motorini*—on which I noticed that a girl on the pillion might be sitting astride or side-saddle and was told that those on side-saddle were unmarried. The trip was soon over, but I knew I would return and even enjoyed the return journey over-night from Milan to Calais, followed by a rough Channel crossing. And so to R.A.F. North Coates.

When I arrived at the camp's guardroom, the duty police knew I was coming but had no idea what I was supposed to do or where I was supposed to be sent, being neither a lorry driver nor a sapper. That was my introduction to the "real" Air Force in post-war Britain and would set the stage for the wider Iraqi experience later on. Eventually, since no one could be found who had any idea of why I had arrived and how long I should be there, it was decided that the camp needed a librarian, and since I could both read and write I would be ideal for the job. Or, as it turned out, the non-job. I cannot remember exactly how many library-users entered the building in the six weeks I was in charge of it, but it cannot have been more than three individuals.

The library was better stocked than I expected, and not only with books; there were also a good number of records, mostly of classical music. I had learned some piano at school under the ruthless eye of a Miss Greaves, so by then was able to "produce" at least some parts of Beethoven's Moonlight Sonata. But my musical knowledge was minimal, so at North Coates there was much to be heard and learned. For me especially pleasing were the symphonies of Sibelius and Bruckner, punctured though they were by the roar of ordnance exploding on a not-so-distant beach. I knew that the slow movement of one of Bruckner's symphonies had been played as a lament for Hitler on German Radio after the Führer had supposedly "died heroically at the head of his troops in defense of Berlin." So despite explosions, my time in Lincolnshire—a county to which I have never returned—passed peacefully enough, and as I duly noted, being demobilized had grown nearer by at least six more weeks: as it would be put in the "mob," I was "getting some in." A bit more leave followed, then the train journey to Bodmin and the Russian language, military-style.

The JSSL was located in a camp on the edge of Bodmin, facing a low hill with twin peaks, to be inevitably compared with a woman's breasts. Beside us "intellectuals," two other units were stationed there, one of paratroopers, the other of the Devon and Cornwall Light Infantry. Of the latter we saw and heard little, though noted that being a light-infantryman entailed doing most marching "at the double." The paratroopers were equally remote and more legendary. It was said that relations between the officers and the "other ranks" in para-units were more friendly than elsewhere in the army—because each soldier was responsible for securing the parachute of the man who was to jump in front of him. It was said that during the Second World War a hated officer might realize too late that his parachute had been inadequately secured—not but what a faster than planned fall might also occur apart from any malice.

Our instructors in what was an almost total immersion course—apart from an enigmatic Mr Bancroft who endeavored with considerable success to explain the complexities of Russian grammar in English—were drawn from Eastern Europe, as their inimitable accents revealed when they spoke English, which they rarely did. To "White Russians"—who were White not from Belarus (White Russia) but "White" in the political sense and living in exile from their homeland since the 1920s, were added a smattering of Poles, Czechs, and Bulgarians, the last being generally regarded as deserving the unpleasant reputation Bulgarians seem often to have acquired.

What all shared was a notable incomprehension of the attitude of most of their military pupils. They assumed that we would be keen to learn—and we almost all were, though hardly from patriotic motives—but they also assumed that we ought to display a visceral hatred of Russian communists. This we did not, rather we found the Soviet propaganda films to which we were regularly "exposed" comic rather than sinister—and the lies we read in *Pravda* and *Izvestiya*, though informative in their way, were a regular source of entertainment: all this in the spirit of the occasion in Oxford at roughly the same time when students greeted the visiting Khrushchev and Bulganin with a hearty rendition of "Poor old Joe"—which "B and K" took as a display of youthful enthusiasm for their Communist ideology.

The high-point in the propaganda comedy was a well-known "documentary" called "Meeting on the Elbe," a river where, as a result of Roosevelt's overruling of Churchill and some of his own generals and allowing the Red Army to advance thus far, we met the cheery and highly disciplined Soviet troops—no breath of the millions of rapes they had just committed in and around Berlin—with on the western bank a largely black, drunken, drug-sodden rabble, the Americans. It was hard to believe that this was taken at face value back home in Russia, but there is apparently much evidence that it was.

There were also more local "entertainments" from time to time. One fine day a huge number of cigarettes (some said thousands) were stolen from the NAAFI. The military police could find no trace of them, so the authorities handed the investigation over to the civilian police—who within a few hours arrested two of their military counterparts.

Spurred on by such entertainment, and at least for me by the fascination of the language itself, we learned quite a lot of Russian—passing A-level en route—and were enabled to understand something of why Russians regard Pushkin as their greatest writer, his *Queen of Spades* being on the syllabus. There was no time to read Dostoevsky but our instructors unanimously assured us that his Russian was far superior to Tolstoy's; indeed for Tolstoy many of them evinced considerable aversion. Only decades later did I realize that Dostoevsky's scathing anatomy of the mind of the revolutionary nihilist must have evoked their appreciation of his novels.

Apart from study and some occasional more obviously military activity, there was plenty of entertainment, even in Bodmin. The town pubs served a potent scrumpy cider and I found that my capacity to hold it was greater than that of most of my fellow "airmen"—bringing with it the obligation to drag the legless back to camp. On one such occasion I found myself arriving back at the same time as the NCO in charge of the billet, who had also been drinking heavily—and presumably fornicating as well, since he kept muttering that "this is the last time I'll go out with a virgin; it's just too much trouble 'getting your end away.'" I was not sure how far the "trouble" was moral, but supposed it to be more physical.

Not far away was the north Cornish coast, its Atlantic breakers offering some fairly elementary but highly enjoyable surfing of a summer weekend. And on the occasional forty-eight-hour pass it proved easy to hitch a lift or a series of lifts to and from London (hence on to home), for many drivers still honored the wartime convention that it was right—even a duty—to offer lifts to anyone in uniform.

And so about nine months passed and another decision was to be made. For the next stage of our military journey there were two options, and in an important respect we could influence the choice. Those among us who might have thought of themselves as the "superior" group could proceed to London to work toward more specific interpreting skills, and near the end of their military life would be transferred to Germany to exercise these skills as junior officers. The "inferior" group would move to R.A.F. Wythall to learn the more technical vocabulary needed to comprehend Russian military personnel carrying out their various duties: these usually involved aircraft supporting tank maneuvers on the ground, and, as was to turn out, exploding the odd atomic bomb in the wastes of Russia's central Asian provinces.

One had to make the decision to attempt officer rank of one's own volition — that is, if you managed to pass the course, which almost everyone did: some, including myself, rather well. But I had no particular wish to be an officer — had indeed a certain hostility to taking on that kind of establishment role — whereas the "inferior" option might enable me to travel to places of far greater interest than Germany, perhaps even to the Middle East. Again it was my time to decide, and I plumped — that is certainly the best word — to play the system by choosing the more plebeian route — knowing that if I refused the possibility of a commission I would never get a second chance. More immediately it meant leaving the beauties of Bodmin Moor for the urban desert of Wythall, a rather squalid outpost of Birmingham, itself no beauty spot and where the inhabitants lived (as in parts of London with which I was more familiar) deprived of clean air.

We might have realized we were in Shakespeare country, the forest of Arden being fairly close, but none of us gave much thought to that as we listened to endless Russian pilots calling in to their controllers, and vice versa, "Rain, Rain; this is Rain 3394": at least that was the English version of a call we heard over and over again, sometimes accompanied by the Soviet National Anthem. In the end, of course, everyone passed and once again the future brought hopes and fears: most even of this "inferior" group still wanted to go to Germany, and when it became clear that the RAF needed two or three for Iraq, my fellow "airmen" were astonished when I immediately volunteered and was accepted. Two others, one of whom had signed on for an extra year in order to get (and save) more pay, eventually joined me. Now proudly styled "Junior Technicians," none of us grieved at leaving the dreary Midlands for our respective destinations. For me what mattered was that again my gamble had paid off.

In March 1956, a few days later, after saying goodbye to my parents in Leigh-on-Sea, I boarded a Lancaster bomber now converted into a troop carrier, with benches fitted to seat the troops. I cannot remember where it took off, possibly from near Gloucester, but it was a bumpy ride with nothing to see through the clouds. Some twelve hours later it was dark when, dressed in our newly-minted "tropical kit," we reached Habbaniyah (formerly, till handed over to the Iraqis in 1955, R.A.F. Habbaniyah) and were soon accommodated. The Lancaster took off again almost immediately for Abu Sueir in Egypt, intended to return from there to England next morning. Instead it crashed shortly after take-off, which seemed not particularly relevant since apart from myself and the two others from my class who were flying with me, I had no idea who else was on board or why. Some part of the explanation for this was to become clearer in the ensuing weeks.

R.A.F. Habbaniyah, built in 1936 close to the River Euphrates some fifty miles west of Baghdad, had originally been a vast complex extending over several square miles, but by my time parts of it had been abandoned. Intended as a major part of the defense of British interests "East of Suez" at a cost of £1.75 million pounds (some £126.5 million at today's prices), it had seen considerable fighting in the Second World War, but in 1955 was turned over to the Iraqis, Akrotiri in Cyprus being substituted; hence there were some 10,000 Iraqi military personnel in the camp in 1956. The Brits (who I soon realized were not officially supposed to be there) numbered only about 500. That included us "Russian people," a maintenance unit and a few pilots who seemed primarily engaged in teaching Iraqis to fly the latest jets: no easy task as the near-peasant trainees seemed to need hashish before getting into the cockpit and consequently were more than once involved in wing-tip collisions.

Our normally quite simple work—listening in on Russian military exercises east of the Urals—was organized in shifts: "mornings" (7:00 AM to noon) and "middles" (midnight to 7:00 AM) the first day. That left the rest of that day free and most of the next as well, the second part of the shift being "evenings" (7:00 PM to midnight), while the final day of the cycle would be "afternoons" (midday to 7:00 PM), and then we started again.

Occasionally there would be a night trip to the DF (Direction Finding) hut, pitch darkness being required if the work was to be done accurately.

This meant a short drive across the desert, and on these occasions RAF personnel would be accompanied by an Iraqi sergeant. I only made the trip once, and all passed quietly, but a friend on another occasion realized why the Iraqi might be required. When they reached the hut he flung open the door, flashed a powerful torch and in an instant pulled and hurled a knife to transfix a large camel-spider to the opposite wooden wall. Camel spiders, we were warned, could be lethal, as could scorpions, though surprisingly I never saw any. As for the direction finding, it seemed that the measurements we provided to identify Russian military activity were coordinated with similar measurements taken somewhere in eastern Turkey and handled by the Americans.

We were not the only "spies" operating from Habbaniyah; quite separate from us—we never seemed to see them apart from work times—was a group of "airmen" who spent their time recording Russian coded signals. I have little idea of the kind of material they intercepted, or at least about those messages they passed on for others to decode, but rumor had it that a fair percentage of their work related to atomic weapons. In any case, the final result would have depended on who wanted to notice what. Much of the voice mail we intercepted was far from routine, and in my view was probably of far greater interest. After listening for a while on some particular wave-length we began to recognize "old friends" among the voices of the tank commanders or pilots.

Much of their conversation was personal rather than military in nature; some of the pilots seemed more interested in going to the "fuckin' cinema" when they returned to earth than in their more immediate tasks. And because many swore regularly or resorted to other forms of "unconventional" Russian in recognizable patterns, it became possible to identify individuals and individual squadrons. But—to my mind absurdly—we were discouraged from recording such personalized information: told that it would be ignored in London even if we did record it, after a while most of us just listened and learned without bothering to report—which might seem to subvert the whole purpose of our activities. But that was what we were told we should do and we began to understand why it was widely observed that "military intelligence" is a contradiction in terms, and more unhappily why in the previous War so many had fallen victim to "friendly" fire caused by faulty intelligence.

As I have noted, the shift system gifted us considerable amounts of free time. Some of the "airmen" would spend much of this lying around in the sweltering huts (which were equipped with utterly ineffectual ceiling fans). Mercifully, in a desert climate humidity is not a problem, and most of us soon got used to the dry heat; in fact when in the evenings the temperature dropped to the eighties Fahrenheit we would often put on sweaters. And in the open desert the extremes of hot and cold by day and night were the more noticeable. In summer the temperature might rise to well over 110 degrees Fahrenheit.

But there was always relief to be found in water. When abandoning the base, the British had bequeathed to the Iraqis an Olympic-size pool (our officers, I believe, also had a more private one of their own) and although you could fry eggs on the concrete poolside, the water was fine, though often crowded, since the Iraqi troops were as keen as we were to cool off, or to attempt to play water-polo — in the nude since neither the Iraqi nor the British authorities included swimming trunks in a soldier's kit.

Much better than the pool, however, was Lake Habbaniyah, which could from time to time be reached by lorry. Here was provided a hut and a few chairs where one could relax in the shade after splashing about in the clear water. There was canned beer too, to which we could add various delights from the NAAFI. But the heat, the exercise, and the beer combined could induce sleep — embarrassing if you woke up displaying an erection when you would find yourself surrounded by joshing mates: "Who were you dreaming of? What's her name? Has she got nice tits?" One of the "mates" had won considerable street-cred a few days earlier by taking from his wallet a photo of an ex-girl-friend's "more private parts" (I quote Milton's anti-monarchist text).

As for me, I had to confess not only that I was unaware of a girl in my dreams but that back home I did not even have a girlfriend nor had gone to a dance, let alone enjoyed its sequel on a Saturday night. So I seemed odder than ever, but it did me no harm. Laughing it all off, I remembered Adam and Eve and wondered whether it was erection rather than nudity that had bothered Adam — though that did not account for Eve. Any theology, however, was at that stage unavailable to me! Whereas my mates failed to attend church parades out of apathy, I considered my dislike of the C. of E. to be principled.

The authorities seemed to have become aware of the problem of erections, which the alleged treatment of our drinking water with bromides had not solved. Hence soon after my arrival a proposal emanated from someone in the Officers' Mess to establish a brothel on the camp that would serve not only to satisfy the lustful, but, under medical supervision, might do so without harm to health. Getting venereal disease was a chargeable offence, though in any case we were made to understand that the local whores were too risky: thus on my sole confinement in the hospital while suffering from dysentery—happily not the amoebic variety—I noticed a characteristically British warning plastered up inside the building: "Flies spread disease; keep yours closed." The brothel scheme had to be abandoned when some of the officers' wives—in King's Regulations (so it was said) the term would be "ladies," while NCO's had "wives" and private soldiers "women"—suggested that if it were to go ahead, it could soon be featured in *The Sun* or *The Mirror*.

That would have done the officer-in-command no good, particularly if (so we thought we had learned from some tapped wave-band) he was in the habit of using an RAF machine to fly to Teheran for supper with a pal in the Embassy. And the "flogging off" (i.e., selling) to the Iraqis of "damaged" lorries claimed to be unfit for inspection might come out too. Or about the education officer selling hundreds of rifles to local "traders." While at North Coates I had been reading Evelyn Waugh's Guy Crouchback trilogy, and now I began to see how it all fitted together in late Imperial times—and at a Habbaniyah which had been built when the Empire's future—bizarrely—seemed not in doubt.

Such dodgy activity in camp more or less echoed what was happening off it. There was still at that time a Hashemite king of Iraq, but the country was run by his prime minister Nuri al-Said as a kind of client-kingdom in what was presumed to be the British interest. Apart from the army—in which it would soon become clear to us that sadism was encouraged and killing was a popular hobby—there was also a significant para-military instrument of government: the Iraq Levy, officially held to be akin to Glubb Pasha's Jordan Legion away to the west. But the two were very different, Glubb's outfit being a disciplined and generally orderly force with connections to the legendary "Desert Arabs" of Lawrence of Arabia. The Iraq Levy seemed rather to be largely a collection of thugs who had been offered the choice — often after conviction for murder or rape — between it and an Iraqi prison. Only a fool would have chosen prison, where torture was standard and the guards — as Juvenal might have put it — might match in character those they were supposed to be guarding. Overall, the client-kingdom seemed savage and corrupt, but when it was abolished with the murder of those who ran it, things became progressively worse, with Iraq falling into the hands of a series of military dictators, each more brutal than his predecessor and culminating in gas-happy Saddam Hussein.

Most people, certainly most of those with any authority, who write about Iraq, seem to omit a very important feature of its society in my time and (so far as I know) to this day. Everyone seems to know about the distinction within Islam in Iraq between Sunnis and the Shi'ite followers of Ali. That is certainly important, causing both political divisions verging at times on local wars and possibly provoking war with Shi'a Iran whenever Sunnis were in clear control in Baghdad. Indeed a mild version of such a conflict broke out during my time at Habbaniyah, thwarting my ambition — still unfulfilled — to visit Isfahan and other Iranian holy cities.

But in many more day-to-day ways the basic division in the country between Sunnis and Shi'as mattered less than divisions between the various tribes within both Sunni and Shi'a communities. One had the impression that what most held a tribe together was hatred of neighboring tribes. This mattered little when all lived in small communities in the open desert dozens of miles apart, getting the chance to shoot at one another only on the rare occasions when perhaps for some trading reason they met at an oasis. But by my time many of the tribes had migrated to the cities, especially to Baghdad itself where an unfriendly tribe might live just around the corner: hence hostilities which the authorities seemed to ignore as long as they could. If, however, the death-toll became excessive and too many properties were destroyed, they would send in armored personnel carriers to restore order by firing indiscriminately at the rioters. That quieted things down, until after a few weeks the cycle repeated itself. The Iraq Levy thus had plenty of dirty work on its hands.

Many of the Brits at Habbaniyah were content to stay in camp; nearby there was nowhere particular to go, Falluja, the nearest town, being strictly out of bounds (i.e., off limits), having then as now a reputation for violence extreme even for Iraq. Nevertheless, my ambition was to see as much of the country as possible, starting with a visit to Baghdad itself. For a comparatively low sum you could hire a taxi to take you across the fifty odd miles of desert; you passed through empty country except for the occasional waystation selling petrol and Pepsi.

Some of the old hands knew the city well, and were lavish with advice on what and what not to do, mostly on sexual matters. Thus I was advised never to sit on a bench wearing shorts. These would be non-uniform as was mandatory off-camp, in accordance with the myth that members of the British armed forces were no longer in the country, let alone major players in running it. If I ignored this advice, I would find within minutes that a girl had slipped up to me and already had her hand on my genitals. My informant added that the less brazen would wait for the foreigner (there were a number of businessmen in Baghdad and elsewhere in Iraq, particularly, as I later noticed, in Mosul) to make the first move, which would be a straightforward *"Shufti qush"* (Show me your cunt), to which the reply with hand outstretched for baksheesh would be, *"Shufti zubriq"* (Show me your cock).

Baghdad had been a considerable cultural and artistic center in the days of the Abbasid Caliphate, but much of its glory came to an end when in 1248 it was captured by Tamburlaine, who destroyed every building except for the "Golden Mosque" (so-called from the gold on its dome), leaving piles of skulls to mark his passing. So three of us set off across the desert, the Golden Mosque being, along with the Archaeological Museum, our principal target. We had not realized, however, that the mosque being Shi'a, infidels were not permitted to enter, so since it was located on one side of a large and dirty piazza we thought we could pay someone to allow us up onto the flat roof of his house; from there we could look down on the courtyard in front of the mosque. This we did satisfactorily, having ascended three steep flights of stairs on the way up.

But then there was the matter of the descent. I was in front and had descended one floor, when I found myself confronted by the home-owner pointing a large knife at my stomach. You don't think on such occasions. I just walked straight by and the other two followed, not particularly hurriedly. The knifeman did not move. His aim had probably been more cash than a killing, but once at the foot of the stairs we raced off at top speed in the direction of the Archaeological Museum. There a different sort of surprise awaited us.

I knew that Agatha Christie and her archaeologist husband had been (perhaps still were) working in Iraq, where Christie was reputed more or less to hold court in the desert. I assumed that their presence would ensure that the museum would be in good order, but that proved not to be the case as many of the objects supposed to be there were absent. Though I wondered whether they had been sold off to Latin-American millionaires, I was told that they had been removed from the "open shelves" for their own protection: which might well have been the case, since in that ill-monitored and dirty building it would have been quite easy to remove a few of the smaller pieces.

Failing at the Museum and having an hour or two to spare, we thought to go to a local cinema, as much to watch the viewers as to follow the film which was in Arabic with limited English subtitles. But it was a rewarding experience. Set in San Francisco, the plot recorded an attack on the city by a monster from the sea, a huge dinosaur-like creature of the height of some of the skyscrapers, whose intent was to kill the terrified population. As we soon realized, killing was what the audience had come for; they cheered and roared their delight every time the monster grabbed and ate a Yank, especially if the victim was caught trying to escape. At the time I put such enthusiasm down to the standard anti-Americanism recognizable if less extremely elsewhere. On later reflection I concluded that its real explanation was the support America had been giving to the incipient state of Israel. Most Iraqis wished Israel to be annihilated and the Jews massacred.

In sum, the world of Arab Islam as viewed in Baghdad seemed quite unlike the heroic Bedouin culture portrayed by Lawrence of Arabia and much loved by the "Camel Corps" in our own Foreign Office. It was more like the world of the Turkish Pasha who, when Lawrence was captured at Dera'a in Syria, beat and then sodomized him — that is, unless this event only occurred, as some suppose, in Lawrence's turgid imagination. Apologists for the local society — in camp and later — dismissed my criticism of aspects of the Islamic world more generally revealed by contemporary Baghdad, telling me: "Oh, most Arabs regard Iraq as the arsehole of the Arab world." I was not entirely convinced, though clearly this was hardly the society of Lawrence Durrell's Alexandria trilogy.

Enlightened at the cinema but far from sated with the local world, we taxied back to camp, and a few days later managed another trip, not this time to Baghdad but to ancient sites fairly close by: to Babylon, then Ctesiphon, capital of the region during the Parthian and Sassanid periods and hence more than once sacked by the Romans. The ruins, then attracting few visitors, were quite impressive, though I knew little of their history, and my companions even less. As for Babylon, it had rather little to show, though not as yet suffering from Saddam Hussein's mindless "reconstruction." But the name exerted a certain fascination on us all, though we were hardly aware of why it did, being largely unfamiliar with the Old Testament or the Apocalypse.

Such limited explorations whetted my appetite for more, but leave was limited and only one longish trip would be possible. After abandoning the idea of Ur of the Chaldees to the south, I settled on Mosul both as a possibly interesting city with a mixed Christian and Muslim population and as a base for further taxi trips: Nineveh, Assur, and possibly Hatra, some seventy miles away to the southwest across the desert in the direction of Syria.

So we booked three first-class tickets at what seemed a very reasonable price on the Baghdad–Mosul overnight train and woke up fighting fit, which might soon have seemed an appropriate metaphor. We knew little about Mosul and there were no books in the camp library which might have helped us find out more, but I at least was aware that it was indeed a mixed community: Shi'a and Sunni, Arab and Kurd, and Christians of various sorts. Indeed, the "various sorts" both from Mosul and elsewhere in the region had reached us at Habbaniyah in the guise of traveling salesmen and were called "Assyrians"; they were said to be mostly Monophysites or Nestorians, though as yet I knew little about what these denominations indicated theologically.

So we wandered about the town where most of the mosques were closed and the churches hard to find, ate rather well in one of the street cafés and decided to pass the evening at a well-advertised nightclub. Approaching its doors we found a large dustbin-like container into which we were invited, with a certain menace, to throw our weapons. We explained that we were unarmed and, being allowed to enter, noticed that the bin was already more than half full of knives, revolvers and a variety of sawn-off shot-guns. They were evidently taking no chances.

Comfortably enough seated, we found that the show had begun and was in a broken English, that being assumed to be the common language of the fair number of both Iraqis and visiting oilmen or other businessmen; these were mostly Germans with a few Americans. The entertainment seemed to be song and dance routines, the performers mostly — and especially the girls — European. The standard was low and the dancing largely suggestive, and after an hour or so the audience, or some of them, joined the performers on stage. We did not move, reflecting on the possibility of theft at least, grievous bodily harm at worst, although others were less easily deterred. Hence the most amusing part of the evening began, and having watched the barely clad girls dancing with the overweight businessmen for the next half hour until the show came to an end, and with no weapons to pick up as we left, we returned to our quiet and surprisingly clean hotel for another good meal and night's sleep.

Next day was on the road, first across the desert to Hatra (which lacked any formal road); that took over two hours. The city, a significant Parthian fortress in the early centuries of the Christian era, had withstood several Roman sieges and was eventually destroyed in the third century by the Sassanids. There had been a certain number of excavations — and more were to come — but most of the site had been covered up and as reward for our sunbaked trip — being now July, the temperature was about 110 in the shade — we found little above ground, though a photo I still possess records me sitting astride a stone lion parked outside the main gate to the ancient city.

So we soon turned back to try for Nineveh and Assur — in the so-called valley of the Christians — within the same day. The heat seemed to grow worse and our water supply began to run low, so when at last we reached Nineveh, the water being unreliable at best, we poured Pepsis down our throats in considerable quantities (I think that I drank thirteen — which at a distance may seem almost incredible) — but we had survived. We had heard Iraqi tales about people who gave misleading advice to desert travelers, their idea of a good joke being that they would die of thirst.

Neither Nineveh nor Assur had much to show above ground, but while walking around near the former we got into conversation with an irrigation expert surveying his handiwork in one of the fields. The system we have now put in place, he told us, means that irrigation here is as good as it was in the time of Hammurabi (1900 BC). We congratulated him and hoped he would improve on his predecessor, which elicited a weary smile. We returned to Mosul, to take the train next day back to Baghdad, thence taxi to Habbaniyah and we were back at our benches as though nothing had occurred. It was the last trip I was able to make at any distance from the camp.

I had hoped for more. Every month or so a convoy of trucks set out from Habbaniyah for Amman in Jordan and would wait there for about ten days. Custom was to ask volunteers to "ride shot-gun" on one of the trucks, then allow them to spend their time as they pleased until the convoy returned. I volunteered, but on the horizon a larger and more fateful war than local skirmishes with Iran loomed, for in July 1956 the Egyptian President Gamal Abdul Nasser nationalized the Suez Canal. Britain, France, and Israel thought he could not be allowed to get away with it, so the Iraqi frontiers were closed in anticipation of an upcoming Western invasion of Egypt; the convoys ceased to flow westward and so disappeared my possibility of visiting the Holy Land and Jerusalem, target of my willingness to volunteer. Nor did I realize that the coming war would show my time at Habbaniyah to have been during the last days of British power "east of Suez," or that I was living on this spot through the fag-end of the whole British Empire. Indeed the "culture" of Habbaniyah as I experienced it might seem an appropriate end to our imperial adventure.

Thus did time roll on toward my being demobbed; the phrase "chit peachy"—meaning release-slip soon—might at last have taken on meaning were it not for the closing of the frontiers. I was supposed to be demobbed on October 1, 1956, and for some reason this act could only take place in Gloucester. Of course, it would have been of little use (and unintelligible even in RAF terms) to be demobilized several thousand miles from where one would want to go back to civvy-street—and times had changed since the days of the end of the Second World War when, if you chose to be demobilized and paid off in the Far East, you could, by exchanging of currencies, reach Blighty richer than when you started. In any case I was in a bit of a hurry.

I and a few others were told that if we could get back to Gloucester under our own steam, we could be duly demobbed: try your hand. This I managed without much difficulty by "hitching" a plane to a transit camp at Akrotiri, the "new Habbaniyah," in Cyprus. From there in a day or two it was easy enough to board another plane to Britain, hence to Gloucester, where I could officially pass from active to reserve service. Many demob-ees would ceremonially burn their greatcoats on Gloucester station, but I did not pause for that ritual, being intent only on getting back via London to Leigh-on-Sea as quickly as possible. I was expected to "sign in" at Trinity College, Cambridge, in four days' time.

So it was tight, but that did not worry me. Unexpectedly and with the help of a little luck and cunning I had managed to enjoy and profit far more from my National Service than I could have expected. I am sure I was not missed; the senior military people by now had become weary of training recruits for a short time and then being unable to make much use of them, and wanted a more professional Armed Forces, while National Service was to end in 1959. What was more important for me, though I did not realize it at the time, was that I was now to matriculate at the venerable University of Cambridge, and at its academically most prestigious College, as a very different (even though the same) person from what I would have been had I signed in at eighteen. Thanks to "the mob" I had gained a little experience of life — that being (as Aristotle pointed out) a necessary prerequisite for trying to understand it.

CHAPTER 4

The Fenland Don Reserve in the Later Fifties

Much learning does not teach sense.
— Heraclitus

Education is the process of casting false pearls before real swine.
— Irwin Edman

We [women] thought we were the first of the free; we found we were the last of the frumps.
— Margaret Drabble

I had managed to check in at Trinity on time, and first was to find my rooms, which turned out to be in Whewell's Court, a Victorian structure named after a nineteenth-century philosophical master of the College and located on Trinity Street opposite the College's Main Gate. For the next two years I was now possessed of two rooms on the ground floor with a gyp room which could be used for any cooking — and, in the sitting room, a fire with a Perspex front which will soon figure in the story. The loos and bathrooms were underground and had to be reached by a walk (it would be a run in the cold of winter) to the next staircase. All fine and traditional if primitive, and it was pleasing to find my name painted at the bottom of the staircase outside my rooms. I soon found that I was allotted some of the time of a "bedder" who would indeed regularly make up the bed and clean the rooms when they became intolerable — also (this I realized not from personal experience) to report any undergraduate who appeared to have unduly "entertained" a woman in the bedroom. My bedder was fattish and genial; she told me that her family had worked for the College for generations, the men often as porters.

Our ceremony of matriculation followed shortly, we undergraduates wearing our dark suits and "Geneva" bands, topped off by the gown, Trinity's being uniquely short and blue, hence known as a "bum-freezer." It was still the 1950s, and gowns were compulsory not only for ceremonies but for meals—all taken in the majestic College Hall, presided over by Holbein's portrait of the founder (or actually re-founder) and substantial benefactor, King Henry VIII—as also for all lectures and supervisions as well as passage into town beyond the College gates. Thus "gown" was clearly demarcated from "town." Such rules were enforced by "proctors" who roamed the town at night to make sure that behavior was acceptable, that bicycles were marked to indicate College, and that the ten-o'clock curfew was maintained. At that magic hour College gates were closed and those outside, if hopeful of avoiding penalty by entering in the morning, must resort to climbing in: an option easier in some colleges than in others. Terms lasted for eight weeks, of which every night had to be "kept," no more than two exceptions being allowed. I never asked for an exception.

I had no objection to any of these rules; indeed looked on them, in words recorded from a visiting American girl, as "cute and feudal." What I regarded as less "cute"—as did most male undergraduates—was the statute then allowing one woman to study at the University for every ten men. Even that had not long before been regarded by many as an unwarranted concession, and I was soon to learn that until the end of the Second World War the women who did "come up" to the two women's colleges, Newnham and Girton (the latter safely located a couple of miles out of town) were not permitted to "proceed" to a Cambridge degree, having to content themselves with one courtesy of Trinity College, Dublin. Quite recently, in 1954, a third college for women, New Hall, had opened its doors, though only with a handful of students, in premises on Silver Street previously occupied by Darwin, whose aging niece, Gwen Raverat, could still be seen, paint-brush in hand, looking across the Mill Pond to Mill Lane Bridge and Coe Fen.

There was a pomposity and complacency about Trinity College, which happily was punctured at times, as on my second day in residence when someone managed to climb on to the roof of the Dining Hall overlooking Great Court, the largest such court in all "Oxbridge" (though this term was hardly used in the 1950s) and paint thereon the word CAFE (presumably to be pronounced "caif"). This complacency was in many ways academically well-deserved, but had an odd effect on people like me who had come to Trinity's hallowed halls as the first representatives of their school. I would soon discover that many of my fellows in the College knew one another before they came up, having been to the same higher-ranking public school; several of them seemed to know some of the dons too, thus immediately being (if smart) admitted to an inner circle.

Being outside this circle did not bother me, but it meant that I made few friends in the College itself apart from my fellow Classicists, of whom about a dozen were admitted each year. Looking back on it I realize that most of my closer friends (though not the closest) came from other colleges and became known to me through various clubs which Trinity students generally did not frequent: above all the Rambling Club and the Round, the latter a group engaging weekly in English Country Dancing which I found appealing and entertaining, and where I was introduced to some beautiful traditional music, whether in more formal mode as compiled by John Playford, dance-master to Charles II, or in more populist versions saved from oblivion by Cecil Sharp.

That was for later; first was a return to Latin and Greek of which I had read nothing over the past two years. Our supervisor for the year, Alan Ker, immediately issued a reading list which looked formidable: one substantial Greek and similarly substantial Latin text every week in term time: we started (cold!) with Aeschylus's *Agamemnon* and the first book of Lucretius's *De Rerum Natura*. Another instructor went through the list of lectures organized by the University, and dismissed most of it as not worth bothering with: "He doesn't know much about this"; "He will bore you stiff"; "This one might be worth trying." The principle on which he worked was a largely good one; namely that you can read in five minutes what you can listen to in fifty, which fifty might be wastefully spent. The University intake countrywide then being small — about five percent of the youth each year — no one wanted (or expected) to be spoon-fed, and of this some of the dons at Cambridge took advantage, knowing that most of their pupils could get a reasonable degree however badly they were taught. Had C.P. Snow's *The Masters* been written by then, I would have recognized the Classics Fellow who pronounces that "there is no reason why the arrival of the young gentlemen should in any way impair the pleasures of our society."

I tested the lecture list out and quickly realized that our instructor's evaluation of much that was on offer was correct: good themes were reduced to trivia; on literary texts most lecturers seemed to have no interest in the quality of the material, only in the state of the received text and the possible sources of the author's work. I constantly discovered that well known poets would disappear into their sources if I stayed long enough to come to that conclusion. Of those lecturing during my first two years, that is, for Part One of the Classical Tripos, only two seemed to know how to lecture: the Professor of Greek, Denys Page, and Moses Finlay, a communist refugee who found Cambridge a pleasing port in a storm, having been driven from Columbia University by partisans of Senator Joe McCarthy. As for the rest, I began to think of them as mere collectors of sources—just as (I would claim) a collector of matchbox tops might be interested in which country each box came from. I appreciated the (perhaps apocryphal) story that one eminent Latinist, having finished a course on Horace's Odes without evaluative comment, concluded—by now to the astonishment of his hearers—that "This poem [the Bandusia Ode] is, gentlemen [ignoring any ladies present], the finest poem in the Latin language." There was heard almost a breathless gasp, and another when this rare judgment ended with: "Macaulay."

In my case it hardly mattered whether I attended any lectures or not (and the same could have been said of most of our "supervisions"). The bulk of the course on which we would be examined was translation from and into Greek and Latin, and I could do that comparatively easily once I got back to it. There were no set books in Part One and only two or three essay papers, which could be easily disposed of by chutzpah. The translations from Greek and Latin were put together in papers requiring that we translate five "unseen" passages in three hours, some of them being quite difficult. It was known that Pindar would regularly appear on the Greek verse paper, so the man who lectured on this particular poet could expect a sizeable audience, though after a first trial I took the risk of avoiding him. The most striking lecture series, however, was surely that offered by an ancient historian who read from a prepared script about Aristotle's *Constitution of Athens*, apparently without noticing in the front row a student following the reading almost word for word from his father's record of the same performance some decades earlier.

The advantage of the vagueness of the material to be examined in the essay papers, where plenty of choice was always offered, was in enabling me to read whatever I wanted across the whole range of Classical literature—I tended to concentrate on comedy and satire—without needing to worry that I might be confronted with a set of essay topics on all of which I was ignorant. The loose format of the syllabus, therefore, suited me admirably, but only because I had been taught so well to read Greek and Latin at Sir Anthony Browne's. Had I reflected on the matter, I would have realized that the system in its present form could not survive much longer.

Nor did I realize that the structure of Part One represented the last stand of the losing side in a cultural battle among Classicists, nor that beneath this obvious battle lay a second more fundamental one. The losing party were those generally older Classicists whose dream was to nurture another generation of Renaissance humanists or eighteenth-century gentlemen (perhaps destined for the Foreign or Colonial Office) who could read (and quote) Classical authors of the "Golden Age" with ease, and themselves produce stylish copy of such authors: "humanism" indeed meant such ability. The winning side were those who followed Gilbert Murray, an earlier Regius Professor of Greek at Oxford, and a number of his Cambridge supporters and friends, not least Newnham's formidable Jane Harrison, in viewing a Classical education as concerned with Greece, not just Greek and with Rome rather than just Classical Latin.

In the nineteenth century it had been possible to get a degree by completing only the language-based Part One of the Tripos, and many did, but by my time there had been established not only what was supposed to be the wider cultural approach in Part Two but a minimum of the same, represented by a general essay paper, in Part One. Before too long all this would be swept away, and Greek and Latin culture (of which of course the languages were an important part) come to dominate the Tripos. Inevitably, that meant that by the time of writing many people who teach Classics at British Universities know far less Latin and Greek than did my schoolmasters, not to speak of most of my Cambridge instructors.

In Trinity the older way was still strong: thus for us, though by no means for Classicists in other colleges, verse composition was regarded as necessary, although the University no longer required it. The ghost of A. E. Housman, perhaps the greatest Latinist of the twentieth century—ferocious scourge of linguistically inadequate colleagues and distinguished poet more or less on the side—haunted the College, still represented in fleshly form by his devotee and one-time star pupil, A. S. F. Gow. Gow had been a Classics Master at Eton before returning to Trinity, where he wrote a memoir of Housman in which one reads that at the first of the master's lectures a crowd of "tourists" appeared but at the next only Gow himself and one or two other serious students.

The spirit of Gow (as well as of his master) not only seemed to haunt the next generation—that is, those who were my immediate teachers—but was made more substantial by tales of Gow himself: as that when his magisterial edition and commentary on Theocritus appeared, he had been greeted on the street by a colleague with: "Ah, Gow, I see your Theocritus is out," to receive an abrupt, "What's wrong with it?." Famously Gow, by now of advanced age, never attended meetings of the College Council—breaking this rule once a year to cast a solitary vote against the College May Ball which, being held in Neville's Court, must disturb him in pursuing the duties of a College Fellow.

Not all Trinity Fellows were so dutiful. One of the figures who graced our days in what we referred to as the FDR—the Fenland Don Reserve—was the Reverend Simpson, once regarded as the upcoming star of modern history, whose first volume of an intended three-volume account of the life of Louis Napoleon had secured him a Life Fellowship, but was savaged by reviewers—a fate by no means suffered only by bad books. Simpson, indignant that his genius was thus challenged, decided to abandon the project. Indeed, he abandoned every project, though retaining the Fellowship from which he could not be removed. In my time he could be seen of a summer morning clipping the hedges on a path running alongside the University Library. I do not know when he died, but by that time Trinity had decided that Life Fellowships on terms such as his were not in the College's interest.

Underlying the strange and soon to be altered Classical Tripos, disputes about the nature of a true humanism were not the only "hidden agenda," and a second, more fundamental one was visible to the perceptive undergraduate: namely that humanism, however understood, was to be the requisite religion-substitute. In the spirit of a Matthew Arnold more consciously followed in other departments, Christianity with its baggage of superstition and credulousness must surely be replaced. Few at that time—most being too conventional—would express such sentiments openly, nor was Christianity in England as yet in obvious free fall, but anti-Christianity was latent, even if semi-unconscious, in most Classical dons.

Yet convention—and even Anglican belief—was still strong enough among the undergraduates to ensure a small but continuing presence of worshippers in the College Chapel, most of these being from the North of England, members of the Cambridge Intercollegiate Christian Union (CICCU); this purveyed a variety of Anglican belief that was low Church, but in my view no better for that. The vicar of Great Saint Mary's, the University church, namely "Great Saint" Mervyn Stockwood, was their most visible standard-bearer in the world beyond the College, while within the College we could boast among the clergy a stylish former boy-friend of Princess Margaret. That left me cold; I knew how unpopular that princess had made herself in the Armed Forces.

◦∞∗∞◦

Apart from study at Trinity and more generally, there were Girls, an obvious interest I had hardly known up to this date. But the options within the University might seem discouraging, and many wealthier and posher members of Trinity—often, it seemed, named Jeremy—preferred to look outside, bringing at weekends from London girls who usually seemed to be called Susan, and though the word "air-head" was not yet common currency, it might have summed many of them up. Inevitably they evoked lewd stories. As of the two air-heads trying to buy knickers, one of whom was worried about which was the back and which the front. "Look," says the other, "It tells you here," pointing to a label reading "C. and A." (the name of a now long defunct London department store but taken as referring to "cunt" and "arse").

Or of the two debutantes, one of whom tells her friend that she is soon to be married. "Oh, my dear," says the friend, "Who is the lucky man?" Comes the reply, "He's in the King's Africa Rifles," to be followed by, "Oh darling, are you going to marry a *black* man?" "No, no, darling. In the King's Africa Rifles the officers are white; only their privates are black." To close with, "Oh, Susan, how madly contemporary!" Hearing such tales, my growing opinion that sexual activities, though an important part of life, are also often comic and liable to bring the "high and mighty" down to earth—hence being subject-matter of many of the more amusing jokes—was confirmed: as an "airman" it had occurred to me that it would be odd to be in bed with the Queen!

As I have already observed, at the University itself there were only two substantial women's colleges and if one had no previous acquaintance, the only chance of meeting any of their inmates was either at University societies or at the lectures which I had largely ceased to attend. Somehow, nevertheless, I got talking to a girl from Girton College who was certainly not an air-head but rather an ultra-rationalist (which at least meant she was not religious), and had, as I found in due course, a life-size portrait of Bertrand Russell on the wall of her room. But like most rationalists (at least the ones I have met over the decades) she turned out to be dull, earnest, and boring—though I never found out if she justified a current piece of undergraduate advice, "Never go out with a girl who wears a vest."

In any case our acquaintance did not last long. We went to a couple of interesting and well-acted Greek films at the Arts—I particularly remember *A Girl in Black*. We also tried *The Seventh Seal* after which I preferred to avoid the transgressive neo-pagan *angst* of Bergman. Then, without risking the Rex—"Sex at the Rex"—which tended to offer a popular soft porn, usually starring (better, exposing) Brigitte Bardot—the vested one decided that I might be a distraction. I was a bit annoyed at this for a day or two, but then began to wonder why I had ever wanted to take her out in the first place. After that I lost track of her only to learn years later that she had got a good degree and married a doctor. I was inclined to feel sorry for him.

If erotic interest was so far non-existent, intellectual companionship certainly was not. Most of the Classicists (and some of the other Trinity-types) were highly intelligent and some must be counted among the smartest people I have ever met—smart, if not always wise. One of them was Henry Blumenthal, son of a Jewish family who had escaped in 1937 from Leipzig, where his father's five brothers remained too long and hence died in Auschwitz. We met on leaving yet another of the monstrously dull lectures to which we were "exposed"—this one on Ovid—and on which he too largely gave up.

Henry had been at Mill Hill, a "superior" school to Brentwood in snobbery terms, and had won a Major (as distinct from my Minor) Scholarship to the College. Like me he had "enjoyed" an interesting and maturing National Service, being bilingual in German and hence recruited to interview in Berlin people who had crossed over from the Soviet Zone and wished to make themselves acceptable to the Western military authorities. Only their ideas of how to win favor might come unstuck. Knowing nothing of the West except that it was anti-Communist, they would invent a Nazi (and so anti-Communist) past which they assumed would be acceptable, some even boasting of atrocities as (they alleged) members of SS death-squads.

Henry told wryly how, when he and the other interpreters were being trained for their work, an officer had warned them about this habit of making up a lurid Nazi past, and had remarked that "You people might well feel inclined to put the boot in" — only to add with a smile that it would be better not to do that as it would be a chargeable offence. An odd characteristic of Henry was that he never evinced any interest in things Jewish; he was to be an English gentleman, or so his kindly parents presumably hoped. He had one sister who caused anxiety as inclining to anorexia.

So Henry and I walked back to Trinity, starting a friendship which was to last until his untimely death. We were to travel together during our undergraduate years and even after. Now we retired to his rooms in Great Court (his entitlement as a Major Scholar) for coffee and a lengthy chat about the pretentiousness of many of the dons and their assumption that we were still more or less schoolboys. We were, as all undergraduates then, *in statu pupillari*, but interpreted this as being apprentices in academia rather than still kids. And I at least was coming to think of the dons as a self-satisfied group who knew a lot, regarded themselves as a justly privileged élite and, with few exceptions, wanted to be left alone to get on with their personal interests. These for many included research, though at that time Cambridge regarded itself as primarily an undergraduate institution, and comparatively rare were presuppositions, derived in part from Americanization, that graduate studies and research are what academia is really about and that undergraduates know too little to be spared the time of the more able dons.

Henry and I (with sometimes one or two others) developed the habit of leaning over Trinity Bridge before proceeding to Hall gowned for the evening meal. The food was notably inferior to that of the Armed Forces. The dons, of course, did a good deal better—unsurprisingly, given the wealth of a College which among its other assets would acquire a substantial stake in Felixstowe's container port. It was claimed that one could walk from Cambridge to London on Trinity land.

So life settled down into a recognizable pattern, enabling me to read extensively across ancient literature with virtually no "secondary" sources. Indeed, these were discouraged by supervisors, the advice at Trinity being to follow Housman (again) and think in terms of "*Ratio et res ipsa*": namely, look at the text and think about it—perfect advice for undergraduates in the humanities but now increasingly forgotten. To a self-imposed ban on secondary material in these first two years of the Tripos I allowed very few exceptions: one was Syme's *Roman Revolution*, which I had already read at school but found helpful well beyond Roman history; the second was Gilbert Murray's *Rise of the Greek Epic*, which made me think seriously about how people and cultures develop and change over time. The third and perhaps most influential, whether I agreed or came radically to disagree, was E.R. Dodds's *The Greeks and the Irrational*.

Although I hardly realized it at the time, Dodds's book has two possibly conflicting themes: the first to show how difficult it is to establish what he thinks of as a rationalist tradition in Greece— though I thought (and still think) that there was a marked tendency in his book to view "rational" in a post-Cartesian sense, with consequent viewing of Greek thought through an Early Modern or Enlightenment lens. The second theme is summed up by the author's comparison of the progress of Greek "rationalism" to a horse in a steeple-chase balking at the last fence: that is, the Classical world eventually lost its nerve and gave way to religious revival in Christian form. Dodds is not sure who fails, the rider or his horse, but as a progressive hopes it was the rider and that when he (or rather "we") next come to that fateful fence, we shall not falter a second time. As an undergraduate I was impressed by this, being "rationalist" enough to think Dodds on the right lines—it never crossing my mind then that the failure at the last fence might better be described as a running into a brick wall.

Apart from Henry, my other close friend in the College, and the first Roman Catholic I had ever really known, was to be Denis O'Brien. Denis had been a pupil at Cardinal Vaughan's School in London, which he too hated but where he was also well prepared in the Classical languages, so we shared something of a schoolboy past as well as the variety of National Service which followed, Denis also learning Russian and (allegedly) playing the prince in a Russian version of *Hamlet*: this he himself later denied. I cannot remember how I first got to know him but I was certainly interested when he invited me to the Catholic Chaplaincy and introduced me to the exotic figure of Monsignor Gilbey, scion of the gin-making company. Of half Spanish origin, Gilbey persistently refused at any price to sell the chaplaincy-building in the middle of Cambridge when developers were buying up and—with the connivance of a number of colleges—even vandalizing the area around him: hence the charming chaplaincy building stands to this day and has expanded into premises alongside.

Gilbey was famous beyond the Catholic community and a popular if puzzling figure within it: famed in particular for refusing to permit women undergraduates to use the services of Fisher House lest they distract the males and discourage possible vocations to the priesthood. Nevertheless, among those males—though most of them disagreed with this policy—he was popular and indirectly a great evangelizer. In his view the first priority of a chaplaincy should be the chapel and the second the bar; he had a great gift for hospitality and it was at the bar that Denis introduced me to him.

Denis was not only the first Catholic I came to know at all well but also one of the oddest, not only in that he had a real interest in the philosophical aspects of religion, and in philosophy in general, but in that he combined—and has continued to do so throughout his life—his devout Catholicism with an uncatholic attitude to morality. Later in life I would recognize this as a star example of a mental compartmentalization to which I shall return later in this autobiography. Thus Denis would maintain that morality was no business of the Church, which turned out to be convenient. It seems Monsignor Gilbey had expressed to him the hope that he might have a "vocation"; this Denis always denied. In our undergraduate days he was my principal intellectual sparring partner and one of such antagonists in our later professional lives. Anna, who met him through me, once described our intellectual clashes as between a blood-axe and a rapier, Denis, of course, being the rapier. But for a while my encounters with Catholicism were limited to the Chaplaincy bar. And soon a new but not unexpected distraction came to my attention

---

I had been in Cambridge less than a month when events in the Middle East brought back memories of an over-heated Iraq. On October 29, Israel struck at Nasser's forces in Sinai and two days later Britain and France joined in. This, when I left Habbaniyah, had widely been assumed would be the case—indeed disputes about which plans for dealing with Nasser should be adopted were well known there long before the invasion occurred. Nor did it surprise me, in view of the parlous state of Empire I had witnessed, that the Americans were quickly able to push the show off the road (i.e., put an end to the war), thus ending British power "East of Suez."

The whole episode taught me an important political lesson, enabled by my "Iraq experience." Reading accounts of the fighting in the press and hearing them on the radio—hearing also the uninformed discussions among the undergraduates—I was astonished at the ignorance that drove public judgments about the war, and even more at the lies emerging from the press as well as from all parts of the political spectrum. It was not to be the last time I was to realize that to understand political events it may be essential to be familiar with them at first-hand. Of course, a reporter with an agenda can pretend—with lies—to have seen things at first hand: in a later war I recall a *Guardian* reporter claiming that he had seen with his own eyes a group of Israeli soldiers beating up a Palestinian prisoner, though, as it turned out, he was fifty miles away at the time. In 1956 Cambridge it became difficult to talk about the war intelligibly because much that was true was rejected out of hand by those who had become victims of media manipulation. Undergraduates (and probably dons), thinking themselves smart, often seemed more gullible than the less privileged.

As it turned out, the immediate effect of the Suez fiasco was to enable the UK to get rid of Anthony Eden, while being too distracted to give the Hungarian revolt against Communism the attention it deserved. In Cambridge Hungarian refugees were welcomed, enabling us to pat ourselves on the back for political straight-dealing but contributing very little to the country from which the refugees had fled—in the case of more than one I know of clinging to the underside of a train. In more recent times the phrase "virtue-signaling" would have seemed appropriate.

One effect of the political education which Suez enabled me to acquire was that I lost interest in two political clubs which could have attracted me. I had, of course, already dismissed the Conservatives as blind to social justice and the Liberals as bland wafflers; this left the two left-wing societies, one being the Socialist Club which after attending just one meeting I abandoned, as seeming to be a bunch of champagne communists playing at supporting the working man but rather hoping to feed him with ideological slogans. The Labour Club seemed better: less crudely extreme yet essentially, like most student political clubs, only wanting to talk to themselves, or to promote themselves as future politicians, rather than to explore politics in any depth.

Many student politicians seemed to confuse University politics with real politics, which might lead to unfortunate results if ever they entered real politics. But the Labour Club did give me the opportunity to listen to one or two of the better politicians and ex-ministers, especially impressive being the ageing Emmanuel ("Manny") Shinwell. (He in fact was to last many more years, dying only after completing a century.) So in the end politics at Cambridge had become for me a private affair, none of my Classical friends being particularly interested. Until, that is, I joined the Rambling Club where, among other advantages, I could talk politics with some of the group without the need to discount too much posturing.

I cannot remember why I decided to try the Rambling Club. Perhaps, having heard the name and liking rambling not only among mountains, I just decided to see what it was like. It met every Sunday in term time (which guaranteed that few if any of its members went to a church, since after the ramble was over, we would spend the evening first in a restaurant, then in someone's room chatting and singing). The Club had existed for some years and included among past members a number of the well-known, perhaps the most noteworthy being the anti-Big Bang astronomer and cosmologist Fred Hoyle. Rambles began at 10:30 AM sharp on Mill Lane Bridge (MLB), on the parapet of which chalked words would inform late-comers where we had gone.

The first ramble of the term was by tradition to Eltisley, about sixteen miles away with an attractive tea-room — returning by a convenient bus. Lunch would, if possible, be in a pub, and the parts of the walk along roads were made the more pleasant by the shortage of petrol due to Suez, which meant that "farmers, parsons, and politicians" were the only regular car-drivers in the countryside. After the evening reunion all would be recorded — at times with a satirizing or scurrilous economy with the truth — in the Club's "Archives."

Nor were Rambling activities limited to term time; out of term I would join walks along Hadrian's Wall at a snowy Eastertide, as well as to the Lake District, the Torridon Hills in Scotland and the island of Skye with its formidable "Cuillin" ridge. We even managed to reach "the Twelve" beautiful if midge-infested Pins of Connemara in western Ireland: "It's a glorious day, the air's full of midges," as one of the locals put it. Another, greeting a friend emerging from Sunday Mass, introduced me to what I would later think of as "tribal Catholicism," when he enquired, "What did Father preach about today" — and learned that "He preached about the pope." "And what did he say about the pope?" "He said he was a good man." To celebrate such memories, we decided on a Club tie. I still possess mine: green with an embroiderd tortoise.

The Rambling Club was not only devoid of churchgoers but also of members from Trinity, certainly being regarded by some there as "prole" — though I did induce a fellow Classicist from the College, himself an Old Rugbeian, to try it out. Nor were there many "humanists" among its members; this helped its unpretentiousness, most "ramblers" being natural scientists, medics, or engineers, with a high proportion (though membership in any one year was never more than about twenty) being from the Midlands or the North of England. Of each twenty or so ramblers, roughly twelve would be men and eight girls (the phrase "young women" had not yet come into fashion), mostly from Newnham, though I remember an active couple from Homerton, the teachers training college (not yet formally part of the University). It was a new and pleasant experience to meet a group of new girls (and later some of their female friends) but I fell in love with none of them; the female medics seemed hard and I wondered what sort of doctors they would become. However, they generally did very well in Tripos.

After I had joined the Club, I became a regular member, along with Don Truman, one of the first undergraduates to be allowed to take Part Two of the Natural Sciences Tripos with specialization in biochemistry, also his friend and fellow pupil at Wyggeston Grammar School near Leicester, David Moulds—then a rather uninterested Classicist and later lawyer—and an engineer from Kings, Charles Frederick, who was embarking on what was to be a successful career but died comparatively young. A small graduate component appeared from time to time, again almost all scientists, but they seemed of a more boring scientific breed, though more interested in country-dancing at the Round than their successors. They included a pair of married couples.

Sundays apart, the first year passed pleasantly and uneventfully, while the summer term included on Sundays, as an occasional alternative to rambling, punting on the Upper River up to Grantchester. As the year drew to a close, some in Trinity looked forward to the coming May Ball (predictably with a "Susan") but this year I had no intention of going, indeed had no partner to go with. That did not bother me, since after some comparatively easy "prelims" (eleven three-hour papers in five and a half days) had been completed, indeed even before, Henry Blumenthal and I started to plan some summer travelling.

⸻

Greece might have seemed the obvious target, had not an opportunity provided by Franco's government decided us to put Greece off for a year, while we took up the Spanish offer of a kilometric ticket which, if purchased in the UK, would give us 5000 kilometers of railway travel for about ten pounds. Though neither of us was aware of the full horrors of the Spanish Civil War and its murderous sequel—battlefields apart, roughly 40,000 were executed by the Republicans and some 200,000 (according to later estimates) by the Nationalists—we were both eager to see something of a fascist state from the inside, even apart from its obvious artistic heritage, and were quite prepared to put up with the minor inconvenience that, our tickets being third class only and most of the railways being single-track—our trains would have to pull off on to a siding every time an express full of the more affluent members of the New Order needed to overtake us. This, as we came to realize, meant that a ten-hour journey might take fifteen, also long delays in a tunnel where after a while the oxygen seemed to be running out. But it was worth it, not least with hindsight, and we reckoned we might have enough time and money left to be able to cross over near Gibraltar and see a bit of Morocco.

So in late July we set out, and soon realized that the climate was very hot indeed: "*O, que calor,*" heard repeatedly, was one of our first bits of Spanish, and heard the more the further south we advanced. Our intended route was Barcelona, Valencia, Malaga, Algeciras (thence to Spanish Ceuta in Morocco), thence to Cordoba (for the mosque turned cathedral), followed by Granada, Seville, Merida, Madrid, Toledo (for the paintings by El Greco), Avila, Burgos, Salamanca, Segovia (for the Roman Aqueduct), Altamira (for the cave paintings), San Sebastian, thence Bilbao and home via France. Looking back it seems astonishing that we managed to complete this circuit.

One of our first meetings with Spanish Fascism was with the Civil Guard, or rather with one of its officials, the police chief in a small town north of Barcelona on the coast where we decided, having come down from France, to spend the night before proceeding next day to the big city. We were sitting on a bench overlooking the sea when we were approached by two young men who turned out to be Israelis. (We would suspect them later of being engaged in arms-smuggling.) One of them turned out to be the son of a man who had known Henry's father in Leipzig before the war.

That of course broke the ice and they asked us where we intended to spend the night, and when we said we had not thought about that yet, they offered to show us somewhere to go, and took us to what turned out to be the home of the local police chief who welcomed us cordially, and whose wife gave us a good supper—no moldering lettuce leaves swimming in cheap olive oil that we would come to recognize as part of the diet of the average Spaniard—then took us on a tour of the town, or rather of its bars.

After we had sampled various sorts of local cocktails at about half a dozen of these, Henry thought we ought to pay for the next drink and ordered some sort of banana-flavored liqueur, for which he was asked to pay far in excess of the price on a very visible list. When he challenged this, an argument ensued, Henry speaking a broken Spanish with an Italian flavor until the policeman realized what had happened and came over to the counter. "They are my friends, you understand," he informed the bartender. "Ah, I am very sorry; it's on the house" was the immediate response. It was a good introduction to Spain.

When we reached Madrid—having noted that every church in the country had an inscription somewhere on its walls in honor of Primo de Rivera, founder of the Falange—Henry's wallet was stolen, with little money inside but unfortunately containing his passport. Knowing that if we went to the British Embassy to get some sort of replacement we would need to have previously contacted the police, we made our way to the nearest police station where we were greeted in a friendly manner. We explained that the wallet had been stolen, indicating approximately where this had happened, and were told that though it was unlikely it would be recovered, if we came back in three days they would have retrieved the passport. This we were hardly prepared to believe, but we came back at the appointed time and the passport was indeed found. On our asking why the officer had been so sure that the document would be recovered, we were treated to a broad smile: "You must understand that we found the passport on the ground very close to where you told us you had lost it. Clearly the thief, realizing what it was, immediately threw it down and ran." "But why?" we asked. "Because being caught with a foreign passport is a capital offence in Spain," was the reply, accompanied by a further smile.

Although we soon realized that the Guardia Civil were everywhere in evidence, our most difficult experience with them was on a local train from Seville to Merida. To our surprise we were checked carefully before being allowed to board by two plain-clothed men who indicated from behind the lapels of their jackets that they were police and eventually let us board. There were almost no other passengers, and the train took about fifteen hours to complete its ten-hour journey. Our immediate companions were a group of about a dozen men chained together with armed guards in close attendance: we assumed them to be political prisoners but failed at the time to realize the possible implications. In later years I began to wonder whether they would not shortly have been shot; Franco's determination to eliminate his enemies had not abated, indeed continued until his death in 1975. During the Civil War some compared the Caudillo with a nineteenth-century General Narváez who, asked by his confessor on his deathbed whether he had forgiven his enemies, replied, "I do not have any enemies; I have had them all shot."

But we were leaving Seville with other Spanish memories. Ever since entering the country we had been made aware of the cult of bull-fighting, since every place we visited invited us to come to the bullring and watch the skilled and ritualized slaughter of "6 MAGNIFICOS TOROS 6": under which screaming headline we could read the name of the matador displaying his skills with beneath it the names of two others, apparently expected to perform at a lower level. We also noticed in hotels and on various public notice-boards, a reproduction of a famous fight (I bought a replica of the poster on a piece of rock which decades later got lost when we moved houses) in which the famous Manolete had died while hoping to celebrate the FESTA E FERIA DE SAN AGUSTIN by killing a couple of large black bulls. The ring was not the amphitheater in which he normally performed, but a dusty square in the little village where he had been born and where he slipped on the sand and was gored: arguably a great way to go in front of the home crowd!

As a break from antiquities, we had decided that Seville was the place to partake of the *Corrida*: Andalucía being one of the most distinguished venues for bull-fighting, the colossal ring at Seville should display the "sport" at its best. So after deciding that in the searing heat it would be worth buying tickets for *sombre* rather than *sol*, we took our seats to watch six bulls duly executed after being tormented and provoked by *picadors*, as is customary. But the audience, though at times cheering, eventually decided the performances were no better than average and the leading *matador* was awarded merely an ear. The others got nothing.

So we joined the crowd streaming past the exits toward a celebration of the killing in an open space in front of and inside a large bar. Clearly the base for the real *aficionados*, it was appropriately squalid: perhaps the Spanish equivalent of one of those British pubs whose character could then be identified by the words "Knock 'em down, drag 'em out." As we left, I muttered to Henry that "Bizet's *Carmen* it ain't"; even the local Carmens, though bearing floral bouquets, seemed otherwise down-at-heel.

> Toreador, oh, don't spit on the floor.
> Use the spittoon, that's what it's for...

This parody of Bizet might have caught the spirit of the gathering better.

We would discover that bullfighting, still upheld by many as the real Spain, was already being challenged, especially by the young. On several occasions while chugging along on some local train, Spanish students tried to explain to us in a competitive broken English that not bull-fighting but soccer was the Spain of the future — which left us uncertain as to what any more general future of the country might be, fascism seeming far better nailed down than it would before long to prove to be, and though I welcomed that change when it came — it had almost arrived by my next visit to the country in the early 1970s — it was to bring with it cultural variants of a less desirable sort, though similar to what was happening in other Roman Catholic countries; some of these changes I might have welcomed in 1957 but would come to regard as disastrous fifty years later when the arrogance of youth had subsided.

For in 1957 the problem in Spain seemed to be in no small part due to its Catholicism. I have already recorded the omnipresence on church walls of the cult of Primo de Rivera, but that was only a contemporary part of the story, and I was as yet unaware that time-serving had become a feature of varieties of clergy representing a Christianity already in decline in Europe. I had inherited, of course, a generally British mistrust of Spain with its "Inquisition" and auto-da-fés, being deceived by "Whig" historians to suppose that similar practices were not widespread elsewhere, including the "Merry England" of Elizabeth I. That said, Spanish Catholicism, as we met it, did seem downright gloomy and superstitious, its past glories best typified by the ghastly porphyry structures of the Escorial palace-monastery of King Philip II outside Madrid, which I recall as one of the more sinister buildings I have visited. By 1957, however, I had not learned that less than 10 percent of Spaniards attended Mass. Or that in the Civil War itself those who did attend might be blessed before the coming battle while going on to sing:

> Give me my blue beret,
> Give me my rifle.
> I am going to kill more reds
> Than flowers in April and May.

Nor that the rifle might be a present from Schicklgruber.

More than politically disturbing might seem such celebrations of Francoist Catholicism as the blazing bonfires and ghostly Corpus Christi procession we watched with some shivering in some small place I have now forgotten. Nor did I know then of the local entertainment in certain parts of the country of throwing goats off church towers. Though looking back I would no longer assume superstition to have been so entirely in charge, I suspect it played a too prominent part in religious proceedings. Of course, an alliance between Church and State was what Franco longed to revive, and in 1957 I had little idea of how many Spaniards still opposed it and why. The deprived anarchists, communists, and fellow travelers who hated the régime had little idea (apart from atrocities of their own) of what they would replace it with. But that was (and is) part of a wider Western problem as to what is the best form of democracy and whether it should be mere egalitarianism with atheist, if "liberal" — ambiguous word — underpinnings.

After Andalucía we did not stay long in Morocco, barely scratching its surface after crossing over to Ceuta — still in Spanish hands — where a business associate of Henry's father looked after us and took us out in the evening to join the local *passeggiata*, of segregated lines of young men and young women walking back and forth along the main drag without contact unless an occasional "nod and wink": fertility ritual of a soon-to-pass culture with, again, no equivalent replacement in sight.

Thus after five weeks of Fascists, El Greco, Velasquez, Goya in the Prado, Morisco culture in Granada and Cordoba, Roman remains in Merida and Segovia, single-track railways and poor food, we crossed back into France, some of our prejudices apparently confirmed but a certain knowledge added. Indeed with hindsight it seems I had learned quite a lot but understood little: was not that, I was coming to think, all that was required of a mid-century apprentice in the Fenland Don Reserve?

So back to another year at Trinity with much the same routine, except that this year I attended even fewer lectures and wrote even fewer essays and verse compositions. But I continued to talk, to read Latin and Greek and occasionally to attend lectures in other departments: I particularly enjoyed hearing F.R. Leavis destroy one of Elizabeth Barrett Browning's *Sonnets from the Portuguese* — it turning out to be inane if not unintelligible — and David Daiches starting with Jane Austen ("the immortal Jane"), then after a student objection, realizing he was supposed to be discussing James Joyce's *Dubliners*, continuing, apparently off-the-top-of-his-head, with a detailed and fascinating account of "Ivy Day in the Committee Room."

On another memorable occasion the Trinity Classics Club was addressed by Denys Page, then Regius Professor of Greek and a Fellow of the College. Page was a distinguished editor of Greek texts, but this time he "entertained" us with stories of his immediate post-war military assignment to investigate the activities of various German academics, among them Classicists, during the Thousand Year Reich. I already knew that some of them had been highly sympathetic to the New Order, and not least to its antisemitic aspects, but was still impressed by the detailed realism of Page's account. I had always thought of him as a "hard man," as I am sure he was, so I was taken aback when after retailing a number of his discoveries he admitted that he had had nightmares about them for the next ten years. The spirit of Schicklgruber was still, it appeared, operating, and I was far from the only one affected by it, albeit in my case in a rather limited way. Blumenthal, who was in the audience, had of course suffered — and was to suffer — more.

A further very different but still memorable incident that year involved my room's heating system. One night, I think in February, I woke at about 2:30 AM feeling that the room was preternaturally warm, so got up, opened the door into the sitting room and found the carpet was on fire: it seemed that the Perspex fire-screen had melted and a spark had started the blaze. So far little damage had been done and a couple of buckets of water quickly dowsed the flames. So after confirming that there was no further damage I went back to bed and to sleep, intending to report the matter in the morning.

The porter to whom I spoke seemed unsurprised, merely asking, "Is the fire now quite out, sir?," and when I assured him that it was, he said he would look into it and have the heating restored. That he did within a day or two, and later told me that they often had trouble with the chimneys, not least because they had a large ledge in them on which things could be stored and forgotten. The last time they had them cleaned, he added, they found some twenty University Library books; luckily it was summer and the fire had not been lit for some time.

Part One of the Tripos awaited us in May, but we did not bother much about it, and in that Easter break I completed the walk along a snowy Hadrian's Wall with some of the Rambling Club, being lucky enough to come across the Black Bull, a pub which every year on Good Friday dispensed a splendid mulled ale for free. And that year the Rambling Club continued to fill up my Sundays, most of its membership remaining stable but with one curious addition: Jill Tyrer—or as for some reason she often seemed to be named, "Miss Tyrer." Jill was the daughter of a prominent judge who lived near Cambridge. She maintained that he was a collector and avid reader of books on torture, adding that this interest carried over into his professional life in the form of a regret for the floggings which in the "good old days" had been inflicted on violent young men in Romford and elsewhere and on disobedient sailors.

Jill had been sent, as was to be expected, to the Perse Girls School for which she evinced considerable dislike: not so much of the teaching staff, despite the predictable snobbery, but for the girls and their flirtatious mannerisms. She told me that she had developed the habit, when one of the girls would boast of how many boys had had their hands inside her blouse at a school dance, of asking—infuriatingly as it usually turned out—which one she had gone to bed with.

Jill did not apply to go to University but took a job at the University Library where, being sprightly and comparatively good looking, she attracted much unwanted attention, usually from middle-aged men. Apparently she was regularly asked to be kind enough to get a book down from a high shelf, giving the man holding the ladder a chance to look up her skirt. Though I was never in love with her (we never kissed, let alone, as some insinuated, had an affair), I found her company refreshing and utterly unpretentious, though her contempt for convention was even by my standards excessive.

Such attitudes put her at the center of a number of urban myths, some of which might well have been more substantial. There was a story that being caught out by an intense thunderstorm in the Peak District National Park with a group of ramblers (none in our own club) she avoided getting soaked by simply taking off her clothes (other presumably than her boots), stuffing them into her rucksack and putting them on dry when the storm had passed. An incident which I did witness suggests that this was quite possibly a reality.

Sometimes in the winter, if the weather was particularly bad, Jill preferred not to cycle home after the ramble and then return later in the evening: hence two or three times she asked me if she could come back to my room to clean up. I had no objection to this and on one such occasion, neither the first nor the last, I left her in my room while I walked across the court to return a book to a friend. When I returned five minutes later—perhaps she had thought I would be away longer—I found her naked to the waist and rinsing herself down at my wash-basin. She turned as I entered, said "Hi" in a slightly nervous voice, perhaps fearing that I might try to take advantage of her nudity, and resumed her ablutions. I said "Hi" and sat down at my desk to look at a book about Bronze Age Greek Art which I was reading in connection with some essay shortly due. The first page I opened contained a picture from a fresco in Heraklion of bare-breasted Cretan maidens considerably better endowed than was Jill.

Jill having restored her bra and blouse, we set off for the Kismet, an Indian restaurant on Northampton Street—one of the first in Cambridge—where we were to meet friends for supper. On the way she said she hoped she had not embarrassed me and I replied that she hadn't, which seemed to satisfy her and the matter was dropped. But it might tend to explain why she was not particularly popular among the girls in the Rambling Club and was regarded as predatory by some of the males. But I always liked curiosities, and she was certainly that, nor in my view was she a predator.

In the summer term that year some of us in the Club decided that since punting on the Upper River—technically here the Granta—was expensive, it would be a good idea to buy a punt ourselves, which we did. It was named Captain Fred, was more or less seaworthy and parked by Charles Frederick on King's

Backs, to be launched and pulled over the rollers at Mill Lane when required.

Part One passed without much incident and was preceded and followed by a number of parties in crowded rooms where the "Cambridge Two-Step" was the only dance possible and some — but again not me — waited for the May Balls. By now I had other more pressing concerns. Near the beginning of the term Denis O'Brien and I had decided, for reasons which I cannot now remember, to translate — or rather to produce a modern version of — Aristophanes' comedy *Thesmophoriazusae* — *Women at the Thesmophoria* — a satire on Euripides as a supposedly crude misogynist on whom the women of Athens want revenge.

Bowing to a more recent fashion we called our version *Angry Young Women*, which meant we needed a group of girls to form the chorus if the play was to be staged the following year, we hoped during May Week. And through various connections Denis managed to round up enough for auditions which would take place early in the next academic year. Among those who appeared was Anna Vogler (though she called herself Anne at the time, concerned that Anna Vogler might sound too German), who had agreed to a friend's request that she audition on condition that the friend buy a collection of inevitably lousy poems which Anna had undertaken to sell for some visitors from the new University of Keele.

I liked the look of Miss Vogler the moment I saw her, and she was obliging enough to come out with me to a couple of films when she had finished her finals. She was one year ahead of me and now in English, having elected to escape the dullness of Classics Part Two's literary offerings. I felt undisturbed that she was ending her term with a second May Ball; assuming that she had accepted some fellow's invitation before finding him yesterday's man, and before leaving Cambridge, being soon to embark on more travels, I wished her all success with the Tripos results. We exchanged a few letters from our respective homes and I told her I would pick up mail at the Poste Restante in Athens, where I soon intended to be. By then I would know about my Part One results.

⟨∞∗∞⟩

Henry and I had already worked out our forthcoming trip in detail; this time we were to be accompanied by two other Classicists, at least to begin with. Again it was an ambitious itinerary and included parts of Turkey and Yugoslavia as well as much of Greece—and not least an intended ascent of Mount Olympus, on the pretext of looking for Zeus. A visit to Holy Mount Athos required permissions to be obtained in advance, which involved asking Trinity's Senior Tutor, John Morrison (an expert on Greek naval affairs; his work in this area would culminate in the building and launching into Aegean waters of a "Greek" trireme) to write something we hoped would secure the required documents. He duly obliged, informing "whomever it might concern" that we had a "profound interest in the later manifestations of Greek culture." This was not entirely untrue, since we were thus hoping to take the unusual step of a "pilgrimage" to the heart of Greek (and wider) Orthodoxy.

Greece was at that time to be approached by train to Brindisi—still a squalid port in the south of Italy—then by ferry, usually overnight, across the Adriatic and through the Corinth Canal to Piraeus, the port of Athens, which route we took and within a minute of disembarking I met my first "modern Greek," who had a question for me: "Wanna meet my sister, very nice, very clean?" Not wanting in the least to meet his "sister," however clean, we bussed into Athens, found some cheap accommodation near the center and, among the very limited number of visitors, mostly students from Germany, followed the usual tourist route: Acropolis with Parthenon, Theater of Dionysus, Pnyx, building works of Herodes Atticus, the National Museum—still rather ill-kept but full of wonders—and Evzones marching before the then still royal palace. Just before we left, came the hoped-for letter from Anna: she had got a First and Newnham was willing to pay for her to continue as a graduate student; she would be in Cambridge next year and, I felt, the omens were good. My companions were rather surprised at my enthusiastic reaction to her message.

After a few days, and having added the Byzantine church at Daphni to our tally, we set off northward for Delphi, by one of the local buses which formed almost the only means of travel in the more rural parts of Greece. These tended to run twice a day: early in the morning, between four and five, and in the afternoon much less conveniently after the more or less obligatory siesta. Delphi was even less visited than Athens and there were no other guests at the hostelry where we arrived and after some preliminary viewing of the Tholos picked out edible delights from what was cooking in the kitchen: I came to like particularly the stuffed peppers and the moussaka, but was careful about the inevitable water-melons (*karpouzi*) which tended to provoke "looseness." (So did the often-ill-washed salads.)

Delphi, nestling under Parnassus—which we had no time to climb nor any obvious means of protection against the wild dogs which lurked on its slopes—lived up to all expectations and these had to be symbolized: as one of us proposed when in the early hours of the next morning and clad only in his shoes, he raced around the stadium, completing the circuit to earn our applause. He commented that he would not have envied Greek runners doing it without sandals in the warmer parts of the day. Somewhat later we sadly moved on. I have been to Delphi only once since then and would now be afraid to return lest I be unable to see the site for coaches disgorging their human contents to be herded around the wonders—only to forget where they were minutes after being bussed away.

So down to Itea, crossing the water to Patras and on to Olympia which—apart from its glorious bougainvillea to which we woke in the morning—proved rather disappointing, except to the more archeologically-minded. One of those was in our company, and, like many another archaeologist, seemed (as we liked to put it) to find more interest in Phidias's chisel than in his statues. Next stop was the then rather remote but attractive little mid-Peloponnesian town of Andritsaina, starting point for a walk a mile or so up a dirt road under construction (mostly by females; the males were presumably occupied at sipping ouzo in the bar) to the even more remote, indeed entirely isolated temple at Bassai.

After walking past the road-workers, we were lucky at Bassai, not only in that there were again no other visitors but because the temple was soon to be shrouded in plastic coverings for years, if not decades, while "restoration-work" got slowly underway. We munched our sandwiches on site and drank too much of our water, then decided not to return to Andritsaina but to walk across the hills to the coast, where we could pick up a train going toward Pylos. We had no compass and knew that the local maps were useless, but also in which direction to walk and that our target should be the village of Phigaleia. We estimated it would take between two and three hours to reach it.

But when a couple of hours had past and we seemed to be getting nowhere, we thought we had better enquire of the next shepherd we met, who indicated that Phigaleia was about half an hour away and pointed us to the relevant path. As we followed it, seemingly coming no nearer to the coast, we were puzzled — until we reached Phigaleia, however, when the puzzle was solved: there were two Phigaleias, Upper and Lower, the latter being more than three hours away, and though down a road of sorts, not to be reached that evening.

Not that that needed to worry us, nor did it worry the locals who seemed delighted to greet us and told us in a mixture of Greek and broken English that we were the first strangers they had seen in the last year, apart from an Austrian student who had passed that way about nine months earlier. We were welcomed into local homes, offered comfortable if sparse accommodation, were able to buy a good local supper and then join the celebrations for our arrival for which, it might have seemed, all the villagers turned out. Perhaps surprisingly, the celebrations did not center on an old man (such we had seen elsewhere) returned from making money in Detroit or Cleveland and now holding court in the village where he had been born and where he planned to die. That said, ouzo flowed freely and we found ourselves invited to toast Greek-English friendship, albeit in the dubious form of Archbishop Makarios of Nicosia in Cyprus, responsible for the deaths of British soldiers on his island.

Indeed we knew that the Greeks had foolishly rejected a proposed new status for Cyprus as a separate country and had sent troops and a General Grivas to form the Ethniki Organosis Kyprion Agoniston (EOKA), meaning National Organization of Cypriot Fighters, an organization dedicated to uniting it with mainland Greece. It was a piece of typically nationalist idiocy (reminding us of what had happened to the Greeks of Asia Minor after the First World War) which was to leave Cyprus neither as part of Greece, nor a separate unified state, but partitioned between its Greek and Turkish communities, now guaranteed to become even more hostile to one another than they already were. But in the flowing ouzo none of this seemed to matter and only very late at night did the party break up to allow us to fall into what seemed by now a well-earned sleep.

Next day we reached Lower Phigaleia easily enough and after a bit more walking found a station and a train going south. I cannot remember where we got off, but Henry and I (I cannot remember now where the others went) were obliged to continue our journey by another local bus that proved the only way to reach Pylos, where Nestor's palace was still largely to be uncovered. It was a beautiful evening with the sun sinking dramatically over the island of Sphacteria to westward, so suggestive of the battle there in 425 BC when the Athenians dramatically humbled the Spartans.

Two blond German students on seats on the other side of the bus were, like us, watching the gleaming skyline and, unlike us, talking volubly and excitedly. I could not understand them, but Henry could, so trying not to attract German attention I asked him what they were almost shouting. "Well, the gist of it," he replied, "is, 'Look at that; isn't it wonderful. Just think. If it hadn't been for a few mistakes it would have all been ours.'" The bus rumbled into Pylos, under an easy apprehension of Schicklgruber's unquiet ghost, and we wondered, "De-Nazification, what de-Nazification?"

Time for moving on again, and we soon found ourselves on the other side of the Peloponnese, and nearing better known Mycenaean sites. Tiryns was rather disappointing, but Mycenae with its Lion Gate was far from disappointing in the setting sun and its *Belle Hélène*: the hostelry beloved among archaeologists until a few years later when the family would be caught smuggling antiquities. Anna had been there with three other girls the year before; one of them had inscribed in the Visitors' book:

> I eat my peas with honey;
> I've done it all my life.
> It makes the peas taste funny
> but it keeps them on the knife.

So on to Nafplio and Epidavros—where at the last minute we managed to get tickets for the *Iphigeneia in Tauris*: in modern Greek and not very well acted, yet fascinatingly revealing of its original setting. And so via Corinth and Acrocorinth—the former notably run-down—back to Athens and nearby Marathon, where—realizing too late that in planning journeyings supposed to be scholarly rather than a search for sun and sea, we had neglected to bring swimming costumes—nudity was the only option for a swim on an empty and stony beach: Odysseus-style but (as someone noted) meeting no Nausicaa.

Thus bathed, we were ready to launch more purposefully onto the "wine dark" sea with Mykonos as the first stop, and knowing that from Mykonos it is possible, tides and winds permitting, to reach the uninhabited island of Delos, sacred to Apollo, center of Hellenistic slave-trading and with temples still in recognizable shape. Our ferry from Athens — in more seaworthy condition than others we were to come across — arrived in the evening, and we were greeted by the white windmills and white-painted houses of a small town then becoming popular though not yet the "gay" capital of the Mediterranean. I remember eating particularly well there and after waiting a day for the tide we contrived to reach lonely Delos.

Thence to Rhodes — this time by a more dilapidated ferry — where we visited the old town and a neighboring ancient settlement at Lindos. And Rhodes had other visitors, the American Sixth Fleet being in town, and its beaches, consequently, covered with empty beer cans so that it was almost impossible to see the sand. Still, it seemed worthwhile to watch the "animals" at play, so we entered the Crystal Bar where a neon sign read: "Welcome to the Sixth Fleet."

The "Crystal" being packed with more or less drunken sailors, we had to fight our way through to order Phix beers ("Fix does you good" was in Greek on an ashtray which I purloined). Our Phix arriving, we were asked for a sum at least three times the proper (and listed) price. Remembering our earlier Spanish incident — though now lacking the assistance of a local police chief — Henry was more direct, telling the bartender that if he did not let us have the beer at the proper price he would inform the sailors how grossly they were being over-charged. Not willing to risk the Crystal being trashed, the bartender reduced the price to below the normal level. That said, his bar did not escape unscathed: next morning, as we walked past, fragments of its shattered windows littered the street.

The next ferry took us to Crete — just barely, since apparently it was kept stable only by lengthy metal bars tied down on the higher side of the deck. Nevertheless, it reached Agios Nikolaos, then a tiny unspoiled village on the eastern end of the island, now a sun-sea-and-sex Mecca. After a pleasant night there we bussed on to Heraklion for its museum and startling frescos of divers and bull-jumpers, then to the adjacent site of Knossos, known at the time to Classicists as "Evansville," after the British excavator who dug it up and tried to reconstruct it. Those were the heroic days of archaeology before its more "scientific" reorganization, but its results were sufficient to delight us and urge us on southward to a second Minoan site, at Phaistos on the opposite coast, pausing en route at the beautiful and then isolated monastery of Hagia Triada.

Thence we were somehow ferried to nowhere in Greece but to the once-Greek port of Izmir (ancient Smyrna). Wandering along its waterfront on a star-lit evening we tried to catch our breath after the hectic last days but aware that we were far from finished with Greece and would return after dipping into goodies of her ancient Muslim nemesis. In fact, Turkey's archaeological goodies are substantially Greek too, at least in this part of the country, but the food was substantially better — much Greek food (and music) is Turkish in origin — and substantially cheaper if one knew where best to convert pounds into their Turkish equivalents.

Izmir was to be the staging-post for "Diana of the Ephesians" and her city sprawling massively over the hillside by which the Meander once flowed. We could "do" it in a long day from Izmir, not least because the "city" was entirely free of visitors — not even a German in sight — perhaps because most people, including ourselves, had at that time no idea that it was the supposed last residence of the Mother of Jesus. Alone on the site, we spent many hours roaming among the extensive remains of the theater, the Library of Celsus and much more (which with Anna I would visit again in 2022) before returning to Izmir and taking next day's bus to Pergamum of the Attalids and Bursa, capital of the Seljuk Turks whose memorials are seen on the green tablets covering the walls of the mosques and mausolea. Finally to Istanbul — to which I would return with Anna many decades later as guest of the Honorary President of the Ataturk Youth League.

For Christians, and even ex-Christians as I was then, Istanbul is a sorrowful city, the stupendous Hagia Sophia, Justinian's masterpiece, being defaced and turned into a museum (and worse back to a mosque as ordained by Mehmet the Conqueror) and most other churches and former churches closed — though we did get into the Chora, located in a squalid part of the city, but revealing stupendous Medieval frescoes. Another old glory of the one-time Constantinople — the Church of the Holy Apostles where many

Byzantine Emperors were buried—had long since been destroyed, and the Topkapi palace was a disappointing memorial to brute power. As for the Blue Mosque, while intended to outdo Justinian's great church, it seemed inside even more like a railway-station than Saint Peter's in Rome.

Thus, although the underground cisterns were to be remembered, we felt little regret at leaving Istanbul, for all the beauty of its location and its palaces along the Bosphorus. We boarded a train which, after passing through the remaining European parts of Turkey, crossed the frontier into Greece. "Welcome to Europe," the Greek border guards greeted us, and we could see their point, mulling it over till we eventually reached Thessaloniki with its museums and Roman remains; the tomb of Philip II of Macedon was still to be unearthed at nearby Vergina. For us the targets were first the Holy Mountain, then, duly purified, Mount Olympus: a mere 9570 feet, but although less than I had attained in Italy, high up and, in the baking sun, considerably more challenging.

Mount Athos rises at the southern end of the most easterly promontory of Chalcidice, south of Thessaloniki, and is a semiautonomous theocratic state under the protection of the Greek government. To enter it, if larger than a mouse, you have to be male—which eliminates any chance for heterosexual love but not, so rumor maintained, for love between older and younger males. You have to enter by boat at the hamlet of Daphni, then walk to the administrative center at Karyes to have your documents checked, where, after waiting some hours in a dusty square in the blazing sun, you are told whether or not you are welcome.

All of which we did, and the decision being eventually in our favor, we received the "pass" which we could show at any of the monasteries and as a result be given food and one night's shelter—that is, provided there were any monks left. In 1958 there were very few under the age of sixty, since Greeks did not want to go while Russians, who in the past had formed the spiritual core of the community, were now prevented from doing so.

We set off for five or so days of wandering through majestic scenery around the base of the mountain, often with superb views over the wine-dark sea. Our reception was mixed: at the Monastery of the Great Lavra, we felt decidedly unwelcome, while at Dionysiou the opposite was the case, and we spent several hours chatting to one of the monks who was very proud, and rightly so, of having sheltered several British wartime pilots who had been shot down over the sea and managed to reach the Holy Mountain. Food depended on whether you arrived on a fast — as in our case most of the time we did — which meant little to consume except bean soup and, of course, ouzo.

The most startling point of our "pilgrimage" was achieved at a Russian monastery, I think called Panteleimon. There were only three very aged monks left, but they welcomed us with enthusiasm and, it being a feast that day, we were seated at a high-table in front of three huge portraits: on one side Tsar Nicholas II, on the other the Tsarina Alexandra, and between them Rasputin. We did not risk asking for an explanation and I have often wondered whether the paintings are still there — or perhaps Rasputin has been replaced by Putin, now become an admired benefactor of the monastery. That said, we did drink a surreptitious toast in ouzo to Rasputin's continuing good health. I don't think we felt particularly holy when we left the Holy Mountain but I will always be grateful for being allowed the visit, remembering the mountain paths, the stars, the sea far below, the ouzo, the aged monks falling asleep during the "night hours" worship.

So to the next and last Greek stop: Mount Olympus. It normally takes two days to climb to the summit of Mytikas, the highest of Olympus's many peaks: on day one we slogged through pastures (where we were photographed looking pretty scruffy under a sign which said — in Greek — "It is forbidden to feed the animals"), then forests and over a few streams, to reach a mountain hut some thousand feet below the summit. It was not particularly clean or well-kept but no others were there and we left next morning at sunrise to clamber across the exposed upper part of the mountain before the heat became even worse. After a couple of hours we reached the summit. Zeus was not there — perhaps, as Homer suggests, he was far away feasting with the Ethiopians — but the view down and beyond the sheer face on the other side of the mountain was stupendous, until the rapidly increasing heat-haze intervened.

We came down much faster than we had ascended, and set off to leave the Hellenes behind, and visit the population — here openly recognized as Slavic — of what was then still designated Yugoslavia. Our target was Ohrid, just beyond Greece and close to the border with Albania—at that time to be avoided. The route took us to an overnight stop in Florina where the only memorable sight was a statue of Basil the Bulgar-slayer in the main square: we wondered whether it marked the spot where he had slaughtered or blinded (a favorite Byzantine subterfuge to avoid the stigma of murder) thousands of Bulgars.

Crossing the border was unproblematic and we found Ohrid on its shimmering lake a cheerful welcome. We could not linger as money was dwindling, hence we passed on by bus via Skopje through the mountains of Bosnia-Herzegovina, thence Pristina and Titograd (now Podgoritsa, its earlier name), eventually to be driven down an impressively steep descent to the Adriatic coast at Bar. We were as yet little conscious of the tentacles of the communist state; even Putnik, the organization through which one was supposed to book all accommodation, but which closed its doors at the absurdly inconvenient hour of 4:00 PM, did not yet seem to matter as there was accommodation and friendliness wherever we wished; the scenery, though not unattractive, was a disappointment after Greece.

Movement now was to be largely by water, with the first major stop at Dubrovnik (plus a side-trip to Mostar and its bridge, later the target of Serb vandalism), then again up the coast by ferries: the island of Brač, Šibenik, Zadar, and eventually (we knew nothing of Diocletian's palace at Split, so passed it by) Rijeka. Sailing northward our awareness of the tyrannical régime increased, firstly owing to a curious blunder (as it can only be described) by its security forces. Mike Passey was a keen photographer, and as we passed along the coast, would from time to time take pictures of the passing villages and boats. On one occasion, as he pointed his camera at the coast, he was assailed from behind by a couple of goons who grabbed the camera and took it off for inspection, later returning it minus the film. We realized that by chance Mike had been about to photograph something of military importance, so peering at the shore (as we otherwise would not have done) we spotted submarine pens cut into the rock. Spying, though, was no longer on my agenda!

In Rijeka we had been warned that accommodation really did depend on Putnik, and we had arrived much later than 4:00 PM, briefed, however, for this circumstance: we must walk up the main street and notice curtains in the windows, the arrangement of which would indicate the offer of a bed overnight. So it turned out and the next day we went down to Pula—all Italian territory till the end of the Second World War—admired the amphitheater, then boarded the train for the frontier.

Here again we ran into the authorities and the last thirteen or so miles before crossing the Italian border took about thirteen hours. At one point we were allowed to stay in our seats while the rest of the passengers were taken off the train and strip-searched in what was supposed to be a hunt for contraband cigarettes, but was obviously mere political harassment, since even the show of cigarette-hunting was hardly serious and when we eventually reached the Italian side at Trieste, one of our fellow passengers picked up a box from under his seat, and opened it to show us proudly a not inconsiderable number of cigarettes. All then got off the train and with this second taste of dictatorship in our mouths we wended our way back to London with Mission Accomplished—and eventually back to the Fenland Don Reserve for what was to be my final undergraduate year. And back to find "Anne."

⋘✳⋙

As it turned out, the academic year 1958–1959 would be a wholly unpredictable stage in my life. Being now a Senior Scholar I could afford a small room at the top of one of the Great Court staircases (though not overlooking the court, or in sight of the tower where Byron had kept his bear), the room underneath being occupied by a retired luminary who seemed never to emerge, whose meals were brought to him on College silver and whose only visitors appeared to be youths widely assumed to be catamites. I was now committed to passing Part II of the Classical Tripos, though I had toyed with changing subject, either to Arabic and Persian, which I hardly seriously considered, or to what was then called Moral Sciences (aka Philosophy) which I decided against in part through following the excellent advice of Alan Ker that the problem with "those people" was that "They spend so much time polishing the epistemological lens that they never get around to looking through it." Indeed, my dilemma was that of many a would-be philosopher in the Fenland Don Reserve smart enough to conclude that if that was all philosophy is about, they had better study something more worthwhile. To know whether or not one "knew" anything did not seem particularly exciting.

So I opted for Group B of the Classical Tripos, supposed to be "Ancient Philosophy," though the name was misleading. The set texts were Plato's *Phaedo*, and the first part of the *Parmenides*, along with the first book of Aristotle's *Metaphysics*. But the *Phaedo* was taught with little reference to Plato's developing ideas and we were assured that the arguments for immortality did not "work" (without much explanation as to how they did not work—and certainly not addressing whether they might be improved). What seemed to matter was not whether the soul is immortal (or, as Plato puts it, "continues to exist in Hades"), but only that Plato was unsuccessful in claiming it to be so. As for the *Parmenides*, it seemed that that extraordinary work had been written merely to show what was wrong with the *Phaedo*—and the general lectures on Plato were particularly trivial, not least because the impression they left was that he had stopped thinking after the *Republic*, which itself was miserably expounded.

As for the *Metaphysics*, it being Aristotle's summary of what had been achieved in philosophy before his own time, it was largely reduced to the question whether he properly understood the Presocratics, or rather the sparse fragments of the Presocratics that we possess. If anything, the Ancient Philosophy course as a whole might have been denoted as an introduction to cultural anthropology à la Jane Harrison and Francis Cornford: in particular an investigation of how "philosophy" arose from more "primitive" thinking. No one who followed the syllabus as interpreted by our lecturers could have formed much idea of the importance of the writings of Plato and Aristotle, yet reading the first book of the *Republic* at school has influenced my thinking more than any other philosophical text.

After Aristotle there was almost nothing on offer, apart from a noble effort by Doctor Peck (almost the only faculty member then possessed of a doctorate) to give us a taste of Stoicism and Epicureanism. Many years later I was to learn of Gilbert Ryle's comment that "In France many people can talk about philosophy [He meant able to name philosophers and give a summary of their teachings] but there are no philosophers." The same could have been said of much that passed as "Ancient Philosophy" in my undergraduate days, though it did seem to be suggested that one should distrust metaphysicians—even if no one forthrightly said that.

Later I came to suspect that metaphysics could point to religion, where our instructors (generally speaking) did not want to go, though (unlike our more recent contemporaries) too unsure of themselves, too conventional as conventions were then understood, to speak their doubts aloud. In their defense I should add that when they were largely replaced by other apparently more seriously philosophical instructors, a new vice tended to replace the older one: namely to claim that the ancients were poor men's versions of some more fashionable moderns. In which case, I came to wonder, why bother to read them at all: at least if one was interested in philosophy rather than cultural archaeology. Yet the defects of the teaching did not mean that the year was wasted, because the students themselves were often greatly interested in viewing Plato and Aristotle on a wider and distinctively more philosophical canvass. I learned much from discussions with them, particularly with Denis O'Brien with whom I still regularly crossed swords.

Yet as I have recorded elsewhere, you could learn in odd ways if you provoked the Dons effectively, for some of them were indeed immensely knowledgeable about the ancient world and even — if in a rather amateurish and unphilosophical way — about ancient thought. Thus I remember writing for Harry Sandbach (to whom I was later to owe much) an especially smart-aleck essay on Heraclitus, whom I tried to read through a sub-Freudian lens. Having read my essay in front of three others, I had to watch Sandbach climb a ladder to the top of his soaring bookshelves, extract a volume — it turned out to be of Plutarch's *Moralia* — and descend, only to commence reading a couple of sentences from it in Greek which I could just about understand. Then he stopped and asked drily, "What do you think of that, Mr Rist?" What he thought, and I immediately realized, was that these two lines had destroyed my essay. All I could do was pass it over to him and invite him to throw it in the wastepaper basket, which he did. Thus I learned that there was an awful lot I still needed to know even at a crudely factual level.

Meanwhile Anna was finding life as a graduate student lonely and rather pointless; she was supposed to be writing a thesis on the influence of things Classical on such Victorian worthies as Mark Pattison, but she got almost no guidance. The professor, whose student she was supposed to be, always seemed too far out of range to see her and discuss what she was doing, thus leaving her to muddle along in the University Library trying to find her own way with no one, faculty or fellow student, with whom to discuss her findings. Inevitably, she soon began to wonder whether there was any point in continuing. She clearly had chosen the wrong field of study, but lacked the necessary advice as to how to choose a better or to handle better what she had chosen.

I seemed to have plenty of spare time without, I thought, too much detriment to my studies, while Anna wanted relief from hers: the result being that we spent more and more time together. In the Lent Term she took on a minor part (which almost through the illness of another might have become a major part) in the performance of *Antigone*, that year's Greek play. She still remembers the few lines eventually allotted to her as Ismene, Antigone's sister. But it soon became clear to me that her problems were deeper. She had decided that the Anglicanism in which she had been mainly raised (though baptized a Roman Catholic) was a poor substitute and she must return to the original fold. That exacerbated problems within her already divided family, where I soon could hear regular arguments about the Spanish Civil War reduced to, "Your torturers were worse than ours": that the mindless core of debate between her secular Jewish father and a Catholic aunt.

As for her mother, she had decided that the Anglican Church had advantages, among them permission to deny hell and approve contraception, while as a "High Anglican" she could suppose she was still a member of the True Church. When Anna decided the reverse, trouble was inevitable, and was made worse by the fact that my own non-religious prejudices added petrol to the flames, causing our growing relationship to be punctured—though then restored—in religious controversy. Not that I approved of contraception or had too much concern about hell, though Schicklgruber and his mates seemed quite reasonable candidates for the latter. I remember telling Anna that I wanted to make love to her, not to a piece of rubber; I also remembered from my childhood that condoms, though often, in reference to their inventor and first distributor called "frenchies," were also called "rubber johnnies," which seemed an unnecessary abuse of my not uncommon name.

Some of my contemporaries seemed less concerned with such niceties, while in the perspective of Margaret Drabble, some of the girls were looking decidedly less frumpish. And some of the boys welcomed that—as one of my Trinity cohort seen of a bright summer afternoon sunbathing naked with his girl-friend on a flat roofed section of one of the College's extensions. Another was living with his pub-owner mistress in a hostelry in Trumpington. An unfortunate third, caught by his "bedder" early in the morning in his college room *in flagrante delicto*, was immediately sent down; the offender not being of the right set, humbug prevailed.

As for myself, in the early days of our courtship I was very much concerned not to seem too eager, and it took a long time for me to risk the first kiss, but when I did, following it up by saying "I've wanted to do that for a long time," Anna delighted me by replying with a subtle and enticing smile, "So have I." The embrace that followed quite convinced me that eventually we would be married. In the meantime more ecclesial matters had to be sorted out, so Anna, on the recommendation of Monsignor Gilbey, secured the help of an ascetic Dominican—also a Dante-specialist and Catholic humanist—Father Kenelm Foster, while I carried on more or less as usual. I continued to ramble on Sundays which was impossible for Anna with her new churchly obligations.

She did, however, join the Easter trip to the Lake District and further developed her love for the mountains, Miss Tyrer keeping discreetly out of our way and beginning, to my surprise, to take an interest in Don Truman. Characteristically, as Anna reported to me later, she never donned pajamas—nor anything else—when settling down for the night in the various Youth Hostels at which we stayed.

So we entered on the final term of my undergraduate career, Anna being inclined to promote our courtship on the one hand, though fearing she could have a vocation as a "religious" on the other. From time to time she would come over to Trinity before eight o'clock (the official time for swimming off the so-called "Backs") for a dip in the Cam from a flight of steps in front of the Wren Library. Occasionally other swimmers joined us. And at about this time I could easily have been killed. Anna was waiting in my room for me to return from some business in town, and as I passed in front of Trinity's Great Gate, the hook of a crane fell to the ground about a foot in front of me. This I told to the porters (who showed little interest), after which I was able to inform Anna that I was happily still alive. The incident again left me with the impression that perhaps I had survived for some future purpose which some agency hoped to prevent.

By now Anna had given up her graduate program—an aunt blamed me for encouraging her to do this, which was strictly untrue—and was taking small teaching posts, (one for butcher's apprentices who needed to acquire some rudiments of written English) to enable her to continue living in Cambridge, thus avoiding recourse to what seemed to me her viper's nest of home in London. Our courtship progressed in a series of advances, until, both of us realizing that a wedding was the obvious next move, I was introduced to Father Kenelm for marriage instruction. Neither Anna nor I wanted cohabitation, in my case for two reasons: immediately because Anna would come to regret it, but more generally because I thought such arrangements unjust in principle, distributing anxiety about pregnancy unevenly between the "partners." I had as yet no idea that marriage was more than a "deal" between two individuals: that it is also (as everyone in antiquity knew) a civic act for the benefit of society.

Thus, after Anna herself, and my earlier introductions to intellectual Catholicism through Denis O'Brien, entered Father Kenelm. Though suspicious of him in advance, I liked him from the first moment I met him. And he seemed to like me, though at times must have found me immensely irritating. Though not being a man to suffer fools gladly—especially, as I later discovered, clerical fools—he could be patient when dealing with arrogant young men, and while "talking" apparently about marriage, we roamed about the intellectual world of Dante, Petrarch, Aquinas, and at times Manzoni, on the last of whom Kenelm failed to write a last book.

Meanwhile *Angry Young Women* was marching toward its satisfactory denouement in May Week, with Denis stealing the show in the not inappropriate role of epicene poet. It was performed on Trinity Backs and one of the chorus—the daughter, so I learned afterward, of the University registrar—fell into the river: this passed as an intended part of the theatrical proceedings. Meanwhile I wrote my finals and came out pretty confident that I had suckered the examiners—as turned out to be the case—and Anna and I prepared for our last act in Cambridge, the Trinity May Ball, after which she was to go to Italy to be *au pair* in what turned out to be a very respectable academic family's summer place at Santa Margherita Ligure.

But first the Ball itself, magically set under the arches of the Wren Library. To Anna's surprise I managed to arrange for flowers to arrive at her lodging in time, and in the intervals of the dancing to arrange a Greek-style supper in my room with olives and yoghurt (rare in England in those days), to be followed by the customary strawberries with cream and champagne. Anna's quite modest dress looked far more elegant than the "gown-less evening straps" (as they were dubbed) attached to a number of other females, more especially the "Susans." It was tiring but delightful and Anna assured me much better than the year before. Soon afterward she set off for Santa Margherita Ligure as an *au pair*.

Denis wangled a fourth year to make sure of getting a First, while Henry, surprisingly falling short, chose to make up the difference by starting a PhD: on which more anon. Denis was now moving in elevated and rather posh Catholic circles. One of his "set," being an artist, had invited a Newnhamite friend of Anna's to pose in the nude (an offer she declined) and was reported as telling all and sundry of a wedding he had just attended: "Such a lovely couple! I've slept with both of them"—a side of Cambridge life that appealed to me far less than its military equivalent, and which in the 1960s was to become as fashionable among aging dons as among undergraduates.

Soon after the ball I heard that I had obtained, out of ninety odd candidates, one of six Firsts in Part Two, which did not surprise me and was soon to prove of considerable worth. John Morrison, still Trinity's Senior Tutor, asked me what I wanted to do next, intimating that it might be worth my while to hang around a bit, register for a PhD and perhaps pick up some kind of Fellowship. But I had no particular intention of becoming an academic, moreover had decided on leaving Cambridge behind, so I told Morrison that I had greatly enjoyed being there for three years but that now was the time to move on. This evoked great surprise: "If you leave now, you will never get back." I had not the heart to tell him that I had no wish to get back.

Many years later, when the Lawrence Professorship in Ancient Philosophy became vacant, several competent scholars suggested I apply for it. Our son Tom added his voice to theirs, though I told him that I knew that the electors had determined to choose a woman, and that if I applied I would not even be shortlisted. This Tom refused to believe in view of my academic credentials, so I told him that I would apply and he would see what I meant — as I did, but as predicted was not shortlisted. Rather (and after two invitations were rejected), the University appointed the third female candidate (of German origin) who, having made herself unpopular with staff and students, returned to the United States after some three years, when a normally equable (female) don I knew commented with a sigh of relief, "At last we're rid of her!"

I had not entirely given up the idea of academic life and applied to two universities in Africa, but looking elsewhere too, got an interview with the BBC for a job deciding what should be broadcast on its news programs; probably my Iraqi experience helped me to reach the short-list. Interviewed by a committee chaired by the boss of Schweppes, Sir Frederick Hooper, I was asked how, if I were prime minister, I would attempt to solve the Mau Mau crisis in Kenya. Not knowing that Sir Frederick owned large portions of the country, I suggested that the first thing to think about was a redistribution of land. So that was that.

Then came another apparent miracle. Harry Sandbach received a letter from the Head of the Classics Department at University College in the University of Toronto, telling how they had fired an incumbent teacher of ancient philosophy who among other absurdities had tried to reduce all ancient thinkers, poets included, to followers of Hegel. His final mistake had been to extend a forty-five-minute lecture to over an hour and a half, eventually inducing one of the most senior professors to leap out of his seat, and in rushing for the exit, trip over an electric cable and plunge the room into darkness. I only heard these details later, but what Sandbach asked me — despite the fact, as he later told me, that he had entered in my college notes that I was "totally unsuited for the academic life" — was whether I would be willing to go to Toronto for a year to fill in while they found a more permanent replacement for the Hegelian.

This I accepted on the spot, with no awareness that I would be there for twenty years — and more to come. That meant leaving my parents and many old friends behind, including most of those in the Rambling Club, so I closed my "rambling" activities with a crazy overnight walk from Cambridge to the lowest point in England — near Grimes Graves — where we built a "reverse cairn," i.e., dug a deep hole. Then, at a final meeting with several members of the Club, we wished one another "Have a good life." I was never to see most of them again, and I have no idea what happened to the by now waterlogged "Captain Fred." As for Miss Tyrer, she married Don Truman, had a child and was then divorced. Don, before he died, had told me that she had cystitis on their honeymoon: bad start. I saw her one more time, some thirty years later, at a Rambling Club reunion: she had become a psychologist and told me that I had hardly changed.

Before leaving the UK for what I then supposed would be a year, I was to meet Anna at Santa Margherita Ligure. There, on the station platform, I proposed to her and was accepted. She introduced me to the family Travaglini for whom she was *au pair* and seemed to think her new status would improve her street-cred with them — as it certainly discouraged unwanted attentions when we moved on to the south of Italy. That first evening however was of Santa Margherita's feast day, and we spent it watching the fishing boats decorated with colored candles and a myriad of such lights bobbing on the ebb tide against the night sky. Again the omens were good.

So on to Naples, where we met Henry and put up in a characteristically noisy and rather grimy hotel to be used as a base for visiting Pompeii, Herculaneum (then in a squalid suburb and ill-prepared for visitors), the astonishing National Museum which housed the most valuable of the treasures of Pompeii and surrounding sites, then the volcanic waters at Pozzuoli (its caves full of fat Germans getting over-heated), and finally Vesuvius. We walked up the first part of the ascent by road but then Henry and I made the mistake of scrambling through the ash and rubble of the final cone while Anna more wisely stayed on the road and was there when we eventually reached the top.

Leaving Henry in Naples, Anna and I set off by train for Salerno and the Greek temples at Paestum (we missed Amalfi), before boarding another train and eventually finishing up in Palermo, the first stop on a rushed visit to parts of Sicily: Palermo itself, with its Norman Palace and the nearby cathedral at Monreale, Selinunte (where the temples were being rebuilt), and on to Segesta where the magnificent structure did not need rebuilding. Walking up to it along a dirt-track we had what I took to be a typically Sicilian experience when a man on a horse came up to us and told us that if we would walk up that little hill over there he could show us something very important. We duly followed and our guide, pointing to a village in the far distance, said, "That is where Giuliano was born." Giuliano was a well-known brigand and Sicilian separatist eventually killed in a shoot-out with carabinieri.

And so on to the Valley of Temples at Agrigento and finally a pilgrimage to the late Imperial villa in the middle of the island at Piazza Armerina near Enna, the former a famed Mafia stronghold, the latter best known for a Roman mosaic depicting girls in bikinis. There Anna was stricken by a stomach bug. Our hotelier asked me whether she was pregnant; I was not sure he believed me when I told him she was not. Then on to Syracuse where, sitting in the remains of the theater, we read a letter from Anna's mother who, informed of her daughter's engagement, declared that she must return immediately. This she had no intention of doing and we finished our little tour of Sicily at Taormina — under an Etna shrouded in mist — before taking the train for an approximately twelve-hour journey, intending to reach Milan but at the last minute diverting to see the great Byzantine churches and monuments of Ravenna. The emperor Justinian in glory with his wife Theodora, daughter of the keeper of the Imperial bears — pious and heroic but formerly a strip-tease artiste whose act culminated in antics involving seeds and geese — still stands out in my memory. I remember that at the baptistry of the Arians Jesus is shown (most unusually) circumcised — and also the sheep proceeding eastward in the apse mosaics of Sant' Apollinare in Classe.

We had little money left and decided to blow the last of it at the Café Teodorico near Ravenna station — happily it no longer exists — on a chicken supper. But when the animal arrived we could hardly find meat among the bones so we asked for a replacement and Anna told the waiter emphatically that we were not going to pay for the bones we had been offered. (She acquired from me the name "Pollo" as a result.) When the waiter realized we were serious he called the carabinieri, and we accompanied them to their station and recounted our complaint, whereupon one of them took occasion to tell us that he had had poor food in England when he was a prisoner-of-war. We commiserated with him about that, but we had plenty of time to argue and in the end he told the restaurateur to bring us a second bird, which turned out to be marginally better than the first. We then took a train to Milan, then I took another—which was full of work-seeking Calabrians—overnight to Calais, and hence home, while Anna went back to Santa Margherita Ligure.

She returned to England a week or so later. I met her at Victoria station, at which unromantic place I handed over a ruby engagement ring which I had scraped up enough money to buy. A few days later, as we had decided against being married in haste, she watched me board the "Homeric" at Southampton for my first trip (and last by ship) to the New World. I had borrowed fifty pounds from my father for the fare.

CHAPTER 5

The Long Sixties
ACADEMIA AND CATHOLICISM
IN A BRANCH-PLANT STATE

Rist was a somewhat combative Englishman notably lacking in deference towards the University administration.
—W. H. Nelson, in *The Search for Faculty Power*

Professor Rist, whom the minister has obviously listened to, made an argument that I disagree with strongly... he said that the students who will get elected to the governing council will try "to have the university become an ideologically committed university" which is the antithesis he felt of a free university.... He implied that parity...will mean that students will have "a right to say who teaches and what is taught."
—Tim Reid (Liberal, Scarborough East) in the *Legislature of Ontario Debates,* July 22, 1971

This [nominally Catholic] administration is going to do for sex what the previous one did for golf.
—Arthur Schlesinger, Jr.

The "Homeric" (registered, as I remember, in Panama) was not a happy ship. I knew enough Italian (with even a bit of dialect) to recognize that the comments of the Italian crew about the German officers were far from friendly. Nor was the weather on the North Atlantic friendly, the roaring winds compelling us to stay below decks for large parts of the bumpy voyage. The food was poor, and the number of passengers small; the only one I can remember was some kind of proto-hippy from California who knew a lot about drugs and told me that in North America the poor were regarded as wicked: latter-day Calvinism, as I presumed. But the "Homeric" got us across the ocean and one morning I woke to find it edging along the Saint Lawrence below Québec and "dreamboats" racing along the waterfront road. After some six days at sea, we reached Montréal, disembarked and had our documents checked. That done, as a "Landed Immigrant" I was free to catch a train to Toronto (now seemingly pronounced "Tronna").

My new city was not the cosmopolitan metropolis it later became, but seemed like a provincial town complete with "blue" laws, being still largely inhabited by descendants of the original settlers in Ontario: the Scots who gave the orders and the Irish who carried them out — though many of these latter were Protestants and the Orange Lodge, once all-powerful, lingered on, albeit its popularity had begun to wane with the advent of the motor-car: previously it had been the only place in rural areas where the young of different sexes could readily meet and court. With the coming of the automobile, the back-seat was to replace the Lodge for more advanced courting.

In Ontario there were by now immigrants from beyond Ireland and Scotland. The English mainly arrived after the Second World War, also thousands of Italians, mostly from Calabria, many of whom hoped to use Canada as a staging-post to the now largely closed United States: a popular myth had it that when they got off the train they still thought the streets of Toronto were paved with gold, but next day realized that many of them were not paved at all, and the day after that they were to pave them.

But the University (of which as yet I knew chiefly that insulin had been discovered there) was very different: already a vigorous intellectual community greatly profiting from a number of refugees from the Nazis and Fascists. Six subjects, including Classics, were taught in colleges, of which there were then four: University College, a secular institution with a substantial number of Jewish students; Trinity College, Anglican and socially up-market; Victoria College, a bastion of the United Church of Canada — which is to say an amalgam of Methodists and Presbyterians — and Saint Michael's which was Catholic. The religious foundations had been associated with the central University under the University of Toronto Act of 1904, but by 1959 their affiliations — apart from Saint Michael's — were beginning to fade.

In the University College Classics department there were two distinguished refugees: Gilbert Bagnani, one-time proprietor of an art gallery in Rome, was unapologetically "Renaissance Man" — or in his own terms a "farmer among scholars and a scholar among farmers." He owned a farm at Port Hope, having left Italy to escape the Fascist régime. Fritz Heichelheim had been a *Privatdozent* at Giessen whence he was expelled — luckily for him — in 1933. The uniqueness of these two I have recorded elsewhere. Overall, I soon concluded that the faculty members knew less than their parallels in Cambridge but understood more. Despite the unintellectual Protestantism of earlier days, the atmosphere was exhilarating with many faculty members keen to teach and publish and sometimes even able to admit that they might be in error: the University of Toronto seemed to be an interesting place and I soon began to think that I might aim to stay there for more than the one year.

When I arrived on campus I found accommodation with the Dean of Men at University College who, being due to marry at the end of the year, was happy to collect a bit of rent in the intervening months. For me it was ideal, since I could live on campus and eat meals in the Howard Ferguson Men's residence, where for lunch there was a high table, while in the faculty common room I could readily expand my acquaintance with colleagues in the six College departments.

At my first such lunch I enquired of the Polish waitress, "What is a 'Salisbury Steak?,'" to be told that it was "ze sweepings off ze slaughter-house floor." I was beginning to learn Canadian — or more broadly North American — English, soon understanding that my salary, generous by British standards, was paid in "bucks." Less appealing was that "going to the loo" was referred to by both sexes as "going to the John" (presumably in pioneering times only men were supposed to use public conveniences), but to sign my name I might be required to write down my "John Henry" (an allusion that apparently confused a nineteenth-century American folk-hero with the Declaration of Independence signer John Hancock). Polish English might continue to seem puzzling. I recall that an engineer who had worked all day on my non-functioning office radiator, concluded: "It's vine now, so long as you don't abuse it." To my question, "What do you mean, abuse it?" he replied, "You know, turn it on." The radiator still did not work.

Apart from the lunches there was also interesting company in the evenings: a group of senior graduate students and (mainly) younger faculty acted as "Dons" (in a different sense of the term from that with which I was familiar) to look after the various sections of the residence under the general supervision of the

Dean. One of these, an exuberant Western Canadian, had just returned from Budapest where he had taken part in the Hungarian uprising; another was a brilliant (and eventually tragic) ex-Catholic New Englander direct from graduate study in English at Harvard and already making a name for himself as an expert on eighteenth-century novelists, especially Samuel Richardson. A third, from California and also an ex-Catholic, was thinking of finishing his doctorate at the Pontifical Institute of Mediaeval Studies but was being seduced—as were many Catholic "intellectuals" of that era—by the nihilist *angst* of Heidegger. An older English psychologist was dubbed "a guy with an eye for a thigh," but seemed to be psychologically competent.

I was set to teach nine hours of undergraduate classes a week: on Homer, Thucydides, Plato's *Republic* (which I would teach for some twenty years), and some limited instruction in Greek Prose Composition, still obligatory for Honors Classicists. I noticed that also in other departments the syllabus was rather conservative and with a strong historical character: the English department still (though for little longer) demanding Anglo-Saxon—and starred, outside University College, Northrop Frye, Marshall McLuhan, and Kathleen Coburn, and within University College, the formidable editor of the Army Debates of 1648, A.S.P. Woodhouse: more generally a power in English studies. Modern language departments also had compulsory courses on Medieval and Renaissance authors. For philosophy, the department was the largest in North America and exceptionally variegated, with a strong emphasis on the early modern period: Descartes, Spinoza, Leibniz, Kant. It also took ancient philosophy seriously, which in later years would turn out to be good for me.

All this I tried to communicate to Anna in weekly air-letters to which replies always arrived on time and from which I read of her immersion in her post at the North London Collegiate School (NLCS): an institution which she had been deterred from attending as a girl—and whence she probably would have gone to Oxford. She now found herself teaching daughters of champagne socialists, given names like Cressida. She also was having a hard time living at home over religious differences as she prepared to be received into the Catholic Church.

As soon as I began to think I might like to become a genuine "academic animal," I knew I had two problems: one that if

I taught as badly as I had been taught at Cambridge I would have no chance of staying beyond the year; the other that I was now living in a world where, unlike England thus far, professors even in the humanities usually needed a doctorate. This I had no chance of getting, and certainly would have found doctoral programs hard to tolerate. The alternative was to write: first articles and then a book of sufficiently recognized quality to procure me tenure.

I needed to get to work on these two problems, in which I was encouraged by my colleagues who generally seemed to like me, and especially by the Latinist Niall Rudd and by the older Greek historian, William Wallace, with whom I played chess—and routinely lost—after evening Classical meetings and who had a considerable knowledge of popular ballads, some mildly lewd, as the limerick

> There was a young man from Khartoum
> Took a Lesbian back to his room.
>   Said he "Now, my dear,
>   let's first get this clear:
> Who does what, and with what, and to whom."

I prepared my class-notes carefully, working long into most evenings, and I began to think about what to write, here coming up with what would have seemed a strange conclusion to my Cambridge teachers. My decision to read Plotinus resulted from two earlier interests: the first being my love of Plato—which led me to wonder what happened next in the Platonic tradition—and the second, my interest, aroused by Dodds's *Greeks and the Irrational*, in the transformation of the Roman world into a Christian Empire. When I started to read Plotinus's *Enneads* I recognized immediately a master metaphysician and began to wonder why I had never heard any of my Cambridge instructors speak a word about him. Perhaps that was a case of not wanting to know, since Plotinus's metaphysics might point them in a religious direction—as it had Augustine.

I began to read and to write: first an article on the dating of Plato's *Timaeus*, rejecting some of the arguments of G.E.L. Owen (which had become the orthodoxy of the time). This was published in *Phoenix*, the journal of the Classical Association of Canada, albeit an outlet which I was advised by Heichelheim as a young scholar to avoid. The article received — at least for a while — almost no attention unless from some who commented that only *Phoenix* would have published it. But I followed it up with several more articles on Plato and soon on Plotinus, on whom I was lucky because only two writers of note in English (Dodds and A.H. Armstrong) seemed to be interested in him, and though things were different in France, the amount of "secondary literature" was quite limited.

So bits of an upcoming book were regularly shipped off to Anna who typed them out, the result eventually being *Eros and Psyche* (her suggestion for title) which was published in 1964. It did quite well with reviewers and was to be translated into Italian; Italians still seem quite fond of it. Interesting in light of my future thinking is that it led to my involvement in a dispute about love which had developed after the publication of the Swedish Lutheran Anders Nygren's *Agape and Eros*, a book which was said then to be read more widely in Protestant seminaries than anything apart from the Bible, but which I regarded as massively misguided, thus finding myself on the "Catholic" side in the dispute. Nor, were I to go back to *Eros and Psyche* now, would I change much of the content, though the presentation would be substantially altered: it looks oddly bitty and amateurish — because that is what it is!

It was not all work and no play during that first year. The residence "Dons," dubbing themselves on Fridays the "Thank God it's Friday Club," regularly set out for an all-you-can-eat buffet downtown and I soon began to accompany them. It was good company and at times offered surprises, as the occasion when Jack McLeod, the Westerner back from Budapest, was sounding off and gesticulating with vigor, tipping his chair back in the process, the result being that he fell backward into the lap of a woman at the next table and spattered her in her faux-fur coat with a bowlful of soup. Never at a loss with the ladies, McLeod apologized profusely, offered to pay for cleaning the fur, and began mopping things up. That worked; he was instantly forgiven and a fascinating conversation with the next table was set in motion, the subject being the tedium of Canadian politics.

Christmas came. I could not afford to return to Britain and so began a habit of attending the meetings of the American Philological Association, which that year took place in New York. A colleague who was driving down offered to take me along, and brought me safe and sound through a blizzard on the New York Freeway to my first experience of "God's Own Country." It gave me a chance to look around New York, where I appreciated the art galleries and especially the ride on the ferry from downtown Manhattan to Staten Island and back.

The conference itself was a mixed bag, most of the papers, especially those given by older scholars, being hardly original (I was warned at one point not to attend any paper given by anyone over fifty: either it had been published already or the author was now "senile"). One paper—though not given by a man over fifty—particularly irritated me, and as I emerged from the room where it had been presented I joined a group of some seniority who, to my surprise, were praising its worth. I dissented and was asked to explain my objections, which I had little difficulty in doing, but then warming to the task and looking for some fun, alleged that the "original" bits had been published in the 1880s in a German periodical—I could not exactly remember which. To my surprise, several of the professionals claimed to have read it. I did wonder afterward whether the revealing of such a minor piece of academic dishonesty justified the means adopted.

Not long before the end of the academic year, my spirits were boosted by an unexpected meeting. I was invigilating, and the exam ran late; a few of us invigilators, while cleaning up at the end, got chatting. One of them was Father Charles ("Charlie") Leland, a member of the English Department at Saint Michael's College (Saint Mike's), and as it was late and their lunches lasted longer than those at University College, he invited me to join him across campus. So began a friendship to last for decades, until Charlie's premature death.

Leland was an American whose mother had died when he was young, after which he had been raised at a military school in Michigan, then studied at Oberlin College, and from there passed on to Oxford (and later to Oslo where he learned Norwegian), and having converted to Catholicism had joined the Basilian Order, being a newish member of their English department in Toronto, where he also taught Ibsen, some of whose plays he was later to translate. He was my first introduction to the better side of North American Catholicism, being a born teacher, devoted to his students and devoid of any clericalist pretension.

Before meeting Charles I accepted without much thought the general opinion in University College that Saint Michael's was "pastoral," that is, not particularly intellectual — which in a way was true, but not entirely. And associated with the College was the Pontifical Institute of Mediaeval Studies (PIMS), founded by Etienne Gilson, paid for by the Basilian Fathers, and intended to promote serious work at the graduate level in Medieval theology and philosophy within a much wider cultural context.

Once admitted to the Saint Michael's circle, I was to meet many good scholars and find many good friends, especially at the Institute — while it lasted: these included the paleographer Reginald O'Donnell, the philosophers Armand Maurer, Joseph Owens and (later) Eduard Jeanneau, canon of Chartres Cathedral and editor of the works of Scotus Eriugena. There was also Ignatius Eschmann, OP, whom I scarcely knew, but who earned my respect when I learned that after Pope Pius XI published his encyclical *Mit Brennender Sorge*, he had preached several anti-Nazi sermons in Cologne Cathedral, thus angering both Nazis and many German bishops who still thought that by kowtowing they could save Catholic schools. Already previously arrested, after the last of these sermons Eschmann had been whisked away through a back door of the cathedral as the Gestapo entered through the front. He eventually reached Toronto where he was appointed at the Institute, as was later the Medieval polymath Leonard Boyle, of the Irish Dominicans at San Clemente in Rome and later Prefect of the Vatican Library, where after admirably succeeding in further opening up the collections to scholars but being naïve in business he was eventually thrown to the wolves. Anna and I were to attend his funeral when his devoted staff all turned out to pay their last respects and his ecclesiastical superiors were invisible.

I soon came to realize that Canadian Catholicism had obvious weaknesses — being of different kinds before and after the reforms of Vatican II — but could also boast some Catholic humanists, and only after its decline did I recognize how much the Pontifical Institute had contributed to the humanity both of Canadian Catholicism in general and of the University of Toronto in particular. Father Charles was later to become almost one of the family, not infrequently joining us at our Sunday lunches at which he would speak highly of "Mother's roast potatoes."

Professor Leonard Woodbury, the cautious Winnipeg-born and Harvard-trained head of the Department of Classics who had taken me on, eventually decided that I was worth having for another year. I would want to thank those colleagues who helped him arrive at that decision: decision-making, as I came to realize, being immensely painful for him. This character trait had earned him the unflattering nickname of "Tiberius," after the emperor. Secure of cash for a while and somehow confident that even the next year might not be my last, I decided not to risk the North Atlantic again, but fly by Comet airliner—a mark of the jet-age to come—which, with the still requisite stop in Montréal, would be back to London in less than eight hours: back, that is, well in time for a wedding on July 30 and the honeymoon in Norway's Jotunheim mountains to follow.

Other later flights were not always to go so smoothly: on one an engine failed a couple of hours beyond Newfoundland and we had to return to Bangor in Maine. On another I was seated next to a Sikh with an empty seat beyond him on which no one would sit: that being because a Sikh had recently blown up an Air India flight from Vancouver. With the passengers all seated elsewhere, the Sikh—who had thus far said nothing—indicated to me by moving his lapel that he was a member of the Toronto Metropolitan Police. On a third occasion, with Anna on the last seat with British Airways, I was about to take off on an Air Canada Boeing when the captain's voice came over the intercom telling us to get out of the plane; it was feared there was a bomb on board: there followed a rush by the cabin crew for the doors, thus hindering the passengers from getting out. We eventually emerged (some who had come from the West Indies in short-sleeves), into a blizzard with outside temperatures well below zero. After the plane had been moved to a remoter part of the airfield, where our baggage was dumped and became covered with snow, it was concluded that the bomb threat was a hoax. We eventually managed to find our own baggage, it was restored to the hold, and we set off many hours late; some of the passengers were Indians headed for a wedding in Delhi which they must have failed to attend. The behavior of the cabin crew gave me further reason (beyond Air Canada's tendency to lateness on North Atlantic flights) to follow the advice of the travel agent from whom I regularly bought my tickets: "I take it you don't want to fly Air Canada, Sir."

Anna had already arranged most things for the wedding: the church was to be Our Lady of Dolours in Hendon, the celebrant was to be Father Christopher Miller, a German Benedictine who, with the assistance of her grandmother, had managed to pass the years from 1939 to 1945 in London, still acting as prior at the German Benedictine house in Hendon which had been long established to teach English to German monks due to proceed to Tanganyika, the former German colony later styled Tanzania. For the limited reception after the church ceremony — alas, no dancing — Anna's father had secured through a Jewish acquaintance a pleasant enough venue at a reasonable price. Don Truman was to be my best man, and we drank my health the evening before in a pub in Leigh-on-Sea while more or less simultaneously the bride-to-be was smoking her last (occasional) cigarette; she knew I hated them, always happy to hear them condemned in American song:

> Cigareetes are the bane of the whole human race.
> A man is a monkey with one in his face.
> Take warning, dear sister, take warning, dear brother:
> A fire at the one end, a fool at the other.

Happily all went well "on the day" and as man and wife we left the reception in good time — or, as Anna complained, early — and returned to her home to change into hiking kit for the journey to Bergen; it was to be Anna's first flight. As we got ready, I was amused that while she was changing her bra, with a little assistance from me, her mother entered the room and withdrew like a terrified rabbit. And so, also too early — but I am always nervous about missing planes — we set off for Heathrow, thence to Bergen, which we reached after a rather bumpy flight well after midnight, and thence wending our happy if weary way to our wedding-night hotel — where we were assigned single beds, so elected both to sleep in the one. And though it is said to rain in Bergen on three hundred and sixty days of the year, the weather was dry.

Next morning, our union consummated, we wandered around the old town and on the following day boarded a steamer up the Sognefjord. As we embarked a Frenchman addressed Anna as "Madame," which pleased her mightily — though in fact by then "mademoiselle" was dropping out of use in France. Anna had been in Norway before, with a group of Newnham girls, but they had only managed one real mountain, Surtningsui. This time our aim was to take in Norway's two highest peaks, Glittertind and Galdhøpiggen, the latter at 8100 feet generally believed to be the higher, though there were Glittertind-supporters to dispute this — the disagreement seems to depend on whether you count the snow on top, but no matter: we were going to achieve both.

And in beautiful weather we reached both summits and much besides: empty moorland, jagged peaks, rushing waterfalls, extraordinary stave-churches, the Sognefjord snuggling at the foot of precipitous slopes. The mountain huts were well maintained, the food good, as too the company, though the crowded accommodation meant that the unitive aspects of marriage had to be more appreciated in the open: in that beautiful countryside better still. Once we fell out — inevitably — about religion, though we normally managed to keep our disagreements about religion and related matters to ourselves, and by the time we sailed back to Bergen, thence by air to London, we felt fit in body and soul, and waiting for whatever fortune would throw our way.

And there was indeed a certain hitch with our plans for Canada. We had intended to sail, Anna having not yet experienced the North Atlantic. A dock-strike prevented that and, booked into a London hotel we awaited a plane from Varig, the national airline of Brazil, to come after flying that nation's president. It would be Anna's third and longest flight. The plane eventually arrived and after seven hours we were in Montréal, weighed down with possessions, the most cumbersome of which, a sewing machine, had been adapted to North America's 120 volts.

Immigration at Montréal was easy enough, despite long delays, and Anna's documentation puzzled one of the officials, who noting ethnicity (from the father) to be Jewish and religion Roman Catholic, remarked on this surprising combination. Anna, fearing some impediment, explained, "My father is Jewish, my mother Catholic (omitting other complications)." "Pardon, Madame," he concluded, "It just is a bit unusual." Then we were released to catch a train to "Tronna."

We were first made welcome in the home of Alec Dalzell, one of my colleagues from Trinity College, and remained there for the few days needed to find a basement apartment at 1466 Avenue Road, opposite the posh girls' school Havergal College (where they always said "Hurrah" at sporting events rather than the more

Canadian "Hooray"). On our first day Anna was introduced to a Toronto Sunday of that era when we took the subway — as yet almost a toy line running up only from Union Station to Eglinton — down to the campus for Mass at Saint Basil's Church. On board were mainly ladies with hats and prayer-books, heading, we assumed, for the United Church of Canada. Any who got out at Davisville, the first stop, might notice a sign warning that "Trespassers will be electrocuted."

I had already regaled Anna with comments on one United Church temple actually named "Saint James Bond," the explanation being that the church had originally been on Bond Street downtown. I think it was this same church which, following the non-conformist practice of informing their hoped-for congregations of delights in store for them the following Sunday, displayed a two line notice:

> What hell is like.
> Hear the new preacher.

Our first civic duty in our new home was to vote in a local referendum as to whether restaurants should be allowed to serve alcohol with a meal (though assuredly not without). Which introduced Anna to the Ontario "liquor" situation, a hangover from Prohibition days. In the province liquor could only be obtained at government-run stores controlled by the Liquor Control Board of Ontario (LCBO), and after payment would be handed over wrapped in a brown bag presumably intended to suggest that there was something wicked about wanting it at all. The Ontario Temperance Federation retained legal counsel to oppose every application in the province for a license which would enable "liquor" to be served in clubs or theaters.

That obligation was taken seriously. When an entrepreneur, Ed Mirvish, bought a down-town theater — the Royal Alex — his application to sell booze was opposed on the grounds that the bar, being on the top floor, might cause drunks to fall down the stairs, endangering their lives and those of other theater-goers. Nevertheless, in our local referendum it was voted by a fair majority to allow restaurateurs to sell the corrupting fluids with meals: a small step in the right direction.

Anna hoped for a teaching post and almost literally walked into one not far off on "Armour Heights," namely Loretto Abbey, a Catholic girls' high-school run by the Irish branch of Mary Ward's order, in Canada styled the Ladies of Loretto. Anna was to teach English, Italian, and French—for which she had no formal qualifications and we were astonished that there were no French-speakers available. Then we realized that though one could hear a number of non-English languages on Toronto's downtown streets, French was not among them. Ontario would have disowned the visceral hostility to French one could meet in Alberta—where speakers of "joual," the Québec version of the language, might find themselves told to "Speak White"—still it was far from popular in Toronto, the girls at Loretto Abbey generally evincing little desire to learn it.

On the whole Anna enjoyed her year at Loretto Abbey, particularly in the winter, when, being a novice at ice-skating among those who had almost grown up on skates, she had the girls tow her around on the ice until she more or less got the feel of it—no doubt amusing her charges as well as learning a new skill—at which skill I had more limited success, if in part because I purchased the hockey skates necessary for the national game (then usually played only by males) which was almost a religion: indeed religious terminology was used, as in: "Only God saves more than [Philadelphia's] Bernie Parent" or "Jesus saves and [Chicago's] Bobby Hull bangs in the rebound."

The cult was topped, as these quotations indicate, by the National Hockey League (NHL) where, though many of the teams were American, most of the better players were Canadian, usually from Québec or the tough Northern Ontario mining towns and often French-speaking. Ice hockey was admired for the sheer speed at which it was played, but also for its violence, especially at the professional level. Few of the hockey "greats" survived without loss of teeth at best, and all clubs would send at least one player onto the ice whose prime purpose was to protect his team-mates from "high-sticking," "spearing" and other fouls which might put you into the "sin bin," i.e., the penalty box—while himself intimidating the opposition. Coached by Fred Shero and captained by a minuscule but fearless Bobby Clarke, the Philadelphia Flyers, at whose rink could be read "Winning is not the chief thing, it's the only thing," were masters of these dark arts, playing what the commentators would call "a good physical game."

We were still in Toronto for the first of several series of games between Canada's national team and their (mostly Red Army) Russian counterparts. The series being tied at two–all and the last game being played in Toronto, Anna witnessed, when collecting children from school, the entire city hushed and cars halted while their drivers huddled over their radios. When almost at the last moment a Toronto player, Paul Henderson, scored the goal which won the series, the roar from normally silent Toronto car-drivers might have been heard for miles, Canadian restraint morphing into something more generally American!

Skating and ice hockey being not the only Canadian winter pastimes, our modest success with skates encouraged us to try skiing. We took a coach a fair way north of Toronto to a Sundridge bitterly cold in March, booked into our hotel and took to the slopes — but with no success. After fitting our skis and moving around easily enough — and with Anna showing some promise — we moved to the ski-lift where I got my skis almost inextricably mixed up with the cable. Half-frozen, we returned to the hotel and made no further attempt to ski, taking instead to snow-shoes.

Meanwhile, at Loretto Abbey, Anna would find things could be difficult when teaching English to seniors. For poetry in grade twelve she was issued a book divided into three sections: the first of English poets and generally worthwhile, the second of American poets and also often worthwhile — but the third was of Canadian poets and a rarely good collection. That her teaching concentrated on the English poets did not please the nun in charge of English who informed her that she was to teach equally from all three sections. This nun was youngish and decidedly chic now that the Order's old-fashioned habits had been updated by Christian Dior — though not long after to be abandoned in "sixties preference for 'civvies.'" Exception was also taken by parents to Anna's recommendation of some contemporary novels — among them the obviously attractive and "relevant" *The Catcher in the Rye* — on the grounds that such presented immoral situations.

As a result — as also of the view that a newly-married woman should be getting on with having a family — Anna began to doubt that she would be teaching at Loretto the following year, and was able to make another arrangement. Hence on the termination of her post she was able to tell the headmistress that she had obtained a lectureship in Classics at Saint Michael's College. There the Classics department was the domain of Father James (Jim) Sheridan, a priest under his own recognizance, a witty and conservative lover of the Latin language whose pronunciation of English seemed to become more deeply Irish the longer he stayed away from the "old sod."

I cannot remember how Anna came to Sheridan's attention, but they got on—later she used to say the responses in his persistently private Latin Masses. (He claimed that Gaelic was his mother tongue and therefore his native language or vernacular, which was not strictly true since his father was the "native speaker" and his mother not.) Sheridan, however, did not have the final word on appointments and at "Saint Mike's" at that time there was only one laywoman on the staff—in the German department, and of mature years—though there were besides a bevy of none-too-well qualified nuns both of the Loretto Order and that of Saint Joseph.

Anna wondered how Father John Kelly, the American-born president of the College, would like the idea of her being appointed, but as it turned out she need not have worried. Father Kelly, a man I came rather to like—typically for an Irishman he loved horse-racing and betting and from whom I once took twenty-five bucks by winning a bet about American foreign policy somewhere or other—spoke briefly and to the point: "I don't like having laywomen on the staff but, if Father Sheridan wants you, you can have the job." Thus Anna started as a lecturer in Latin at Saint Michael's which she was to reduce to part-time on the birth of Alice and from which she retired when Tom, our third child, was born in 1971.

Which brings us to the reproductive side of marriage. Anna thought we could have four children, while I, who knew nothing whatever of babies, being an only child with no young relatives in sight, supposed we should stop at two. Nor was our start auspicious, since Anna endured two miscarriages before Peter was eventually born alive, despite having got the umbilical cord around his neck during delivery. Anna was aware of the nurse listening in with a stethoscope shaking her head in answer to a query from another: meaning she could not hear the heart! And two miscarriages had previously taken place in England, where Anna was seriously misdiagnosed. The correct situation of an inverted womb had been ascertained by a Registrar — to be immediately and before a group of students overridden by the eminent consultant, who, as Anna recounted, pronounced after examining her, "And there is no inversion."

In that Cambridge maternity hospital, while Anna was recovering from failing to keep her second unborn child, a woman in the next bed (visited by her Anglican vicar) had had an abortion — still illegal in the United Kingdom. Which did not improve our view of the medical profession. Back in Toronto, however, Anna was referred to a Doctor Harper (later to become a good friend) who immediately recognized the cause of the by then two miscarriages (as had the English Registrar). After exercises to correct the retroversion, pregnancy ensued, until eventually and triumphantly, after considerable lying-up, our son Peter was born.

One of the effects of these medical experiences was that I recognized that, as an aunt of Anna's put it, the Catholic Church was the only bastion still protecting the unborn. I had always condemned abortion, regarding it as a simple matter of the unjust killing of an innocent human being, but of course had found few advocates of such a position among my colleagues. Eventually I was to become a founding member and sometime Chairman of Canada's first pro-life organization, then styled the Coalition for Life. As for Doctor Harper, he and his wife Jody remarkably had six daughters, while his brother and sister-in-law had six sons.

Nor was pro-life the only area in which I began to move into a more public domain. After becoming one of the founders of Oxfam Canada (then still uncorrupted by abortionists), by the end of the 1960s I was a member of a committee called Canairelief which worked to supply humanitarian aid during the civil war in Nigeria: my first contact with a country which Anna's brother Jonathan, having children out there while working as an engineer, was obliged to leave soon after fighting broke out. I had also managed by this time to visit the Pyrenees — my last "expedition" with Henry Blumenthal. We looked in on Lourdes, which impressed me more than I would have expected, especially in that the "religious supermarket" was kept clear of the actual sanctuary. (I hope it still is.) We also endured the long traffic jam which constituted most of what is officially named Andorra, of which the French state and the Spanish bishop of Urgel are joint sovereigns.

One of Anna's first social obligations was to meet Professor Woodbury and his wife and two young children, and we were soon invited to his home for dinner. By North American custom Anna was regarded as a "bride" for a year and a day, by which time according to tradition she and others in her situation would be assumed to be sufficiently "groomed" to be mothers-in-waiting. So as "bride" Anna was welcomed by a rather aristocratic lady American-style, Mrs. Leonard Woodbury, née Marjorie Bell from Pittsburgh, probably of some inherited wealth, and you could recognize in the way she controlled her two children, a boy and a girl, that her background was Presbyterian or something like it. It must have been a bit of a wrench for her originally to have come to Toronto, at that time for many Americans Canada seeming the frozen north; she told us later that some of her friends had speculated on the possibility of finding polar bears in the city.

Anna and I met near the Woodbury house, and Anna had some difficulty, it seemed, in taking the coming meeting seriously, having, while riding on a bus, been reading an exchange in Kingsley Amis's novel *Lucky Jim* between the eponymous hero and his madrigal-obsessed professor; this had made her laugh so much that she almost fell off her seat, to the astonishment of her fellow passengers. The Woodbury family were not quite like Amis's professor, and nor, I think, am I like Lucky Jim. In any case, the evening went well enough, in view of Mrs. Woodbury showing what seemed to us an excessive concern with her young daughter's dress not "riding up" and Woodbury trying to balance hospitality against the consciousness of being a "god-professor" with power to retain or to fire. I recall some discussion of the changing political scene in Canada, not least in still apparently Catholic Québec.

During my lonely first year in Toronto I had been struck by the oddity of this scene, which featured two main parties: the Liberals, who were anti-British, and the Conservatives who were anti-American. In the West, and with some small following elsewhere, there was also the Canadian Cooperative Federation (later the New Democratic Party) which modeled itself on the British Labour Party and strove for a similar relationship with the Trade Unions. It tended to be led by the now secular sons of Methodist circuit preachers with a social conscience. It first obtained power in Saskatchewan, where, as we found later when we penetrated that part of the world, doctors (some refugees from the British NHS) had posted a notice on the border with Manitoba which read "Welcome to Red Canada."

So all three parties looked like branch-plant organizations, there apparently being little positively and uniquely Canadian about any of them. In the industrial field something similar pertained: the unions being often affiliates of their American elder brothers while the bosses ran branch-plant subsidiaries of such as General Motors. But the economy was in good shape, with the result that in general smart people were not drawn to politics but to law and business: thus a high percentage of Canadian members of parliament, whether provincial or federal, were lawyers.

Nor was the negative definition of Canada and things Canadian limited to the strictly political; it also strongly affected academia. Thus on my first venture into departmental politics, when I attacked a proposed curriculum change and got nowhere, I was buttonholed on leaving the meeting by John Grant, a crusty but friendly older Greek historian from Victoria College, who commented, "You made a real cock-up of that. You approached the question entirely the wrong way." "Oh," said I, "What should I have done?" To which Grant replied, "You should have praised the proposal vigorously, emphasizing that this is how it is done at Harvard (where his was the last PhD thesis written in Latin). That would have killed it right away." Thus I had begun to understand not only more about Canadian society but that Woodbury's view of Grant (once expressed as, "No, no, he's not a misanthrope; he doesn't hate the human race — just the people he knows") — was misleading.

But soon the political situation was to change dramatically, Québec having been taken over by Jean Lesage's Liberals, elected in June 1960, the former leader of the corrupt Union Nationale (and close ally of the Catholic Church) having died in the previous year. Called the Quiet Revolution, it rather resembled the bursting of a balloon. From being the most Catholic part of Canada, Québec was soon to be the least Catholic, and from having the highest birth-rate (viewed as securing *"la revanche des berceaux"*), Québec was soon to have the lowest. Families of eleven or twelve were succeeded by families of one at the most, thus by the turn of the century, thwarting any *"revanche."* Québec was to be the first among "Catholic" entities to enter on this path, being followed by Ireland (and its American and Canadian diaspora), Spain, and even France ("eldest daughter of the Church"). As time passed we would see what effect the reforms of Vatican II were to have on this changing religious scene. Being not yet a Catholic, I did not appreciate the importance of such changes as we first met in Québec.

⊰⊰⊰✵⊱⊱⊱

And so our first married year passed and my post was again renewed, so we decided not to return for the summer to Britain but to look at a very different extension of Europe on what was now our side of the Atlantic, namely New Spain (or specifically the Mexican part of it). Landing therefore in a rosy dawn and at 5000 feet in Mexico City, we visited its Spanish remains, especially the cathedral, built on the site of an Aztec temple, along with various Aztec sites nearby, found the more recent art of Diego Rivera and especially Jose Orozco fascinating—as also the shrine of Our Lady of Guadalupe, where we watched devotees approach it on their knees across a huge stone courtyard.

Then we set out to tour parts of the hinterland by local busses: Puebla, from which is seen the notorious volcano Popocatepetl, Cholula with its alleged 365 churches, each said to replace a pagan temple, Taxco where the ultra-baroque church put up by one Borda, a silver tycoon, bore the inscription "God gives to Borda and Borda gives to God," Acapulco where our host, an ex-sailor who had deserted his British ship and seemed unable to distinguish English from Spanish would offer us the choice at breakfast of "Pineapple or Piña?"—and where, after the briefest dip in the Pacific, I managed to get the worst sunburn I have ever experienced, leading to ructions when Anna in bathing it got water on the bed. Finally we reached Toltec Oaxaca, scene of a religious experience of some note.

We were the only guests at Oaxaca's only hotel, where after watching a "shower" of beetles falling outside our window—landing on their backs for the most part and ineffectually waving their feelers—we sat down at the restaurant. While enjoying our meal, part of which was *huevos rancheros*, we were approached by a Mexican enquiring if we were "Adventists Seventh Day"—being apparently of the opinion that "gringos" (we were always taken for these) were liable to be such. He seemed disappointed to learn that we were not.

No one at that time would travel to Mexico without a bout of "Montezuma's revenge," and we were no exception. But the country never failed to delight and I long wished to return, though that is now most unlikely. Arrived back at Toronto airport, with little luggage, we had difficulty persuading a female customs officer that there was not more secreted away somewhere. But there were still just our two small bags, and a brass vessel the base of which she tapped suspiciously.

⸻※⸻

In the summer of 1963, still trying for a child after Anna's miscarriages, we set out across the continent in a newly-acquired second-hand VW "Beetle," and covered some 9000 miles, the aim being to cross Canada via some pretty wild and largely uninhabited country north of Lake Superior and from there to Winnipeg, where the summer temperature was over 100 degrees Fahrenheit and where we met an acquaintance of Anna's family who had become a ballerina. On to Edmonton and the Jasper-Banff highway along the line of the Rockies, passing the Athabasca glacier, then visiting Maligne Lake and Lake Louise before proceeding across the more fertile parts of British Columbia.

I was especially impressed by the sheer power of the Fraser River and left it reluctantly to reach Vancouver. There in Stanley Park the VW was broken into, perhaps from mere vandalism — or perhaps we had surprised the thieves by an early return — since we lost virtually nothing. In Vancouver — surely one of the most beautifully located cities on earth, with sea, "fjords," and Mount Waddington — we stayed with the Winnipeg ballerina's parents: Gus Skerl, a geologist, and Doris who had been friend of Anna's father in the London of the 1930s. Later both Gus and Doris survived a Japanese internment camp in the Philippines.

After Vancouver we moved south into the United States, this being Anna's first experience of that variegated entity. The astonishingly blue Crater Lake in Oregon — not to speak of the redwoods and sequoias which followed (one of these trees allowed us to drive through it) — was a relief from the massive freeways by which we continued through California to San Francisco and the wine-world around Sacramento, then through Yosemite National Park and a steep evening descent — Anna at the wheel being actually blown downhill — to Las Vegas which we reached to find the temperature still at 107 degrees Fahrenheit: however, there was a pool. Before that we had risked a crazy drive across Death Valley (in July!) with little else on the road and towels on seats roasting from the sun. The engine roared, but being air-cooled kept going. The one man-made structure visible was a gas-station and bar where we found a desolate trucker whose over-heated engine would not permit him to continue until evening. A jar on the bar counter displayed a rattlesnake in formaldehyde.

Passing through Flagstaff, Arizona—where the VW needed some repairs to its transmission—we eventually reached the Grand Canyon. Though as yet we were unable to descend it—that was to come many years later—the vast panorama was more impressive than we could have imagined, or than I can describe. A less welcome surprise was Anna's being denied a drink at a campsite bar on the grounds that she was underage: a compliment but an unwanted one, and her passport, which would have clarified the matter, had been left in the car.

After passing Reno, Nevada—its hotels advertising "cheap rates for divorcees"—we came to Salt Lake City. Driving through Utah we noticed the beautifully tilled farms, home still, perhaps, to polygamists though marital pluralities had been banned when the Church of the Latter Day Saints received in the 1880s a revelation informing it that polygamy was, temporarily at least, now off-limits, thus enabling the state to be recognized as a fully-fledged member of the Union.

Non-"saints" are not allowed to enter the Temple, though are offered—and we accepted—the opportunity to visit the adjacent museum. Here, after viewing the "evidence" for the falling of the famous gold plates for John Smith in Palmyra, New York, we could follow Brigham Young as he led his followers to their present stronghold in Salt Lake City—"behind the Zion curtain," as I later saw it phrased on a T-shirt for sale at the airport. What impressed most were inscriptions around the top of the museum indicating prophetic intimations of the coming of the Saints. One of these purported to be from Aristotle.

At that time, though regularly teaching ancient philosophy, I did not know Aristotle's text as well as I later would, but thinking the inscription implausible and possibly bogus, I called one of the staff and asked if he could give me the reference. He said the director would be able to do so and went off to fetch him, but it seemed he was nowhere to be found, so all I could do was give my University of Toronto address and be assured that he would contact me—which, however, he failed to do.

Nor was this my last journey "behind the Zion Curtain." Many years later, I was invited to give a series of lectures at Utah's Brigham Young University, where I found what suggested an explanation of what appeared to be the false Aristotelian claim. In talking to faculty members all would seem typical of what one would find on other campuses—but should the conversation move to religion, we seemed to be on different planets. There would appear a total disconnect between the academic and the religious mind: a star example, I suppose, of the compartmentalization I was later to discuss in *Confusion in the West*. This was, however extreme, and the compartmentalization absolute. Thus, I knew that Mormons banned alcohol and caffeine-based stimulants, so was surprised to find Coca-Cola fountains all over the campus. It seemed that for the Saints financial advantage might have overruled the ban on stimulants in this one case. Since, however, integrity seemed lacking, perhaps something similar might have been related to the late revelation against polygamy—and to what seemed the apparent non-text of Aristotle.

After our sojourn in Salt Lake City we toiled through the flat "corn-belt" toward Chicago and eventually home—with a brief visit paid to Father Charles's sister's family in Blissfield, Michigan.

⸻

And so we commenced another academic year. I was promoted now to Assistant Professor (though with as yet no certainty of tenure) and Anna continued in post at Saint Michael's. With *Eros and Psyche* soon to be accepted by the University of Toronto Press, tenure would surely be forthcoming and I was already at work on a fuller study of Plotinus for which several articles had cleared the way. Anna was now pregnant with Peter, while beyond the bounds of the University—indeed beyond the frontiers of Canada—the times they were a-changing. On November 22, 1963, William Wallace banged on the door of my office to tell me that John F. Kennedy had been assassinated. Which calls for what might seem—but is not—a digression.

Partly, but not only, because the realities of the Kennedy clan were not—owing to Press collusion—detailed in the public domain, many of us were deluded about JFK. He seemed to have much in his favor and had boldly resolved the Cuban missile crisis; he was a Catholic, apparently in the spirit of the reforming Second Vatican Council which had been working in Rome since 1962, and from which many derived high hopes, some of which would be realized. He seemed concerned with the plight of the Third World and encouraged the young to join what almost amounted to a crusade to improve the lives of millions both inside and outside the United States: "Camelot" seemed to project an inspiring dream, and many thought of Kennedy as a new and even better Roosevelt. The truth, as it was to transpire, was quite other.

John Fitzgerald Kennedy was heir to an Irish dynasty which had been growing in power since the days of "Honey Fitz," mayor of Boston in the mid-nineteenth century. His mother was one of "Honey's" daughters. His father (to the fury of many in the United Kingdom, including my parents), as American ambassador in London before the Second World War, had been conspicuously pro-Nazi (and earlier pro-Franco) and did what he could to keep the United States out of the war, while bringing up his sons to be gross womanizers. And when son John F. Kennedy was named as the Democratic Party's candidate for the presidency in 1960 (and inaugurated in 1961) it was less as representative of the party than of a cabal, orchestrated by brother Bobby, to establish a party within the party. In office his internal policy was a flop, Kennedy failing to get a single reform bill through Congress; all the Civil Rights legislation that eventually passed was the work of a machine-democrat, Kennedy's successor, Lyndon B. Johnson, who, with a twenty-odd year career behind him as House Leader in the Senate, "knew where the bodies were buried" and as president put his knowledge to good use.

From the Catholic point of view the Kennedy régime was a disaster on two fronts. Kennedy had publicly proclaimed that where he found Catholic teaching would conflict with the Constitution he would always follow the Constitution: that gave him the hope for more non-Catholic votes and the pretext for abandoning Catholic moral teaching, not least about sexuality. As Arthur Schlesinger put it, the Kennedy administration "did for sex what [Eisenhower's] did for golf," and as the Kennedy "circus" rolled into town you could see what he meant: "college girls" (often Catholics turned Kennedy groupies) from Massachusetts and environs wandering naked from one hotel room to another; the exploitation of Marilyn Monroe, shared between brothers Bobby and Jack ("I was good for his back"); the story that Jack had to have a new woman some twenty minutes before every major speech; the mafia associations at different levels, one through Frank Sinatra and the "Rat Pack," the other, more directly, through Sam Giancana, Capone's successor in Chicago.

The whole "show" seemed summed up later when younger brother Ted crashed a car into a tidal channel in the neighborhood of Martha's Vineyard, killing an attractive young Catholic woman who had worked on his late brother Bobby's campaign and, even though he failed to report the incident till mid-morning the next day, he legally got away with it: a misfortune, so satirists claimed, requiring him to advertise for a new secretary with "the ability to swim." All three brothers, but Ted especially, were to prove hardcore advocates of abortion, while remaining tribally billed as good Catholics, living out what came to be dubbed "the spirit of Vatican II"—as preached by clerics urging good Catholic girls to read *The Power of Sexual Surrender* and other such soft-porn classics of the day. And the Kennedy circus affected other prominent Catholics too, not least—and more immediately relevant to the present story—in branch-plant Canada—though Canadians would always point out that they were no branch-plant in one important respect: they did not, stereotypically, carry hand-guns in their inside pockets.

The second effect of the Kennedys and their Epigoni was on education in Catholic colleges and universities, including Saint Michael's. In 1967 the presidents of a number of senior and often well-heeled Catholic universities met at Land O'Lakes, Wisconsin. Noting the "spirit of Vatican II" and the successes of the Kennedy clan in securing fame, not least by becoming merely tribally Catholic, and often influenced by the same Irish or Jesuit (or both) theologians—and recognizing that their institutions were often falling well below those of their secular academic rivals (hence being labeled, as was Saint Michael's, as "pastoral")—they thought that they must choose between being more than tribally Catholic and being intellectual, and concluded that they must follow the secular path, especially on moral issues: this at a time when the secular universities were themselves in turmoil. I note this because, 1963 not being 1967, the effects of Kennedy Catholicism had not yet become apparent to many, certainly not to those over the Canadian border.

⊰⊱✸⊰⊱

Anna's pregnancy, which eventually resulted in Peter's birth, was not easy; she suffered much from morning sickness and some bleeding, so there remained a lurking fear that the miscarriages might be repeated. Nevertheless, on the evening of July 22, 1964, Anna went to the hospital (not without a surreptitious dose of something alcoholic to see her through), and at 7:30 the following morning I responded to the telephone to hear the cheerful voice of a doctor (not Doctor Harper who was on holiday) saying "Your wife is fine and your son has arrived (confirming my intuition about the sex of the newcomer) and he has all his bits!" It was a great relief, but brought home that since I knew nothing about babies I would have to start learning fast. Immediately we had to determine the child's full name. We had originally intended Peter John, but very soon we heard that my grandfather, Robert Mansfield — Littlebury Granddad — had died. My father's name also being Robert, we added that to the two names already chosen — meaning that any other child to be born would have to have three names too.

In the event we survived the broken nights, the crying, and the occasional lusty screaming well enough, though Anna might be seen at times holding the baby in one arm while with the other hand leafing through Doctor Spock's baby book. But she did know something about babies and handled Peter with growing confidence, while I gradually came to find him fascinating and often unexpected. 1466 Avenue Road did not allow children, so without waiting to be evicted, we rented a rather derelict house on Duplex Avenue near Eglinton subway station.

The basement proved to be full of junk, which Anna cleared out, and perhaps it was in appreciation for that that the landlord put double glazing into the baby's room — and sent in one "Herbie" to spruce the house up on the outside. Herbie gave us an insight into certain more unexpected aspects of the Canadian scene, being a Mohawk Indian who, having apparently no fear of heights (or much else), often worked cleaning the windows of skyscrapers, that is when not dynamiting anything needing to be blown up. On this occasion the temperature rose to well over

100 degrees Fahrenheit, so I offered him a beer. That he refused, saying that if he drank one he would need a whole lot more, so he would lay off alcohol until he had finished the job — and then binge: the first indication that this metabolism was the norm for "native Americans."

When it was time to move again, we contrived to purchase a mortgage for a property of our own. This was 329 Fairlawn Avenue, a three-bedroom detached house off Avenue Road where we were to remain for the next decade in a neighborhood gradually becoming more "ethnic." There we discovered information about the name Rist, for having repeatedly received election propaganda in Estonian, we enquired of some Estonian neighbors why this was, to be told that Rist is a common name in Estonia where it means "cross": the source of some targeted jests by Anna at having married "a cross."

With Christmas came a visit from Henry Blumenthal, now having secured a PhD — on Plotinus's psychology after Professor Guthrie refused to supervise one on the far more original theme that Simplicius's commentaries on Aristotle were the work of a Neoplatonic philosopher: which is now generally accepted thanks to later work by Henry and a number of other scholars who taught us that the Medieval Aristotle was not the historical Aristotle but a Platonized theist, hence much more easily adaptable to the concerns of Christian, Jewish, and Muslim theologians.

Our son Peter was a Canadian citizen by right of birth, so on Fairlawn Avenue we thought we might as well take out citizenship ourselves, the change of abode having been accomplished with the help of one of Anna's former fellow teachers at Loretto Abbey, Jean Kallmeyer and her lawyer husband Bruce. Both of them were graduates of Saint Michael's and Jean a scion of one of the older Irish-Catholic families of Ontario, one of her brothers being a professor of French at the College. Bruce, though of part-German extraction, was an ardent monarchist.

Now apparently permanently settled, we determined to show off our new son to his British grandparents in the coming summer and booked passages on one of the last of the transatlantic liners still sailing from Montréal — so giving Anna the chance of crossing the "pond" by ship, since air-travel was by now taking over. But it proved a tough journey: Peter was getting over inoculations, especially one for measles, and off his food. We took him to the ship's doctor and when we told him we had had him inoculated, found little sympathy: "Why did you do that?"—to which Anna could only reply, "To prevent him from having measles, I suppose," to be told, "Better if he had them."

Though the weather was cold and raw, we walked Peter around the deck in a harness. Worse was to come in the dining room, where he regularly hurled anything he could lay his little hands on in every direction, often accompanying the bombardment with abundant roaring, thus emptying that part of the room. Yet eventually we reached Britain and sailing near the island of Arran we were rewarded with much beauty as the liner turned south. So disembarked, we were at last able to introduce Peter to both sets of grandparents while from time to time I managed to do a bit of work on an intended book on Stoicism — the Plotinus one being now almost complete — in the Library of the London Institute of Classical Studies. And so, after a comparatively restful summer and aided by various not always adequate baby-sitters, we started another academic year. I had now been promoted to Associate Professor and awarded tenure. The year culminated in July 1966 with the arrival of Peter's sister Alice Mary Anna. Anna's mother flew over to help.

Again the birth was not without incident. Anna had an infection in an armpit and when the baby was born — on July 7, tactfully delaying till after my birthday the day before — they both had to be kept apart from others during what was then the week-long hospital stay, again in Saint Michael's Hospital and this time under the care of Doctor Harper. In the end all turned out well, or seemed to, until we realized that Alice had a very serious squint. It was never satisfactorily remedied, due to what we thought incompetent handling by a leading ophthalmologist. Our poor Alice had two operations and immense amounts of "patching," while her lot and ours was not made easier by the extreme jealousy of brother Peter, who would pretend to kiss her and then bite, and against whom she had to be protected in a play-pen. I remembered that in the *Confessions* Augustine had written that with young children the will to harm is there but the power is lacking; it seemed that Peter was trying to prove him wrong about power!

Alice's arrival affected Peter otherwise too: he stopped progressing in a number of ways, particularly speech, in evident protest against the newcomer. It had already become apparent that he resented being left with the "sitter" while Anna went down to Saint Michael's on three days of the week. (She would conclude she would have done better to go for five half-days, and so be at home each day with our son.) Things came to a head one morning when, the baby-sitter arriving, Peter roared his anger at the sight of her. Fortunately the academic year was ending, and in England we took him to a child psychologist who was able to explicate Peter's hostility to us who had left him with a sitter — whom we suspected of leaving him to languish in his cot — and then had foisted a sibling on him. (Anna was reminded that when her brother was born, she, being almost three, had shocked her mother by suggesting we "throw him out of the window.") At this point (now on holiday in Cambridge) she set herself to devote to Peter the time the baby slept.

By now the specter of "Kennedy Catholicism" was appearing in Canada. In June 1967 Pierre Eliot Trudeau became Minister of Justice, and immediately set about decriminalizing homosexuality and relaxing legal restrictions on abortion. Next year he became Prime Minister as successor to the old diplomat and internationalist Lester Pearson, and "Trudeaumania" (a Canadian version of a similar Kennedy outbreak) enveloped most of the country. And his pro-abortion, though majority Catholic, Cabinet followed his lead, his successor as Minister of Justice — John Turner, also a "Catholic" — heading the charge.

This was the moment when I became one of the founders, soon to be appointed Chairman, of the Canadian Coalition for Life. Our first task was supposed to be to galvanize the Catholic bishops, assumed to be powerful opponents of abortion, into action. We could hardly have been more deluded. I remember going (still a non-Catholic) with others to visit Bishop Carter of London, Ontario, later Cardinal Archbishop of Toronto — his struggle to be honest about abortion has already been mentioned in the Introduction — who was known to be a close friend of Trudeau and to dine with him on a regular basis. But our hopes that this relationship could be turned to good account seemed to be going nowhere, and one of the delegation, Gwen Landolt, a feisty woman lawyer and life-long pro-life activist, began to lose patience, finally bursting out with "Everyone knows you are a close friend of Pierre Trudeau; surely you could put in a word on our behalf." To which the bishop, putting an arm around Gwen's shoulder, replied, "My dear Gwen, you can't imagine I have any influence with the Prime Minister!" As we left the bishop's office, Gwen turned to me and muttered, "I could have spat on him."

Nor was this the only such delegation I joined before myself becoming a Catholic. The second was to Trudeau himself, in his office in Ottawa, and I was accompanied by two others, one of whom was Catholic. We had been surprised to be offered an appointment and suspected that it would not last more than a few minutes, but Trudeau, accompanied by his Québec enforcer, continued the conversation at a quite high academic level for nearly an hour and a half, to the visible irritation of the enforcer. What was incongruous about the meeting, however, was that although Trudeau was happy to debate abortion—even apparently conceding that we had something of a case—he had no intention of changing his mind: however doubtful he may have found the arguments in its favor; he knew that being "liberal" about "choice" meant votes.

I suppose Trudeau thought he would also enhance his position if, being an eligible bachelor, he took a wife, which he did. The bride, daughter of a British Columbia politician, became instantly famed when, sitting at some poolside, she declared that "Pierre has taught me how to love": not that it won her universal favor since rumors swirled as to more lurid love interests, as that she had had an affair with Mick (later Sir Michael) Jagger. This he denied, declaring "I would not touch her with a barge-pole." Yet the urban myth seemed *ben trovato*.

Though Trudeau's marriage increased his reputation as enigmatic, Trudeaumania waned over the years, though never entirely disappearing: that said, I once picked up a book on sale before an election entitled "What Pierre Trudeau has done for Canada," and on opening it found—blank pages. And a Monopoly-type game was named after him in which the aim was to do economically as badly as possible, the winner being whoever became bankrupt first.

It would, however, be false to claim that Trudeau did nothing for Canada, even though in my view his social and constitutional policies were disastrous. While his determined opposition to Québec separatism played a substantial part in its eventual defeat, his major project toward the end of his career was achieved by a cynical deception of the Canadian public. To the clear light of day, his aim was to "repatriate" the Canadian Constitution, which meant that he severed the last (though *de facto* insignificant) links which bound the Canadian Parliament to its parent in Westminster. That was popular but, characteristically, into the Act of Parliament which confirmed it, Trudeau slipped a piece of vandalism—a Bill of Rights—which passed almost without debate and immediately attracted little public attention, though it radically changed the Canadian Constitution. In effect it pointed Canada toward an American-style political régime, whereby Parliament lost its sovereignty to the extent that it was increasingly subject to the rulings of unelected judges in the rights-obsessed Supreme Court. That in its turn pointed toward a more presidential system, again on the American model and based on a three-way division of powers.

In the later 1960s not only was the Toronto skyline changing at a phenomenal pace (going away for a summer could mean that on returning one barely recognized the place), and not only was the city becoming increasingly cosmopolitan, changing from "Toronto the good" into something more indeterminate, but the University of Toronto was improving the quality of its staff, and not least in Classics. In these years we welcomed a number of highly qualified scholars: there was the distinguished Latinist George Goold, a native of London—"slum-boy made good" in Bagnani's pithy phrase—the historians Christopher Jones (known in Oxford as "Papist Jones" until converted to homosexuality by his instructor there), Timothy Barnes (who, in the view of Sir Ronald Syme had the problem of being "so damned accurate") and Peter Derow. These later were joined—after the implosion of Classics at Yale (orchestrated by their administration and handled "on the ground" by Eric "the Red" Havelock)—by Alan Samuel (whose wife Debbie found a job at Toronto's new York University) and Michael O' Brien. Finally came Richard Tarrant, another rising star in the Latin firmament. Though Goold, Jones, and Tarrant eventually would move south, and Derow to Oxford, their impact was substantial.

That said, though it was unclear to most of its faculty, the University was by now facing a growing crisis in that it had recently undertaken an enormous but ill-planned expansion. This also opened its doors to the importing from the United States of some of the problems then ravaging American campuses. Massive expansion inevitably changed the relationship of the academic staff not only to the undergraduates—putting far more of them in larger and hence more impersonal classes—but also to the administration which, with the increasing size of the institution it was supposed to administer, seemed to suffer a gradual separation of its interests in "keeping the show on the road" from the teaching and research concerns of the majority of the faculty. Thus the stage was set for the ideologically fraught years from 1967 until 1971, when the passing of a new University of Toronto Act brought into being a new and more disillusioned university.

1968, supposed to be a quiet year, was the date of my first substantial article on Augustine: an analysis of those problems of predestination and free will which were to provoke me to further comment over the next sixty years, and which, to my surprise, have continued to arouse interest. I had been paying increasing attention to Patristics since starting to think about Plotinus and the development of Platonism in late antiquity, and this could not but draw me to the contemporary Christian writers, first the enigmatic Greek known as Pseudo-Dionysius from sixth-century Syria, then Origen and Augustine. I noted as I proceeded that much of the work in these areas was not only tainted by sectarianism but was often of a markedly lower quality than was regarded as requisite in Classical philology. Partly as a result of my growing Patristics interests I was invited to speak on Plotinus at my first international conference at the one-time Abbey of Royaumont, a little north of Paris, in that same year 1968: which conference was to prove a further eye-opener.

For firstly it was chaotic, due to the organizer's having gone home after learning that the abbey's bedrooms were the Medieval monastery's lockless cells, hence exposing him to the risk of being beaten up by his graduate students. This was the time when rock-throwing students fought it out with the tear-gas-firing police on Paris's streets. Then I found that the younger French scholars were eager to accuse older colleagues (usually wholly unjustly) of having collaborated during the Second World War. Then, when after a lecture by a prominent but boring scholar I tried to ask a philosophical question first in English, then in

French, I was banged in the ribs by his colleague and told in loud broken English, "It is no good asking 'im zings like zat; he don't think, he write." Finally, having to wait in Paris for several hours before flying back to Toronto, I went into a cinema showing one of the first lesbo-chic films — *Thérèse et Isabelle* — to recognize that it was set at Royaumont. All this has been recounted in more detail in "Tracking the Animal Academicum"; suffice it to say here that it prepared me for what was soon to follow at the University of Toronto — and that I was only later to learn that the "distinguished scholar," apparently unbalanced (as were many other luminaries, both clerical and lay, of the French academic scene) by the fate of his traditional Catholicism after the Second Vatican Council, jumped out of a sixth-floor window.

Claude Bissell, President of the University of Toronto, was aware of how the University's over-rapid expansion had rendered its governing structures, including its disciplinary structures, more or less unworkable. What he wanted was to replace the lay Board of Governors and the Academic Senate with a new joint Governing Council, to include both lay and academic (including administrative) members. The problem he thought this would solve was that under the old system the Board debated the affairs of the University without much knowledge of the needs and realities of academic life in a larger and more complex world, while the Senate tried to determine academic policy without any financial leverage. Bissell's scheme had merits and demerits which need not be retailed here.

The immediate problem was that it opened up the question of university governance at a time when part of the student body (plus a minority of the faculty) wanted radical changes in the academic portfolio which could allow the more radical students to control the curriculum, these already claiming that under the present system they "had their minds fucked"(which translated meant that they were being taught truths they did not want to hear). To "correct" this, they demanded a substantial say in the appointment, promotion, and possible dismissal of academic staff.

Up to this point I had not taken much part in the affairs of what was then the Association of the Teaching Staff or ATS (later the University of Toronto Faculty Association or UTFA). As a typical Brit, I tended to think that at Toronto the faculty had far too little control of University affairs, a view largely "academic" since as far as I (and the Classics Department) was concerned, the present arrangements were working reasonably well, and in our secluded section of the University we were as yet feeling few of the discomforts affecting larger departments as a result of the greatly increased size (and consequent depersonalization) of the student body. These new mass educational requirements had already helped to foment student unrest and, soon, violence on American campuses, especially at Columbia and the University of California at Berkeley.

Bissell put his plan for University reorganization to an ill-attended meeting of the Faculty Association on October 3, 1968, and met a hostile reception from a naïve and ill-informed group: naïve because they tended to forget that the fate of the University of Toronto (being a state-funded institution) would ultimately be determined by the Ontario legislature, but also because they assumed that the radical students—whose principal spokesman on this occasion was Bob Rae, later leader of the New Democratic Party (NDP) in Ontario and subsequently Foreign Minister of Canada—wanted the kind of reforms that the faculty would approve. That this assumption was mistaken was clear from the fact that the students were asking for a reformed unicameral Governing Council on which they would have as many members as the academic staff: what would come to be called the "principle of parity."

The danger of that was less the effect on the Governing Council itself, on which lay members—that is, government-approved business men—would still control the ultimate decisions (or so one supposed) but that the principle of "parity" would be extended to the various faculty councils, but especially to the Council of the Faculty of Arts and Science, where primary decisions—especially about curricula—would be made. Here indeed would arise what I later (to the fury of some Liberal and NDP members of the Ontario legislature) saw as the real threat: that a university with free speech and free enquiry would be transformed into an ideologically driven institution in which divergence from ephemeral academic fads would be suppressed, if necessary by firings.

Bissell's proposal was rejected by the ATS almost with contempt, and realizing the dangers that lay ahead, I seconded a motion by Jack Robson (later editor-in-chief of the writings of John Stuart Mill) to break the principle of parity on the proposed Governing

Council and thereby prevent it from becoming a paradigm for faculty councils. Our proposal, along with other moderating attempts to help the President out, was defeated. Bissell had by this time left the meeting and for some days considered resigning on the grounds that he had lost the confidence of the faculty. Eventually he was persuaded by a number of senior colleagues that this was not the case — as was true, though the faculty by their naïve behavior had seriously weakened his position and encouraged the radical students to infer that if they pushed hard, the Administration would give way in the interest of "peace in our time" on campus.

The radicals were right about the mentality which then came to govern the administration but wrong in their assumption that in the end they would get all they wanted on parity. But to defeat this destructive proposal required considerable effort by a small group of faculty, including myself, who yet knew they were speaking for a silent (but often cowardly) majority. To understand the events which followed it is essential to look at something of the context in which the struggle against "student power" took place, against a background in the United States of the Civil Rights movement and the war in Vietnam.

Throughout the Western world the late 1960s were years of rapid and extreme change, especially in regard to sexual behavior, with libertinism, as usual, accompanying radical politics. Part of the explanation was the "feminist" version of Marxism developed by Engels in his demand for the destruction of the traditional family as enemy of the awaited communist state. Part was the influence of Simone de Beauvoir, for whom "woman" was a construction of men, with women needing to be liberated from male "ownership" and free to defy the natural rhythms of marriage and birth of children, with contraception and abortion giving them the means so to do. If, according to "Notre Dame de Sartre" (as Parisian students adoringly dubbed De Beauvoir), a woman's right "to be herself" was impeded by an unwanted conception, she had the right to react against the "aggressor" and kill it.

The consequent morality — we knew an academic woman who kept as a "relic" and in a "reliquary" a cigarette end Sartre had discarded in Les Deux Magots — could be read on T-shirts of the age: "A nymphomaniac is a woman with the sexual desires of the average man," or "Help stamp out virginity." The new female libertinism was endorsed by many males hardly able to believe their "luck" (this could be dignified as a desire for justice for women), while "Make love not war" was added to the slogans of the age.

More generally on campuses—and not least that of the University of Toronto—immature youths imagined that in smashing up a building as a way of calling for more student "power," they were contributing to the world-wide Marxist (or "left-liberal") dream now supposedly becoming reality. At its most implausible this delusion could take the form of handing out pieces of watermelon, as if one were an oppressed black from Mississippi; no humor was intended or perceived. So did hypocrisy blend with self-righteousness.

It is informative to record the different reactions of two groups on campus to the would-be revolution. Old-style Marxists could be hostile and appeal to Lenin's condemnation of "infantile" revolutionaries. Informatively, on one occasion a distinguished Marxist professor found himself obliged to stand on a crowded Toronto subway train; this was Barker Fairley, a near-ninety-year-old authority on German literature, as well as no mean artist and close friend of several of that "Group of Seven" whose work is on display in Kleinberg, not far from Toronto. Noting there was a "liberated" student sprawled across three seats, Fairley tapped him on the shoulder and said, "Excuse me, would you mind standing up?" "Why should I?" came the truculent reply, to be answered with, "Because I want to kick your ass." Even restrained Torontonians on the train beamed their satisfaction as the lout stood up.

If old-style Marxists were often opposed to the "revolutionary" antics they saw around them, Catholics at Saint Michael's College, both students and faculty (including clergy) might behave less than wisely. Buoyed up by the "spirit of Vatican II," many of these backed extreme student demands on campus as well as radical if undefined changes in the Church. Of course, many did not, and least of all Anna's boss Father Sheridan: he who, when clergy in the diocese were told by the archbishop to promote the Catholic newspaper in their Lenten sermon, was said to have mounted the pulpit to declare "Lent is a season of alms-giving and penance. For alms-giving you can buy the *Register*—and for penance you can read it!" He was also heard to observe of what became known as the "sand-box Mass" held in the crypt of Saint

Basil's, with children crawling on the altar steps, "If the bishops won't stop it, the police will."

Discussion often ranged in Saint Michael's dining and common rooms about the future education of clergy and their now-to-be modernized lifestyle. Hence, on another occasion Sheridan, sitting silently at the same table and invited to join a lively discussion with one Father Fink — and with Father Gregory Baum, former *peritus* at the Second Vatican Council but eventually expelled from the Augustinians — was challenged, "What do you say, Father? Should priests marry?," coming up with the instant reply, "Only if they love one another very much" (which fifty years later would not necessarily be taken as a joke). Along the same lines when Father Joseph Owens, a friend of mine and a distinguished Catholic philosopher, was asked what he thought about the future of clerical education, he observed dryly, "Well, if you want to stop them thinking, teach them theology." (Clearly he did not have the old-style manualist version of Thomism in mind.)

To add further joy to the liberal Catholics at Saint Michael's there arrived with great fanfare the Tübingen theologian Hans Küng. Though admired much in the College, his manner attracted an excellent strip-cartoon in the student newspaper, of which the punch-line ran, "I am Hans Küng, the distinguished theologian from Tübingen. People often ask me, Well Hans, with all these wars, famines, terrible deaths, how can you believe in a good God? And I say, Well, search me!" In these same years arrived a more refreshing visitor, the Duke of Edinburgh who, emerging with the University President from the administrative headquarters at Simcoe Hall and looking down on scores of Mounties and assorted other protectors, turned to the President to ask, "What is this, a police state?"

⸙

President Bissell now set up a Committee on University Government (CUG) to decide on the University's proposals for the upcoming new University of Toronto Act. Dominant among its members were a group of student radicals, and faculty who largely supported their demands; some of these were deemed to be going through that "male menopause" perceived among the middle-aged and thus pretending to be "lads" again, which might involve swapping wives or becoming involved in sexual relations with their students, some of whom were happy to provide "services" in return for inflated grades. I was never offered such services, but I knew several who were, one of whom told me that looking through a pile of essays he noticed one particularly thin folder, and opening it up, recognized a photograph of the student (female and nude) with a telephone number scrawled underneath. Inflated grades apart, one of the enlightened Catholic faculty accused me of antisemitism when I voted to "refer," rather than approve, a Jewish student's PhD thesis in philosophy: perhaps an ecumenical gesture.

Soon after Bissell's Committee on University Government was established, Bill Nelson of the History Department and I agreed to propose a series of recommendations to the Arts and Science Council rejecting that "parity" which the Commission—dominated as it was by Bob Rae (again) and Professor Larry Lynch, a devout Catholic from Saint Michael's—would produce. Debate in the Council was feisty and often offensive; I was labeled a fascist on several occasions by people who in my view had more than a little of the fascist about themselves. (As a contemporary definition of a fascist was "a man who wears a white shirt," and since my mother would send me one of these every year for my birthday and again at Christmas, to that extent the sobriquet was earned.) In the end the Council rejected "parity" where curriculum, promotion, or appointment was in question.

The Committee on University Government issued its report in October 1969, at about which time I was elected Chairman of the Faculty Association (UTFA) and immediately persuaded Nelson to head a committee to produce our own blueprint for future university governance—and to ward off any attempt by the administration to yield to pernicious student demands—since we recognized that our quarrel was less with the radical students than with craven administrators (these were ex-academics now adopting a corporate view of the University) always inclining to quiet things down without reference to such academic values as freedom to speak, to teach, and to set the curriculum.

We were also to note the increasing tendency of the more extreme students to resort to violence against professors, whether on staff or invited visitors, of whose views they disapproved, and that the administration made little attempt to control such disruptive behavior. Nelson formulated what I called "Nelson's Law" to sum up their attitude: namely, if an administration were faced with a choice between what is honorable and what it not, it would always look for a path between, so establishing a new base for the acceptance of ever more undesirable demands.

The Faculty Association Council and its own University Government Committee were divided on the merits of Bissell's desire for unicameralism, and this was largely shelved while more urgent matters were debated: primarily how to react to that "parity" which the University Government Committee had inevitably advocated. Hence, while agreeing with Bissell that the old Board and Senate needed reform, we went along with unicameralism and proposed to the now established successor of the CUG—the University-wide Committee, intended to formulate the University's final, and supposedly generally supported, view of its needs—that the new Governing Council should consist of twenty faculty, twenty laymen, eight full-time administrators, and seven students. In the summer of 1970, which saw the end of my term as Chairman of UTFA, the University-wide Committee adopted a modified version of this, with the number of students increased to two-thirds that of the faculty, but parity denied. It was as good as we could get and a lot better than we feared. Then we could only wait to see what the Provincial Government would impose on us.

Part of the discussion on University government, as I have noted, depended on unthought-out views of what should be the proper role of the faculty in a university, and this came to a head at the end of my term as Chairman of UTFA, the unresolved issue being whether the faculty were the core of a university or merely its employees. I took the former view, though with insufficient grasp of the dependence of a university on external political powers. The faculty salary committee when I was Chairman proposed what in effect would be a demand for trade-union style bargaining: which view was not shared by the majority of the staff (especially in the professional faculties) and was rejected, not entirely to my regret, at the end of my period of office.

My interest in UTFA had been to promote it not as a mere bargaining agent but as the only remaining means to uphold the old idea that the faculty—not passing waves of students and certainly not the administration—should control the University, with the longer-term good of students viewed as essential to its agenda. Hence I decided that after the University Act had been finally settled in the legislature, I would devote my time as far as possible to teaching and research and leave the faculty association to others — even though I feared these would have views of its purpose other than mine. By taking a stand on university governance, I thought I had repaid some of the kindness the University had shown me in receiving me into its department of Classics.

Before considering my from now on less contentious role in the University, I must recall an incident which might have deprived it of my services on a permanent basis. In that same year 1970 we decided to take a summer trip along the Saint Lawrence, then to tour the Cabot Trail in Nova Scotia, and then to return in slow stages, via New Brunswick, to Toronto. We did indeed manage to get back, but only, it might seem, by a miracle, for when I was driving on a straight road in good light near Fredericton, a car several vehicles ahead of us suddenly stopped on the roadway, forcing all behind it — including me — to brake hard (too hard, as Anna would point out), so that the truck behind, though braking, pushed us across the road to where, by the extraordinary intervention of Providence, we finished up on a pile of sand, being thus prevented from turning over or rolling into the ditch. The truck that had hit us had by then been rammed by another which overturned.

We were shaken up but safe, for though Peter and Alice a few minutes before had been "horsing around" in the back of the VW Estate, by the time of the accident they had tired and lain down. This also seemed providential. So we limped into a very dull Fredericton and eventually back to Toronto, where the car would be written off. The lady who by suddenly braking had caused it all — as she of course had technically the right to do — claimed it was because a bee had flown through her window! This, as I have already recorded, was not the only occasion when I have been spared injury or premature death, but it was certainly the one which unnerved me — and Anna — the most.

But life would revert to normal and my newly acquired notice in the North American academic community was evident in an invitation to speak at the Berkeley campus of the University of California. To understand Berkeley at that time one should read

David Lodge's *Changing Places*, but I can add a pennyworth of personal experience, my visit being both entertaining and a confirmation of my contemporary nervousness about what was happening in the universities of that time, and in the University of Toronto in particular. The invitation I received from Berkeley was to give a paper to a group of advanced graduate students and faculty on some aspect of Plotinus's thought, and I decided to talk about his attitude to the "Platonic underworld" of his day, which he had come to regard as a threat to rational thinking.

Unfortunately, the title I chose—"Some of my best friends are Gnostics," a virtual quotation from Plotinus himself—was misconstrued, so that when I reached the campus I was met by the organizers who said that we must change the venue to a large auditorium: the word "Gnostic" had apparently drawn a large crowd; when we reached the auditorium we found an audience of over two hundred, none of whom knew anything much about Plotinus. It was too late to rewrite the paper, so I decided to add a few jokes, modify some of the rest as I went along and hope for the best. Somewhat to my surprise the lecture was followed in silence and with apparent attention, and I agreed to answer questions.

I can still envisage what happened next. A huge man got up in the far-left corner of the room, dressed only in his underpants except for a heavy chain around his neck. His question was: "Say, Prof, how can I get hold of some of this stuff?" Fortunately I was able to tell him that earlier in the day I had walked along Telegraph Avenue looking at the bookstalls and there, under a cover which seemed to indicate that the work would reveal mystical secrets of the sub-continent, with possible Zen overtones, was what I recognized as a pirated copy of an eighteenth-century translation of Iamblichus's *De mysteriis*. I do not know whether my interrogator took my advice, but after a few more questions the lecture ended without further incident.

⸻

Back in Canada for the academic year 1970–1971, two events occupied most of my time: first the eventual debates in the Ontario legislature and their conclusion with the passage of the new University of Toronto Act, which concluded my concern with wider university politics in Toronto, though not with administration since in 1971 I became Chairman of the University Graduate

Department of Classics: a job which enabled me to strengthen, as I hoped, the linguistic aspects of the Classical program and to invite scholars who I thought would be especially worth hearing.

Much of the evidence about the academic, professional, and sociological impact of my (and other people's) invited visitors to the Classics department has been recorded elsewhere, but I cannot pass up a couple of particularly informative occasions. The first — a warning to lecturers on how not to start their address — was provided by a large and portentous Englishman who opened up with "I am not a practicing Platonist," provoking from the back of the hall, "You'd be in jail if you were." (It is not so clear that he would be now!) The second is set on a summer evening at the house of a colleague where a prominent visitor, surrounded by academic groupies, was dilating on his cat's having fallen out of his rooms in Caius College Cambridge on to the cobbles below. Anna joining the group at this point and not realizing that what had fallen out was a cat — albeit one with a Latin name to whom a book of considerable scholarly merit had been dedicated — then understanding that the talk was of a cat, made the mistake of saying "Ah, a cat! I had thought it was a human being." Which comment generated the retort "I very much wish it *had* been a human being."

As for the University Act, before it was finally passed in the early part of the summer, I was a member of a group from the Faculty Association who attended preliminary discussions at the Ontario legislature's Committee on Human Resources to prepare the ground for the eventual debates on the floor of the legislature. And now in the public domain, student radicals, encouraged by some senior administrators (though not President Bissell) attempted a final push for "parity" between faculty and students on the new Governing Council. They managed to win the support of various ignorant and ill-informed members both of the Liberal party and the NDP and had some hope that they might win over the ruling Conservatives too, not least because an election was coming up and the voting age was to be reduced to eighteen.

However, the major Toronto newspapers now turned against them and so, after some hesitation, did Premier Bill Davis. Hence when the Minister, John White, presented his upcoming bill to the Human Resources Committee, we recognized that on "parity" we had won, but the government exercised its real power by substantially increasing the number of lay representatives on the new Council, thus bringing a sense of reality to those who still hoped for a largely faculty-run University. The final distribution of seats was twenty-four lay people, eight alumni, twelve faculty, and eight students.

The bill was accepted after some fierce discussions in the committee and in the House, with the impotent opposition lashing out at the University faculty when they realized they were not going to get their way. Their claim was that most Toronto professors were lazy, not much interested in teaching their students, and spent their summers lolling on the decks of their lakeside cottages rather than doing any research: most of which was complete nonsense but satisfied the speakers' lust to lash out at those who had no significant means of defending themselves. But we took it on the chin, only pointing out in committee, via a law professor, Stan Schiff, that the bill itself was legally very badly drafted: according to Schiff, a decent lawyer could drive a tank through it in about fifteen places — which he outlined. The Minister agreed with most of Schiff's observations but said there was little time to make any changes so they would vote the thing through more or less unchanged the next day. Which they did, after listening to hours of more abuse of professors (including me) by posturing opposition politicians. So that was that.

The second and more personal event of 1971 was the birth of our third child, Thomas Charles Kenelm, on June 21 — celebrated when the news reached home by Peter's running around the block shouting "All the men and boys in the world have won and all the women and girls have lost." Not too long after I was able to give him and his sister some relief from the new arrival by taking them to Prince Edward Island, and in particular to the house where one of Alice's favorite books, *Anne of Green Gables* is set. After PEI there only remained one Canadian province I had not visited, and I remedied this that winter by lecturing at Memorial University in Newfoundland, — where one moved about the campus underground to avoid wading through the deep snow.

The birth itself (and I had guessed the sex right in advance in this as in all cases, though Anna said it was hardly surprising as he was clearly exceptionally long), was to be different. For Peter and Alice, Anna had endured the discomforts of epidurals — this time it was going to be "natural," something apparently almost unknown in Canada at that time, but Doctor Harper was happy with it, and, for the first time, I was invited to be present. All went as planned: Tom was born quite quickly, Doctor Harper congratulated me on standing up to it well (not at all difficult), and then asked me if I would like to come and watch a hysterectomy! When he asked Anna if she would like anything prescribed, she suggested champagne. This being unavailable, Harper said they could run to Guinness, which twice each day was duly brought. Perhaps the nurses thought they had an alcoholic on their hands, for on one day only one bottle arrived. But on Anna's complaint, the second duly appeared.

The birth of Tom was a bit of a watershed, nor did he escape the squint problem which had troubled us with Alice; he had to endure three operations, but the end-result was far better than was achieved for his sister. Anna, however, who had already gone on to part-time now thought it best to give up her teaching at Saint Michael's while hoping to continue to write; she was later also to assist Father Dan Callam, CSB as Associate Editor of the *Canadian Catholic Review*. Assuming by now that we would remain in Canada, we were soon to enroll both Peter and Alice in the Toronto French School ("TFS," hence dubbed by French-inaugurated pupils "tes fesses"), believing that they would profit from learning Canada's other official language (disliked though it still was in Ontario and even more further west).

At this time we came across a Montessori teacher "Brad," son of an American pilot killed in the course of duty and who might be a draft-dodger. And through Brad, who acted as a live-in help for several years, we met several of his friends, Catholic, often vegetarian and often pacifist: such as Jim Jalsevac and Dianne, with her autoharp, who for a while became his wife. Brad himself had tried his vocation in a monastery in Winnipeg but had been expelled after being caught playing "Plaisirs d'Amour" on his guitar. As for summer holidays, when not returning to Britain, our usual resort was to the lakes of Muskoka and Haliburton, the Lake of Bays being a particular favorite. There was also the annual "Ex," which we could attend in the fall, and where on one occasion Brad was beaten at tik-tak-toe by a chicken.

By now we had gathered a growing group of friends, apart from the "regular" Father Charles, especially the Marmuras: Mike — a fatalistic Palestinian, son of the Rector of the Anglican church in Jerusalem and himself a professor of Islamic philosophy — and his wife Betty (later a United Church minister). The Marmuras eventually had three children, the youngest of whom, Timmy, proved autistic. And then there were the Grazianis — René, son of a Jewish refugee mother and Dorothy regularly apostrophized as "Dorothy dear" from Wales — who were notable (apart from being, as were many other academics at the time, Wagner-devotees) for owning a swimming pool; hence we styled a rather tubby René "Walrus." Some of their family are still known to Peter.

But holidays seemed to pose a special problem. We did not want to deprive our children of the European culture we so much appreciated ourselves, but the airfares and hotel rates seemed prohibitive. Then arrived, again by apparent chance, a solution. The father of one of my students was appointed the first Canadian ambassador to the Holy See and the son — a man of great talents, not least linguistic — decided to live in Rome for a while with his family. Before he left, we invited him to dinner and over a few glasses suggested that he might find us a pad on the Tuscan coast. He went off and we forgot about it.

The crucial year was 1973, and I had been invited to a conference on the third-century Christian polymath Origen to be held at Montserrat, famous abbey and center of Catalan nationalism. My book on Epicurus had now been published (being only an introduction and written because I could not find anything I judged suitable for undergraduates) and I was, it seemed, becoming somewhat known in Continental academic circles. Nor in connection with *Epicurus* can I let pass unnoticed a comment by Harry Sandbach to whom I had sent the typescript for his sure-to-be-challenging appraisal. On the whole he liked it, but I remember with great pleasure one of his criticisms. At a point where I had written "Philodemus said that...," Sandbach in his small and neat hand had crossed this out and written over the top "Jensen printed that." He was right of course as to the fake text Jensen had produced and I treasured the comment as an enduring mark of his extraordinary knowledge of the ancient world which, while an undergraduate, I had not wit to appreciate. I assumed he did not class me with another ex-Trinity hopeful of the time whom he denoted as "a Wunderkind," adding "Always will be."

While I prepared for Montserrat, we received a letter from Italy reminding us that we had asked about a place in Tuscany. The answer was that the coast was hot and prices were through the roof since the likes of Claudia Cardinale and various footballers from Juventus were having villas built there, but that if we would consider something about thirty miles inland, in a village on the first rise of the Apennines, our friend had noted what looked like an attractive prospect. So I decided that after Montserrat I would fly on to Rome, meet the Embassy's chauffeur, Fernando Carlucci, who came from the village and would drive me up to see what was on offer. The details of all this are described in Anna's *We Etruscans*, so I need only give an outline of how we decided to purchase Pian Rocchetto, a *casa colonica* near Semproniano. And Montserrat must come first.

The monastery there is set in magnificent mountain country and the conference was certainly at a higher level than most. But there were features of it which I only understood many years later. What I did notice was that Montserrat had never been Franco-friendly and that the Catalan national anthem was played in its courtyard every midday. Although Franco was still living, it was an open secret that things would change with his now expected death. Accordingly, Spanish academics from the University of Barcelona were much out to please. But to please whom? Primarily a rather distinguished group of French Patristics scholars who included Marguerite Harl, Jean (later Cardinal) Daniélou, SJ, and Henri Crouzel, SJ, the leading Origen scholar of the day. Most French scholars had refused to take part in academic conferences in Spain during the Fascist period.

What I did not understand until many years later was that many of those present had an ecclesial agenda. The Second Vatican Council had substantially changed structures of the Church which had been in place since the Council of Trent, and part of that change was driven by "Patristics theologians" who wanted to downplay the Latin Fathers, especially Augustine—now smeared as a bastion of the old régime—in favor of his philosophically inferior, though seemingly more "liberal" Greek near-contemporaries. Of these the greatest was Origen, but though (from my "officially" non-Christian standpoint) I much appreciated his thought, I could not at that time understand why scholars at Montserrat seemed to overrate his philosophical powers.

When the conference ended, it was decided to continue the debate elsewhere, first in Manchester. There proceedings ended comically, with Crouzel and an English Methodist drawing up a document to be sent to the "heads" of the various Christian denominations urging that Justinian's condemnation of Origen be discarded. They should have known better, since in the ensuing discussion the first speaker observed immediately that "There is nae head of the Presbyterian Church." Finally a Jesuit—indeed the "mole" of Vatican II, "Xavier Rynne"—remarked wryly that he would be happy to sign the appeal but he knew what would happen when it reached Rome: they would say, "We certainly agree but we cannot go further because of the Orthodox," Origen being still hated in many Orthodox circles.

Montserrat duly enjoyed, I took a plane to Rome and met Fernando who drove me up to Semproniano, thence to Pian Rocchetto, from where, after viewing—with explanations from Alberto Bianchi and occasional interventions from his partners, the Dani brothers Albano and Isidoro, and delighted by its stupendous views over the village and Monte Labbro—we all retired to Albergo La Costarella ("The Spare Rib") where under the watchful eye of the owners, Merope and Menotto Mariotti, I was hailed by Alberto and his partners as a "future citizen of Semproniano." (A fourth partner, a plumber named Brugi and not from the village, was absent, being, it seems, drunk at the time, as was his wont.) Then it was back to Rome, stopping to observe the hot springs at Saturnia and some few "Saturniacs" taking the waters ("thirty-nine degrees Celsius at source"). Thence back to T.O. (as we had learned to call Toronto).

I recognized the huge attractiveness of Pian Rocchetto but was anxious about spending the money, and to Anna concluded with "It's tempting but I suppose we had better not"—to be happily repudiated with "It's the chance of a lifetime; let's go for it." She was right, of course, for Pian Rocchetto was to be a major plus in our lives and the lives of our children and theirs from then to now (the "children" having taken possession of it some years ago). This was one of the most successful decisions of our lives, but money was certainly a problem and I asked my father for a loan, which he refused, obviously thinking the whole project a ridiculous gamble—and not least, I suspected, because it meant dealing with Italians. But by now we were determined, so we re-mortgaged our house on Fairlawn Avenue and bought Pian Rocchetto: a decision which we have not regretted.

The final arrangement was that for a fixed price the vendors would put in electricity, water supplied by a pump, and construct a bathroom, which amenities the old farmer who had owned the place had done without. Not that they were of the highest standard. The pump was always to give trouble and the electrical wiring was, in the words of a German who thought to rent the house, "inadequate even by the standards of a southern Mediterranean country." All this and more can be read in Anna's *We Etruscans*. Though she omits it, there was also suspicion of evasion of a land tax. It was too complicated for me to trouble myself with in much detail, but it taught me something about our new country, remote as it then was from both Britain and Canada: namely that you were a fool if you were too bothered about paying taxes to the *stato ladro* (the "thieving state"). I began to understand something of my father's suspicions, and my enthusiasm for Italy would become more nuanced as I came to recognize an endemic political cowardice and a self-serving dishonesty not limited to its political class; the habit of appeasing the strong whether internal or abroad, had from the early twentieth century become nearly universal.

Back in Toronto the old routine was renewed, but with a new academic interest for me: namely being able to teach graduate courses and supervise doctoral theses (though without one of my own). In the years between 1972 and 1980 I mainly taught Plotinus at that level, directed seven theses and assisted with three or four more in a wide variety of areas, some of the students being the best I was ever to teach while others were interesting in rather unexpected ways. The first of them was a nun, Sister Bernard Malone, who later left her Order and became a semi-professional feminist. At that point she was intent on writing on Saint Jerome, while spending her summers on an Indian reservation in Alberta where, as far as I could make out, she largely occupied herself with stitching up the wounds the locals inflicted on one another in drunken brawls.

Another woman, an ex-Catholic from Chicago who, having already turned feminist, and feeling obliged to lace her writing with explicit and colorfully obscene language, had already exhausted the patience of two of my colleagues. Then a Jesuit came to me for help after being told by a previous supervisor that he was just not up to it. He changed supervisors and went on to pursue a good career teaching (mostly) Aristotle. In a fourth case I advised a student whose education thus far had been only in Canada to do his doctorate in Cambridge. He duly applied and was admitted, only to find that his putative supervisor was (already) drunk by nine in the morning, leaving him with little choice but to return to Toronto to finish his program under my supervision.

Since things were going so well for me academically, I began to receive offers to move to the United States, the first from the University of Nevada, where I was offered the chair of the Classics department with, perhaps, I supposed, as a sweetener, the power, if I wished, to get rid of the other members and start from scratch. That might seem a joke, but the second offer — of a Paddison Chair at the University of North Carolina — was more enticing, not least because of the climate. So I asked the Chairman — we had three children at the time — about education at Chapel Hill, to get the honest reply that we would have a choice: either something private which we probably would not be able to afford unless we had private money, or the state system where the pupils quite frequently carried knives in the classroom. So that was that, except that stories were put about that I had lost interest in the chair for various less edifying reasons. Finally there was Northwestern University in the Chicago suburb of Evanston, which I visited and where I gave a paper, but by then had already decided I had no wish to belong there — and not only because it was in a "blue" zone of the city (though on returning to downtown Chicago I noted that after about a mile virtually every store for several blocks was a liquor "outlet" for the Northwestern students).

At some time in these years I managed a trip by hired car around the Roman sites in Tunisia, while on two other occasions I held the fort in Toronto so that Anna could enjoy a "snow-bird" break: first to Bermuda, which she loved, then to Antigua, which she found somewhat unfriendly but where she was to meet some odd company and to listen to genuine steel bands. And in 1974 I was able to enjoy a visit to the Fondation Hardt center near Geneva, founded (as not uncommonly with such places) by a retired arms-manufacturer (and member of a homosexual circle around the poet Stefan George) to encourage European culture, among other ways by providing a venue once a year for meetings of "experts" to discuss some aspect of the ancient world: in my case the work of the late Neoplatonists Porphyry and Iamblichus.

My memories of this occasion are first that as my plane flew over Geneva, preparatory to landing, it passed above a local hostelry on the roof of which I could read "Auberge de la Madeleine: Sans Alcool." This I took to refer to the penitent Magdalene rather than her earlier persona. That "blue" characteristic was also in evidence at the *Fondation*, whose house at Vandoeuvres was guarded by a grim chatelaine whose apparent primary job was to prevent the visiting "experts" from drinking alcohol. So, accompanied by fellow Canadian John Whittaker, I walked a couple of miles of an evening to have a beer at the nearest tavern.

The meetings also brought a somewhat reprehensible revelation. Each of us gave a paper and answered questions, then we were invited to go to the library to rewrite our papers in light of our further investigations. The results were published eventually as though the revised version was that originally given, and hence some of us refused to stuff our answers to questions with additional and lately recalled quotations. This others agreed to do: one man who had mentioned very few primary sources was able in the published version to pass himself off as possessed of monumental knowledge with an "Off-hand I can remember the following relevant texts." Another academic lesson learned.

A second "academic" trip around this time, though less exotic, was also informative. It was to the University of California at Irvine. I duly arrived at the Los Angeles airport to find that, it being later than 4:00 PM, there was no public transport—or rather there was one coach going in at least the right direction, being bound for Disneyland. Thus by joining a herd of screaming teenagers—mostly from Saskatchewan—I got near enough to my destination to require only a shortish taxi ride. The purpose of my visit, in company with Professor Henrichs from Harvard, was to break the ground for a project which eventually would produce the *Thesaurus Linguae Graecae (TLG):* an encyclopedic book of reference for all Classical Greek texts. We conducted some preliminary discussions about which editions of the Greek would be most appropriately cited.

But of most immediate interest to me was a visit to the Getty Museum at Malibu, where we were welcomed to the full-size replica of Hadrian's Villa at Tivoli—only improved by the Pacific backdrop. The curator who showed us around was, I learned later, to be jailed for illegal dealings in antiquities. As we wandered around his museum, Henrichs, noticing that there was an inordinate number of statues of Hercules of varying dates and from differing locations, enquired, "Why is Getty so interested in Hercules?" To which the reply was, "Isn't it obvious? Hercules became a god!" Soon after, we helicoptered from Orange County back to Los Angeles.

✦

That said, the highlights of the years 1974 and 1975—apart from the birth of our fourth child, Rebecca, in November 1975—were our first two visits, as owners, to Pian Rocchetto. This would be Anna's first sight of the new estate, and after meeting Father Charles at the station at Pisa—he had been doing an American-style rush around Europe—and with Peter also in tow, we picked up a hired car, stuffed them both into it and set off in the blazing sun for Semproniano, which—having lost our way near Volterra—we reached exhausted as evening fell. Here Alberto Bianchi presented us with a huge bunch of keys and we settled Anna and Peter at the hotel while Charles and I bedded down on the floor, I at least feeling less than cheerful, realizing how much needed to be done.

But the next day would seem quite different: the sun shone, the view was at its best and in the village, while purchasing our first essential supplies—beds, bedding, bits of other furniture, a kitchen stove (we found one that could use gas from a "*bombola*")—all were friendly, welcoming, and very practically helpful, Merope at the hotel insisting on lending us sheets. It seemed we were as new for most of them as were they for us, since there were as yet no foreigners in the area, though, we were told, a German geologist came from time to time and a Swedish lady apparently owned a house in the *centro storico*—but she must have come at a different time of the year, as we never met her.

Semproniano at that time was a working village, with a population of about 1500—down now to some 550, it is reduced to a dormitory for a few young and for the old a place to return to and die. It provided only subsistence farming with at that point primitive equipment: we were just in time to see a plough similar to those described by Vergil being pulled by oxen, while donkeys — though supplemented by Piaggio "Apes," the little motor-driven three-wheeled vans — were still regular beasts of burden. Old ladies in black would sit in their doorways spinning and very few women — usually schoolteachers — drove a car.

Many of the villagers still drew their water from the standpipes which, as we learned later, had come to the village in the 1930s on Mussolini's orders after a complaint to him by a feisty local woman. We were witnessing the last days of the "old régime," for by about 1980 the character of the village had changed very substantially, the change being best typified by the introduction of combine-harvesters which one heard at night trundling from one farm to another guided by arc-lights. But one important feature of local life had not changed — as yet. Every summer, around the local feast day of Santa Maria delle Grazie (first Sunday after "Ferragosto" on August 15, and originally in thanksgiving for victory over the Turks at Lepanto) there were celebrations, including dancing in the rather tilted "square" in front of the church or (at first) under the "pergola" of the "Milk Lady" as we called her, who still dispensed her local milk over the counter — and after seeing it run over her thumb, Anna would always boil it. Later it could be purchased refrigerated at the general store of Ivo and Elda Carlucci.

We joined in the dances enthusiastically, these being the days of *ballo liscio* (waltzes, mazurkas, polkas and quadrilles) in the revived style from the Communist Romagna then sweeping the country. My favorite (on the accordion, of course) was *Romagna Mia*, celebrating the "old days" when you gathered at a local *casa colonica* to dance the night away: as was said at the time, "In Italy everyone dances, even the cat" (*anche il gatto*). Alas, that is no longer the case — for soon oldies watched while the young preferred globalized discos.

We soon realized that there were four bars in Semproniano, which seemed a large number for a place of that size, though only two were flourishing, these being denoted communist and socialist, the non-flourishing being Christian Democrat and a fourth of indefinite — some said fascist — political character. Until the Second World War the farmers in the area had been tied tenants of the three families who owned large parts of the province of Grosseto: namely the Orsini, the Piccolomini and a more local clan, the Chianchetti. Then at the end of the war the Communist party pointed out to the farmers, who were all but serfs, that they had guns. Why not seize control of the land they farmed? This they did, and the redistribution was subsequently ratified by the government of De Gasperi.

A result was that the more rural you got, the stronger the communist (or Nenni-socialist) vote: in Catabbio, a *frazione* of Semproniano, it reached 95 percent: a result which need not be secured by rigging of ballots. We soon noticed that there were two doctors, one Christian Democrat, the other Communist and cousin of the Dani family—but the Christian Democrat was little favored and soon left. There were also two butchers of the same name who were some sort of cousins and who, for political reasons, had not spoken to each other, it was said, for forty years. What we were not told was that after the war, in a customary settling of scores, fifteen "Fascists" had been shot in the village, only one of whom, a policeman, might have been anything of a real Fascist. Such scenes, we later became aware, were common in the Red Belt, and more especially in Emilia-Romagna, where orders to kill were given by Stalin and passed into effect by Togliatti (after whom, even now, in almost every town a street is named). Italians, we sadly learned, mostly loved Mussolini until he lost; then they moved in droves to the other frightening extreme.

We had only ten days or so in Semproniano, since further stay with a hired car would have been prohibitively expensive, but we determined not only to supply the house with basics but to begin to familiarize ourselves with the Zona Amiatina and the Maremma Toscana. And of course to dip in the Tuscan sea, noting the scantily dressed individuals seemingly roasting on the sand but scarcely venturing into the water unless to paddle. The topless craze, however, was still to come; surprisingly, we first met it in Morocco a few years later while walking on the beach at the *Plage des Nations* near Casablanca, when Anna drew something unexpected to my attention: "Look at those beautiful girls; they look Renaissance"—as they did, sitting on a rock in the topless style popularized by Brigitte Bardot in *And God Created Woman*. The practice became a near-religion in France and then more generally—even in the gardens of Anna's old college in Cambridge where the student paper reported that "the Dons turned a blind eye, the gardeners didn't." Not as yet, however, in Italy—though later a clerical visitor would deprecate that "It's all so pagan!" Indeed, unlike Venus, most of her latter-day devotees could have looked more tempting with rather more on! We left the beach near Albinia to enjoy Father Charles's "treat" of a fine fish-lunch at Orbetello.

1975 was different. Though Anna was pregnant again, we were determined to return to Pian Rocchetto, and for longer. The first stop this time was Rome, where we spent an evening ending—after a splendid dessert called Monte Bianco in a restaurant which we could never find again—with Tom racing around the Colosseum "being a lion." Peter and Alice would claim that he was drunk on the few sips of wine he had been allowed, which he very vigorously denied.

Next day, after a night in a friend's apartment on the Via Nomentana (where we were once awakened by what sounded like a head-on crash on the street below), Fernando took me to a dealer to find a cheap, large-enough estate-car with which to reach Semproniano and (as would come about) to use for many years. When I explained our needs, the dealer advised me that "In your place, Signor, I'd get a stolen one." This Fernando managed to turn to our account, telling his friend that "The professor could not enter into such a dodgy transaction." All went well from then on and we purchased for a very reasonable price a Fiat 124 Familiare which, apart from making a strange noise denoted by Fernando the "*rumore classico della Fiate,*" proved ideal for our purposes, especially in that anyone with minimum mechanical knowledge could repair it.

Thus fitted out, we set off along the Via Cassia—though we should have taken the Aurelia which, despite its notorious record ("*Nuova strage sull' Aurelia*" seemed a common headline) would have offered a much easier journey. That said, once we had passed beyond the city limits the Cassia provided a special point of interest when, driving into Sutri, I stopped short and woke Anna up to point to a notice reading *Luogo di Nascita di Ponzio Pilato* (birthplace of Pontius Pilate)—a claim entirely devoid of evidence, though paralleled in other parts of Northern Italy. In one place there is a lake from which it is held that the craven governor was dragged down to hell. Sutri passed, we came at last to Semproniano, where our future adventures, having mostly been documented in Anna's book, will receive little further comment here.

⋄∞✶∞⋄

Soon after our return, on November 11, 1975 — now designated International Women's Day — Rebecca was born, holding up clenched fists to celebrate the approaching "empowerment" of at least middle-class women. This too had been a "natural" birth, and I was also present at it: however the Guinness was now limited to one per day. When in the following year I was elected a Fellow of the Royal Society of Canada, Rebecca accompanied us to Québec City in a sling while her three siblings remained in Toronto under the care of Brad and friends.

The Royal Society of Canada was then a rather odd institution, being modeled on a combination of the British Royal Society and the British Academy and suffering from the characteristically Canadian phenomenon of "geographical distribution" — this meaning that the Fellowship required some degree of representation from all parts of Canada and the very diverse intellectual levels of its academic institutions. That led some of those in more intellectually prominent universities to look down on its Fellowship, which could produce amusing exchanges. One of my colleagues, long rather inexplicably passed over for Fellowship, was inclined to dismiss the Society as a "bunch of second-raters scratching one another's backs." So being eventually elected, he was challenged: "I thought that in your view the Society was a bunch of second-raters." "Well yes," came the reply, "It *used* to be like that." Nevertheless, I managed to feel self-satisfied that I had been elected at the early age of forty, though I thought the city of Québec over-hyped, perhaps for political reasons, and rather disappointing.

By now, however, our home on Fairlawn Avenue seemed too small for our purpose, and we moved to a "four-bed" house at a more up-market address on Saint Hilda's Avenue close to a ravine where we could pleasantly wander. We had less-appetizing neighbors, of whom one made it clear that she did not like our children running across her unhedged front lawn; this encouraged Tom to run across it more often. Our immediate neighbor was a Zero Population Growth (ZPG) activist who, after the birth of two sons, would pressure his wife into an abortion and then "substitute" an adopted girl for the dispatched baby. And on our right lived a Mrs. Oster, who had so enraged the gentleman who lived in our house earlier — so the story went — that he had pursued her with a pitchfork, and who would tell us that we should return to our own country (from which ancestors of hers had come). Eventually, while trying to damage one of our flowerbeds, she must have managed to heave a huge log across the fence. After that she spent time in hospital with a damaged hip. Seeing her return by ambulance, Anna, resolved to do the handsome thing, approached to make enquiry after her — to receive the rebuff, "Oh, it's you!"

At about the same time we also had a brief run-in with the local powers-that-were. Schools in Ontario were divided between a Separate School Board, which was Catholic, and a Public School Board which was for everyone else. One day early on, Anna had opened the door to someone from the Public Board who wanted to know what my religion was. I had no religion at the time, though increasingly thinking of myself as a Catholic fellow traveler, so Anna told the official that she was Roman Catholic, only to draw the response that only the man's religion mattered, so she hazarded that in that case he could put me down as Anglican.

Some years later, at a time when we might want to use the Catholic system, I appealed to a tribunal where I was confronted by representatives of the two Boards. The presiding official asked me what religion I was, to which I replied that I was "a Catholic for tax purposes," whereupon he demanded of the Public School man why he had brought the case. So we were from then on Separate School Board supporters, and soon after the law was changed to allow the mother's religion to count as well as the father's. I thought my case influenced this change, and congratulated myself on another act of civic duty performed!

⚜

I was owed another sabbatical year for 1976–1977 and we decided to spend it in Aix-en-Provence where I assumed I would profit from the local university and where Anna could develop her new taste for child psychology by hearing all about Lacan and such like. Indeed she was later to earn a master's in child-psychology from the Ontario Institute for Studies in Education (OISE), where she found one or two excellent teachers, though also a certain Englishman who disliked her Classical background and attempted to reduce her grade — corrected on appeal — and on his death we noted that an obituary in the *London Times* informed its readers that he had done more harm to children learning to read than any other known professional. When Anna had completed this degree she started sitting in on therapeutic sessions at the Clarke Institute but had to abandon that as we left Tronna in 1980.

But before moving to France, since I had as yet seen nothing of the "Islands," we managed a splendid trip to Saint Lucia where our base was its capital Castries. Its Catholic cathedral looked like a fair-sized aircraft hangar, but it was hardly large enough to contain its exuberant congregations. From Castries we explored the island with its high "Pitons," its hidden seaside villages, its tropical rainforests and secluded coves, one of which had harbored Sir Francis Drake lurking in hope of looting Spanish ships, and its ground-level bubbling volcanic springs. We soon learned that it had changed hands between Britain and France more than a dozen times and, to our surprise, that the inhabitants were speaking a version of French.

The highlight of Saint Lucia was a "Pirates Tour" by boat around the island from soon after dawn till dusk, and no sooner were we boarded than the rum began to flow — and glasses could be refilled at any time till we docked at the end of the day. Only from the boat could we grasp the extraordinary and somehow unitary beauty of the whole island, and the boat paused two or three times to allow swimming in the clear waters. Toward evening we realized that here too we were in the world of the Sexual Revolution when we passed a private yacht moving slowly in the other direction. We waved and its entirely naked revelers, both male and female, waved back. After Saint Lucia, Aix-en-Provence might seem somehow dull!

But dull it was not, albeit with music in a very different key. To help with the children we had brought Mary Harper, one of the doctor's daughters, who had just obtained a degree in French and we settled into part of a large house in spacious grounds on the Route du Tholonet below Mont Saint Victoire, which we ascended several times by marked trails of varying difficulty. Peter was sent to the Collège Catholique du Sacré-Coeur, run by the archdiocese of Aix-Marseille, where he learned to swear in French. There was no religion taught because hardly anyone wanted to enroll for it, and it was claimed there was no priest—apparently laypeople would not do—to teach it. Peter's class consisted of youths of varying ages, since the system was to keep boys down if they failed a year, as many did. Not that they were always in class; they might be seen racing up and down Aix's main drag, the Cours Mirabeau, on motor-bikes. Peter did also learn how his schoolmates hated the *"flics"* ("cops"), the son of one of them being in his class and made to suffer for it: hardly surprising since *"flics"* were known to be on the brutal side, especially with Arab illegals working on construction-sites.

Alice's convent school—La Nativité, known as La Nat—by contrast would turn out to be the happiest school she would attend. And being linguistically gifted, she was able to profit from the rigorous teaching of the French language, at which she acquired no mean skill, once astonishing a local mother by speaking in the Provençal dialect which could quite normally be heard on the street. And after some effort on our part, Alice was also able to study the cello with Abbé Lynch, the Cathedral organist, himself a concert-performer on the instrument since he was nine years old and now also director of a distinguished children's choir. As for Tom, having downright refused to learn even a few words of French before we left Canada, he was thrown in at the deep end at his *maternelle*, but after about three weeks of near silence he would burst into French and become quite a leader among his mates. Rebecca of course remained with us at home, but was known when provoked to utter her name in the French manner: Rebeccá.

The Aix branch of the University of Aix-Marseille proved almost useless for me, since it had virtually stopped buying books in the late 1960s; it mattered little, since I had plenty of ideas to sort out for future publications at comparative leisure—comparative because there was so much to see in Provence: Avignon, Orange, Nimes, Mont Ventoux, we "did" them all! Perhaps the highlight was the Camargue region where, at Sainte Marie de la Mer, we turned up for what proved to be a gypsy festival. Hundreds of them—and before Hitler there would have been many more—assembled in and around the church, sleeping in its crypt. Their principal devotion seemed to be to a supposedly black Santa Sara—visible in one of the stained-glass windows of Chartres cathedral—believed to have been a servant of Mary Magdalene when she reached her final resting place in Provence: an event commemorated in her cave—La Sainte Baume—and in the Cathedral at nearby Saint Maximin where she is said to have tended the first bishop (or "bishop") on his death-bed.

The inhabitants of Aix seemed rather "bourgeois" and perhaps regretful of the days of Vichy. Varieties of racism were clearly visible: a son of our landlord asked Peter whether he would prefer to be a Jew or an Arab, the implication being that it was a hard choice, and claimed that Rebecca had "slanty eyes" which might suggest a non-Aryan origin. (It might also suggest he suspected Anna's Semitic side!) Being myself uncertain whether as a Canadian resident, though using a British passport, I needed a *carte de séjour* to spend several months in France, I went to the relevant office, and after two failed attempts to get near the counter behind a crowd of North Africans hoping to be served before the *guichet* would be shut in their faces at precisely the time the office closed, I bawled out my request over the heads of the crowd. The reply was a prompt: "You're not an Arab, are you?" So that settled that. When a local member of the Oblates (OMI) who had hoped to be a missionary in the Canadian Arctic but was refused this opportunity on grounds of health, told us "my Eskimos are here," we could understand what he meant!

So as the heat began to build up in the summer of 1977, we moved on to Pian Rocchetto, to another enjoyable few months before returning to Toronto—though a little disconcerted to find that a relation of one of our guardians had thought Pian Rocchetto a good place to supply sexual services. Bianchi had sorted that out for us and told us how the house had provided entertainment on related lines a few weeks earlier, when a *giovanotto* had driven his girlfriend up our hill in his father's Lancia, but in his haste had omitted to put on the handbrake, so next the car rolled down with their clothes on board, to turn over at the bottom. "Such," Bianchi's wife Valeria observed drily, "the price of love."

Nor was such activity peculiar to Italy. A few years earlier back in Toronto when we had rented our house on Fairlawn, our lawyer had to change the locks and thereby exclude the tenants because they had failed to pay the rent. Thus, when we returned, we had found the house in chaos and littered with dead flowers since the tenants had been using it—illegally—as a flower shop.

It apparently had also become known for sex parties. Back in Toronto ourselves, we tried, through our lawyer, to recover the rent and he obtained a court order that the man's wages should be "garnished" until the amount due had been recovered. Only as soon as the garnishee order was served on the company employing him at the airport, they fired him, leaving us for recompense only the knowledge that he had lost his job! By which time the family had disappeared.

Soon after returning from our sabbatical year I was cross-appointed to the Philosophy Department, enabling me to vary my teaching load further and give the occasional course on ethics. At the same time Anna's first book, a verse translation of the Idylls of Theocritus was published by the University of North Carolina Press. Peter started at Saint Michael's High School, Alice at Loretto Abbey and Tom — who it seemed had a voice — at the Choir School. With my growing interest in Patristics I was beginning to draw nearer to the Catholic Church having, even before my 1968 article on Augustine's account of predestination, published in a *Festschrift* for Theophilus J. Meek, a distinguished scholar of Hebrew grammar, a piece on the sixth-century Syrian Christian writer now known as Pseudo-Dionysius. I had come across Meek as a member of the Oriental Club of Toronto, which I was to find a constant source of interesting information about the world "east of Suez" for my remaining time in Toronto. (Some entertaining details about Meek's retirement can be found in my "Animal Academicum.")

Nor were my experiences in this period entirely academic. I would be twice more approached by knife-wielders: the first incident, outside Massey Hall where Anna and I were about to attend a concert, ending as mysteriously as it began, for after waving his knife and being given a shove by me, the foiled assailant melted into the crowd. On the other occasion I learned more after being threatened with a knife on the campus outside Hart House, the knife-wielder being, the University police revealed, a Mi'kmaq Indian well known for this kind of behavior. It would seem his Native American status deterred the authorities from arresting him.

At a Conference on Saint Basil in early 1980 I was assailed by a more academic lunatic. After a quiet enough paper on the influence (or non-influence) of Plotinian thought on Basil, a well-dressed man leapt up in front of me and started hurling accusations of blasphemy, my sin apparently being that I had ascribed a minor work often attributed to Basil to another hand. Though the Chairman appeared to be paralyzed, the abuse did not last long, some of the graduate students in the audience grabbing hold of the interrupter and ejecting him from the room. I later learned that he was a "Moonie."

While surviving such attentions, I was widening my religious enquiries from Patristics to the origins of Christianity itself: a theme that had lurked since in my boyhood I had observed to the local vicar in Gidea Park that Henry VIII was an unlikely candidate for Founding Father of the Church. As I have already recalled, I had also noticed at school that the vicar's fellow clergy would stress the relationship between the Synoptic Gospels, urging the priority of Mark and the importance of a supposed sayings-source dubbed "Q." I had never believed in Q, realizing that there was no serious ancient evidence for it, though as yet unaware of the (ultimately anti-Christian) reasonings which lay behind its positing. Now I wrote a "logical" deconstruction of the Q-theory and the deductions which people drew from it, my point being that arguments for the priority of either Mark or Matthew both engendered serious difficulties and demonstrated that "which is dependent on which?" is a false question.

I argued that the two Gospels were independent of one another except in so far as their authors were both reliant on a preceding collection of memories of Jesus himself, their own and those of others, and that Mark (as the best ancient evidence tells us) was composed for Christians in Rome while Matthew was aimed at Jewish (or "god-fearing") Christians in Palestine and the surrounding lands. Both conclusions were in line with the ancient evidence, so I concluded that both Gospels were composed in the sixties of the first century after Christ — though I missed the statement of Irenaeus that Mark had written after Peter's death. I still hold to this theory, which to my knowledge has never been refuted, the popularity of the "Markan priority" thesis being (now as then) largely a following of the herd. Or, as one fatuous scholar and cleric put it, all arguments for Mark's priority having been subverted or seriously called into question, since Mark is in fact prior, new arguments to this latter conclusion must be found: a text-book example of how not to do scholarship!

I was beginning to feel more comfortable about Christian origins and in 1980, just before leaving Toronto (on which more anon) took the plunge and "crossed the Tiber," being "received" by Anna's old boss Father Sheridan and presented by Father Charles. My conversion was no "road to Damascus" experience, and had almost no emotional accompaniment. Arguments for God's existence seemed to me to achieve only probability and were thus less significant than other aspects of my experience. As Newman put it, "I found myself in another place," and tried then (and more later), to understand how, in his words, "The whole man moves."

In fact, two "moving causes" were fairly evident, the one metaphysical, the other the impact of edifying personal experiences which pointed out (against all *de facto* totalitarians) that what matters is the individual and (ultimately) his being created as a now fallen "image and likeness of God." The specific metaphysics was of course that of Plato and Plotinus, who convinced me that moral and aesthetic judgments must have some solid foundation and that that solid foundation could only be a transcendent mind and "person." It remained for Christian history to account for the nature of that "person," but I already had an inkling of the notion, best expressed by Plato in the first book of his *Republic*, that the choice finally is between transcendental metaphysics and nihilism. It was not, of course, immediately obvious that nihilism is unintelligible, but I was certainly already of the opinion that skeptics about God were on less rational ground than their religious opponents. Or as I would later put it: "my arguments may be bad, but yours are a bloody sight worse."

The second factor behind my "conversion" was more personal: the most well-rounded, honest, and mentally-coherent people I had met were religious or unconsciously longing to be so: Anna primarily, but also Father Kenelm and Father Charles, and in his younger days Denis O'Brien (though he would later seem to "go off the rails"). My estimate of the integrity of the better Christians, especially Catholics, has only grown stronger as the years have passed and my experience of human beings expanded.

I should add that in no way did I expect that all intellectual and moral troubles were now to be resolved. Father Daniel Donovan was the son of a policeman and a veteran from his boyhood of wars against Prods on Orange Days. Now he was a well-known theologian at Saint Michael's, as well as an assistant at our uptown Blessed Sacrament Church known to clergy as the "Church of Silence" because of the resistance of its congregations to playing any active role in Mass. Father Dan told me that he had been asked by the American bishops to write a report on what was becoming a serious problem in the American Church, namely the moving of pedophile priests from one parish to another. Dan had spent nearly three years on his lengthy report and claimed he had not included a single moralizing word, his conclusion being simply, "If you go on doing this, you will eventually be caught out, thus producing a more difficult problem for the Church than that which would have arisen if you had acted firmly to put an end to the practice." With the knowledge that his report had been archived I had in effect been warned of the massive moral problems which were to confront the Church and its clergy in the years to come.

And so we left Toronto in 1980 as a Catholic family, though in other ways, as transpired, on false assumptions. In 1979 we had been awoken early by a phone-call from the Principal of the University of Aberdeen urging me to apply for their Regius Professorship of Classics. By now we had grown somewhat weary of Toronto and this looked a very attractive proposition: Scotland held out magnificent scenery as well as, we supposed, a chance for me to rebuild a Classics department dating back to the days when a pupil of Erasmus had been its first professor of Latin. I went to Aberdeen for an interview plainly determined in advance. Toronto did not want me to leave and proposed to keep my post open for five years, though I assured them that I would not return. They proving more far-sighted, the offer remained open.

CHAPTER 6

A Scottish Principal Fails to Get a Knighthood

MOTORIST (seeing a signpost indicating two divergent routes to Aberdeen): Does it matter which road I take to Aberdeen?

ROADWORKER (at the crossroads): Nae to me.

TOM RIST, his surname being recognized as he stood outside a building bearing the name of Principal McNicol: (nervously) My father was a bit harsh on Principal McNicol.

Retired professor of French at the University of Aberdeen: Nae harsh enough.

Remember the Golden Rule: he who has the gold makes the rules.
— *The Wizard of Id* (1971)

Packing up to leave Toronto was an epic occasion and afforded us our last exchange with Mrs. Oster next door. A large container was parked outside our house and the driver had detached and moved his cab elsewhere while we, having already sold the house, finally prepared what we wanted to take with us. In the midst of the proceedings there appeared at the door a huge and black policeman to say that Mrs. Oster had complained that the container was blocking her driveway, so preventing her car from leaving its garage. To the delight of Tim Barnes, who was helping us pack and whose roar of laughter could be heard some distance away, I informed the officer that Mrs. Oster did not have a car, whereon he banged on her door to certify that this was the case — whereon she said that she would be prevented by the container from using a taxi. At this point the policeman gave up and drove on to his next assignment.

The route we had decided to follow from Toronto to Aberdeen was decidedly indirect. Thus we started by taking the train — all six of us—west to Regina, thence proceeding by rented car to Edmonton, then down the Jasper–Banff highway along which Anna and I had driven in the old "Beetle" in 1963, with views of the mountains and lakes on the way. We have a photograph of three-year-old Rebecca vastly amused by her mother scraping carrots into a stream near the Athabasca glacier. On to Vancouver, from where we crossed to Vancouver Island, one-time resort of retired Indian Army and Civil Service officials and new territory to all of us. Then we ferried from Port Hood at the north of the island: first by a Canadian boat to Prince George (which I remember with little enthusiasm), then by a superior American one enabling us to reach Juneau in Alaska from where we flew on to Anchorage, city of drunken Inuit with a huge stuffed polar bear decorating its airport. That meant that we had sailed up the "Inside Passage," famed for whales, of which we saw a few tails. The whole journey along the coast had afforded some marvelous scenery at very low cost; a cruise ship would have been unaffordable.

The high point of the trip was by car inland from Anchorage in hope of seeing Mount Denali (McKinley), the loftiest summit in the northern Rockies with an elevation—since it drops straight into the Arctic ocean—higher than Everest. The first day we approached, it was shrouded in mist. That night at the campsite we were troubled by a bear which brushed silently past the side of our tent. Anna, going to sit in the front of the car to watch it and raise the alarm if at approached our tent again, saw it jump up and down on the roof of a neighboring camper-van, alarming the occupants, as we were told next morning. That day Denali was clear and displaying its full majesty to us before we drove back to Anchorage, thence to catch a plane which had originated in Osaka and was packed with Japanese businessmen seemingly identical behind their sunshades, among whom space was found for us, though not all together. Landing next morning in London, we were able at last to reach Anna's old home.

Peter and I proceeded to Leeds where Anna's brother Jon had acquired a serviceable brown car for us, and then on to Aberdeen where a vast house reserved for us on the High Street seemed like an empty barn, above all needing massive amounts of floor covering. Mr Laird, the University employee whose job it was to look after campus buildings, while speaking in a scarcely intelligible Buchan Doric, was generally unhelpful; when Anna pointed to damp spots in the bathroom he dismissed the matter out of hand. A year or so later we returned from an excursion to the hills to find dry rot had advanced substantially and the whole place—no notice having been given to us—was about to be fumigated. It was raining, and we took refuge with our neighbors, the Macfarlanes, who like us were Catholic: he a professor of Medieval—especially Scottish—history, and formerly a tank commander during the Second World War who took advantage of his unit passing through San Giovanni Rotondo to go to confession with Padre Pio. His wife was a devoted worker for pro-life causes, especially those helping unwed mothers to keep their unborn children. It fitted with our experience of Mr Laird that Professor Macfarlane introduced us to an important feature of the Scottish heritage, pointing out that after the battle of Bannockburn (1314)—not least in its being infected by "the blight of Geneva"—virtually everything in Scotland had gone wrong.

That was to come. For now we settled in, with Peter and Alice registered at the Aberdeen Grammar School (once attended briefly by Lord Byron before he was expelled: this was "Gordon country") and Tom at the primary Convent, while Anna kept Rebecca at the local nursery for now. Tom soon enough exchanged hockey for soccer, at which he progressed well though being once "sent off" for swearing at the referee. Yet all four children managed to avoid the "tawse," as the Scots called the small leather whip still common and indeed generally popular among Scottish parents, some of whom might be heard on the street roaring at an offending child, "Do that agin and I'll batter ye." One day the pupils at the Grammar (now comprehensivised) would be given a half-holiday while the staff debated whether in the interests of female equality they should ban beating—at that stage only for boys—or extend it to girls, the latter being the decision taken. However, soon after, the practice would be made illegal by the European Court of Human Rights.

The scenery, however, lived up to expectations and we made several trips to nearby Lochnagar (on the summit of which we once met with the Queen's dentist enjoying his flask of whisky), also to the slightly further and more formidable Cairngorms, all four of whose 4000 feet we managed at one time or another to scale. And we could press on further to the Ptarmigan Ridge near Tyndrum and eventually even reach Iona — where it rained incessantly and we were driven, accompanied by Laure, our French *au pair*, to take refuge for the night in an Anglican hostelry. An attempt to breach the nearby Fingal's Cave was also ruled out by the continuing storms, but we would later manage to add Ben Nevis to our haul of Munros.

By the time we had acquired considerable experience of the Scottish countryside we were beginning to understand more of the Aberdonian world in which Mr Laird and his like had grown up. As Macfarlane had said, it still suffered from "the blight of Geneva," for although the practice of Presbyterianism was in free fall, its effects on the public mentality had hardly diminished and might be summarized as gloom and hypocrisy tempered by alcoholism: typically we would read in the papers that a fishing boat, loaded with whisky, had put out to sea and had caught little or nothing, there then being little else to do but drink the whisky and leave the foundering vessel to be hauled back to port by the coastguard.

Students too were affected by the cold and raw nights (also days), and all too often could be found sprawled in the streets drunk and immobile — unless one of their mates had been able to drag them back home and dump them on the doorstep. To reach our house from the north one had to drive "round the block," and one day, with Tom in the back of the car, I was proceeding along this route when "Watch out, Dad," he warned, "the students are back." Sure enough as I rounded the last corner one of them was stretched full length on the road. Luckily I had slowed sufficiently to stop in time, otherwise I would have run over him.

Two other incidents (if one mythical) can illustrate the problem. The first draws attention to a Presbyterian minister who, according to the Aberdeen *Press and Journal* — famed in the world of journalism for reporting the sinking of the Titanic as "Northeast man lost at sea" — was said to have arranged for his whisky to be delivered in milk bottles. The second was our own experience when we were driving along the Gallowgate in a traffic jam at about three miles per hour when a drunk spreadeagled himself sideways on the hood of our car. It was difficult to decide what to do, but when I slightly sped up he got off and staggered away. At a party that evening I asked a Scottish friend "What would you have done?" "What would I have done?" came the reply, "Kicked him back in the gutter, of course!" Such were events typical of a city with more helicopters leaving its airport (for the oil rigs) than anywhere else in the world, and where along Deeside all the wealthier properties were being bought up by people who at the airport you could find returning from Texas wearing Stetsons but who had little interest in the city or its university.

As for the religious divide, Aberdeen had never been a Calvinist stronghold; in fact a second college — Marischal — had been founded in 1593 because the originally Catholic King's College retained a less than godly Episcopalian flavor: indeed its chapel displays unusual religious confusion. Bishop Elphinstone of Aberdeen, Chancellor of Scotland under James IV, had acquired the bull founding the University from the reigning pope, the notorious Alexander VI Borgia, who hence is memorialized in a stained-glass window in what is now the Presbyterian College chapel. Once we met the new principal's wife as we walked to the Catholic chaplaincy while she and her more fashionable retinue were returning from the aforementioned chapel. She urged us to attend service there declaring that we did not need to be Presbyterians. Indeed, she added, we need not have any religion at all.

And that brings me back to Laure, our *au pair*, daughter of the personal assistant to the editor of the French paper Le Figaro. She had been recommended to us by M. Thiercelin, an employee of one of the French oil companies working on the rigs. We soon realized that Laure was unusual both politically and religiously. She was rather reticent about her father, but told Peter eventually that he "did political work," and it transpired he had been killed in a shoot-out with the French police as member of the Secret Army Organization dedicated to retaining French control in Algeria.

Religiously Laure was of opinion that France was under an interdict because of the execution of the King Louis XVI, coronation being regarded as one of the sacraments. Peter argued this point with her and in the course of their discussions she brought out what she called her political bible, which turned out to be a collection of sayings of Charles Maurras, atheist leader in the 1930s of *Action Française*, which attracted Catholics even though membership was forbidden by a decree of Pius XI.

According to Peter, much material in Laure's "bible" "could have been written by Goebbels," being among other things virulently antisemitic. She had, it seems, acquired her religious knowledge from a Dominican school in Paris, and it implied that she could not attend a French Mass, as we were to discover when we offered to take her to one. English Masses were acceptable, since the English generally were heretics and in any case had not executed a Catholic king. But Peter obviously made some impression since after returning to Paris for Christmas Laure never reappeared. Presumably her formidable mother had concluded she was being corrupted.

-∞∞✸∞∞-

By the time Laure left, we had already discovered that while the countryside — not just the hills but the coastal scenery northward from the Ythan estuary with its seabirds to the Bullars of Buchan — surpassed our highest expectations, the University was not likely to do so. Already after arriving in Aberdeen we had been informed that the principal who had so pressed me to come — doubtless foreseeing the storms ahead — had taken early retirement, to yield place to Professor McNicol, former Dean of Medicine at Leeds and before that personal physician to Egypt's Anwar Sadat. And it soon became clear that he saw his task as cooperating with Margaret Thatcher in forcing the universities into line and in particular to destroy the tenure system which, however problematic, is essential if freedom of speech is to be kept alive on campus in a world which is regularly hostile to it.

The chosen tactic was to identify universities over the whole of the United Kingdom where the contractual links between the university and its faculty were weakest — They varied radically from place to place — and then to penalize financially the weakest in the hope that some tenured but sacked staff member would sue — and lose, thus setting a precedent whereby awkward as well as incompetent faculty could be dismissed. At Aberdeen, though my own position as a Regius Professor was secure — I have the appointing document in which I am hailed above the Queen's signature as "Our trusty and well-beloved John M. Rist" — most of the faculty, including all others in the Department of Classics, were at risk. So the University of Aberdeen was hit by a 23 percent cut in its base-budget over three years.

And soon the attempted cull began. All heads of department received a letter from the Principal inviting us to list our faculty members "in order of expendability." That went straight into the waste-paper basket and seventeen heads of department, including me, sought an injunction in the High Court in Edinburgh to restrain the Principal from sackings. Our lawyers told us that we were certain to win, since the University had broken all the rules about giving notice and more generally of due process. Indeed, we had first learned about the proposed sackings not in the University Senate but in the *Press and Journal*.

I had had no intention of becoming involved, as in Toronto, in fighting the administration, but my Toronto doings were known and in any case I felt protective of my own department, as of faculty posts in general. I was, *ex officio*, a member of the Senate, but in a weakened position. For when the holder of the Greek chair retired, Professor Watt, in the Chair of Latin, distinguished in his field and influential in Scottish education more generally, had made no objection to the "rationalization" of Classics in the form of the amalgamation of the two Chairs, so depriving the Department of a senatorial vote. In the straits to which McNicol was intent on reducing the University, that could matter.

In the event, the closing of the Classics department (along with twelve or so others) was unstoppable in view of the financial squeeze, for although we eventually avoided compulsory redundancies for tenured faculty — the Court in Edinburgh after a year and a half's delay ruling against the Principal's scheme on the evening before it was due to be put into effect — we failed to prevent departments from being run down in the interest of saving money. The Classics Department desperately needed replacements when staff retired and I fought for assurances that they would be made available, but to no effect. When I suggested that Anna might be offered a part-time position to help out, that was rejected with the implication that I was a nepotist. Finally I had to tell McNicol that if he would not agree at least that the number of members of the department should not be allowed to fall below five (excluding myself) — this I thought the minimum required to fulfil its teaching obligations — I had no option but to resign. This eventually I did, being aware that Toronto had kept my job there open.

But I did not give up without a fight. Seconded by, as I remember, a professor from one of the social science departments, I proposed in the Senate a motion of no confidence in the Principal which, surprisingly in view of the generally very cautious and conservative majority in the Senate, passed easily. But there was no power to enforce a decision which implied that the principal had lost the confidence of his faculty, and McNicol simply ignored the Senate vote. However, the whole miserable business, as a result of that vote, was widely reported in the national papers and I can assume contributed to the fact that a knighthood "for services to education" was not bestowed when McNicol retired a few years later. I wanted to be able to include as a "hobby" in my *Who's Who* entry, "Preventing Principals from getting knighthoods." Sadly, that proved unacceptable.

I had done very little writing in Aberdeen and taught very few students, none at the graduate level. The problem of writing was exacerbated by the limited resources of the University library: plenty of old books but few new ones and few journals. My top accomplishment during my tenure was to invite two prominent scholars for the six weeks an endowment provided for: these were Professor Emily Vermeule from Harvard and Professor Manolis Andronikos who had recently discovered the tomb of Philip II of Macedon at Vergina—and who told me "unofficially" that he was opposed to the return of the Elgin Marbles to Greece because if that were to happen the money given annually by the government for archaeology would be spent on constructing a new museum to house them. So far the money has been spent on the museum but the marbles not returned.

As for Vermeule (an excellent lecturer) I remember her telling me that "We have at last got rid of her." "Her" was Martha Nussbaum, at that point holder of what became known as the "folding chair" of Greek philosophy at Harvard: we shall meet her again. Also memorably, when driving Vermeule on a sightseeing trip toward Braemar, we slid on the snowy road into a ditch from which we were eventually towed by an oilman who turned out to be a Mohawk Indian from the northern shores of Lake Superior.

But we would have to leave behind all the beautiful Scottish scenery if I were to continue to do serious academic work. Our final days in Aberdeen would be enlivened by an amusing scene at the Macfarlanes' hospitable house, the guest this time being Cardinal Basil Hume, a longtime friend of the family. As the whisky flowed freely, a conversation between Leila Macfarlane and the Cardinal grew more heated, Leila wanting to know why Hume was so unwilling to promote the cause of unborn children, especially since, by default of the Anglican Church, Catholicism was increasingly being recognized (if less in Scotland) as the voice of Christianity in the United Kingdom. Hume prevaricating (as cardinals will), Leila grew exasperated, eventually telling him that "You would do anything to have a glass of sherry with Margaret Thatcher." Whether for this rebuke or other reasons, Hume's pro-life attitude seemed to improve later in his episcopal life. At this time, however, he still appeared to be living in the world evoked, according to another urban myth, by his neighbor at table when the news of his appointment as archbishop of Westminster reached Ampleforth Abbey: "Congratulations, you will never have a bad meal or hear a true word again!"

That said, evidence of the growth of Catholicism in Scotland had been seen in Bellahouston Park in Glasgow, where the arrival of John Paul II under a rarely hot sun was greeted with tremendous enthusiasm and a massed choir of which Anna and Alice were members. For Scotland it was such an astonishingly hot day that some in the crowd fainted. Then as the papal helicopter took off at the end of the Mass the crowd roared, "Will ye nae come back again?" Jack Glass and a few Protestant fanatics had been kept at a safe distance, their obscenities hurled at the "Anti-Christ of Rome" being almost inaudible.

CHAPTER 7

Augustine and the Enigma of Israel

I like the book but I cannot understand how you could have spent so much time on such a dreadful man [i.e., Augustine].
—Letter to the author from Professor Michael Lapidge

You will be the Catholic presence.
—The late Father David Sanders, OP, on hearing of my election as a Visiting Fellow at Saint Edmund's College, Cambridge for the academic year 1986–1987

The Golan is not God's country, it's tank country.
—Yitzhak Rabin

The decision to give up on the University of Aberdeen came at a high price: what to do next? By this time Peter, having done well in Scottish "Highers" and secured a place at the London School of Economics, would be in London — where he soon came to realize that he had chosen the wrong course. Alice, who wanted to read Classics at Cambridge, had already been enrolled at Saint Mary's Convent School in Cambridge where she could study Greek, which had not been available at Aberdeen Grammar. Sister Christina Kenworthy-Browne, Headmistress at Saint Mary's, had at first declined to accept her — it seemed there were no vacancies — but relented on hearing that we were applying at the Perse Girls' School. As she put it, "I have every admiration for the Perse, but they do expect their girls to *shine.*" We agreed that Alice, with her poor eyesight, should not be expected to "shine," and she became a weekly boarder at Saint Mary's, spending the weekends in London with Anna's mother. Accordingly, we deferred an ultimate decision on where we would live and settled that Anna with Tom and Rebecca would move to a small terrace house in Grantchester—bought with the proceeds from selling our old home in Toronto—which we still possess.

Tom would be sent to the Perse Boys School for a disastrous year after which we removed him. I would return to Toronto, to a joint appointment in Classics and Philosophy with a cross-appointment to the Philosophy Department at Saint Michael's—which arrangement worked well enough academically for a few years. I wanted to be sure, however, that I would spend as much time as possible between terms in the United Kingdom, or in the summer with the family at Pian Rocchetto. Not knowing on which continent we would ultimately locate, I rented an apartment conveniently close to the University on Avenue Road: small but adequate.

The University to which I now returned was far from the exuberant institution which I had earlier known; there seemed a marked disillusionment and a perhaps typically Canadian fear of distinction. And the academic pursuit of truth was now overshadowed by the desire to achieve success, whether in student grades or in professorial appointments and promotions, by what was becoming a world-wide problem: increasingly easy access to other people's work. There were many cases of plagiarism in my succeeding years in Toronto which too often went undetected.

To indicate the mentality of the growing number of plagiarists, it is worth noting a couple of instances. In the first, a student submitted a mini-dissertation which the professor realized had been plagiarized. He called the student in, who, when challenged, insisted that the dissertation was his own work—until the professor took from his bookshelf a copy of a Harvard dissertation of which he had been the external examiner and showed the student the stolen text, whereupon the student got into a rage: "The bastard! I paid him two hundred bucks for this essay and all he could do was copy something out!"

The second example shows similar corruption at a higher level, and now is far from unparalleled. The Department of Classics in Toronto (in collaboration with the Department for Religious Studies) appointed a newly-minted Stanford PhD with a thesis on Gregory of Nyssa. Bernard Barmann evidently knew something about Gregory, though he seemed reluctant to talk about him. Then the Dean of the Graduate School received a letter from Professor Ekkehard Mühlenberg, a prominent German scholar, which ran roughly as follows: "I would like to congratulate the

University of Toronto on the appointment of Doctor Barmann. His work on Gregory of Nyssa looks very promising, in fact he agrees with many of my own ideas in this field; indeed, his argument could have been written by the same person."

In this case the offender (whose published work has since been cited as that of Pseudo-Mühlenberg) was fired and his doctorate from Stanford revoked, but in the growing careerism of the academic profession where appointments are increasingly determined by "networking"—or by the "shape" or "color" factor—rather than by ability, and where many academics may be concerned less with honesty than with pushing an ideology, we must expect such cases to be regularly unearthed.

⁕

Soon after I had arrived back in Toronto, and as a result of a review of a book by Albrecht Dihle on *The Will in Classical Antiquity*, I was invited to reply to a paper on a related theme to be given by Dihle at the Southern Methodist University in Dallas. It was to be a memorable occasion. The first morning, after checking in at the hotel, at breakfast I watched a black waiter skillfully juggling eggs in a pan to make omelets, first asking each customer how many eggs he or she wanted. Confronted by a large business-woman, he put the usual question: "How many eggs would you like in your omelet, ma'am?" He may have been a little surprised by the reply: "Twelve, please."

Proceeding to the campus and along Sorority Row, I attempted to calculate the cost of the exotic and pearl-laden dresses worn by various females going to lectures, later telling a member of the faculty that I had never seen such student affluence on any campus—to be reminded that in the television series "Dallas," "All JR's family came to *this* campus."

Such incidents were merely a build-up for the main event for which I had written my response to Dihle's paper and sent it on to him. But to the annoyance of the organizers, he did not appear. So I set myself to retrieve the situation by playing both parts in the debate: thus, "Good morning ladies and gentlemen. I am Professor Albrecht Dihle and I can sum up my paper as follows...." Then, changing hats, I mounted the podium a second time: "Good morning, ladies and gentlemen. I am John Rist and I would like to make some comments on Professor Dihle's stimulating paper...." I don't recall there being any questions, so I did not have to decide which hat to put on in response to them. There was a fair amount of applause at the end and some months later I received a letter from Dihle, telling me that he had not appeared because he had no reply to my criticisms.

⸺∞✵∞⸺

Back in the Cambridge area the following summer we decided to shift from Grantchester to a larger house in Dry Drayton: another mistake because the village, deserted by its commuters in the daytime, was riven by disputes between locals and "incomers." A minor irritation was that our nearest neighbor was forever polishing a boat parked on his front lawn, an activity we dubbed "lawn-boating."

Looking for a replacement for the Perse Boys for Tom, Anna had visited a few Catholic boarding schools with him, and on returning from Ampleforth learned of the death of Father Kenelm from pneumonia. Apparently on his way to hospital he had been talking to the ambulance attendant about Dante and would die still reading the poems of Gerard Manley Hopkins. Not that his death took Anna entirely by surprise; she had attended his last Mass and seeing that he could hardly continue, she suggested that he should go to bed. He was not so sure, having a lecture to prepare, so she referred the matter to his devoted acolyte, Brother James, who replied — almost as though Anna had made an indecent suggestion — "I don't know about *going to bed*." Father Kenelm's lecture would be read by another.

But Kenelm cannot be forgotten: one Christmas at Blackfriars Cambridge he did not look happy, and I greeted him, "Enjoying the feast, Father Kenelm?," to receive the reply, "I was, until I heard my confrère preach!" On another occasion he asked me out of the blue what I thought of Heidegger and when I answered that I did not know much about him but that what I knew I did not like, he replied, "Some of my confrères think he is the Aquinas of the twentieth century." Then he mused (as he often did) before continuing: "You know, when I was a scholastic we spent too much time on Aquinas; our philosophical education was too narrow." Then he stopped and mused again: "But it still seems a bit odd when some of my confrères don't know who he was!" Kenelm would always speak what he believed to be true: a "vice" uncommon among the clergy. And he did not suffer fools gladly. He was a great man.

For the coming year we had decided — after Anna and Tom had journeyed from one Catholic boarding school to the next, looking for somewhere where uniform was informal, cricket not mandatory, Latin taught, and beatings banned — that the best option was Ampleforth, on the grounds of the Benedictine Ampleforth Abbey. It was just about possible for us to pay the fees, partly because I had a North American salary and partly because in 1984 both my parents died within a few months of one another and I inherited some money. This time, however, we got things right: Tom settled down in Saint Edmund's House under the guidance of Father Edward ("Boot") Corbould, OSB, and while soon getting out of the Latin which his mother had prescribed for him, he was eventually recognized by an excellent English teacher as a coming Shakespeare scholar. He was to pay tribute to the Benedictines when choosing Benedict as a third name for his son.

Amid all this I accepted a lecture tour to Australia, comprising Sydney, Melbourne, Macquarie, Newcastle, Canberra, and finally Perth. This worked out very well after my hosts realized that I was offering serious academic papers, apparently not the case with some previous visitors, one of whom had insisted on every possible occasion that he must be taken bird-watching. Before leaving the Southern hemisphere I also managed a trip to Auckland on the North Island of New Zealand and to the somewhat disappointing geysers of Rotorua, besides a display in which some forty different varieties of sheep were sheared. When I returned to Australia and told my hosts I had been in Auckland, I would get the reply, "Were they closed, mate?"

Perhaps my most informative memory of the southern hemisphere — not least in that it was to point to the unjust charge later brought against Cardinal Pell — was an exchange with a taxi-driver who took me on arrival from Sydney airport to a downtown hotel. Noticing a police car pulled up beside us at a traffic light, I enquired, "What are the police like in New South Wales?" "Best money can buy, mate" were the first words I heard in the country after the formalities at the airport.

Returning from Australia, and remembering how twenty-five years before we had honeymooned in Norway, we determined to go back, taking with us Father Charles who knew Norwegian and had helped in a parish in Oslo. We decided to bypass the

Sognefjord and head for the more southerly Hardangerfjord—only to realize that scenically it did not compare with the Jotunheim mountains. Sitting one day in our hotel dining, we were approached by a Norwegian intent on berating us for a recent disaster in a football stadium caused by hooligans, about which we knew nothing, though he seemed to imply that somehow we were responsible. This incident tended to confirm the opinion of a businessman friend that of all nationalities with whom he had had dealings, the Norwegians could be the most unpleasant. Had I by then read more Augustine, I would have understood such behavior better!

Returning sadder and somewhat wiser to England and deciding that Dry Drayton had been a mistake (being a "dormitory" village, isolating for Anna in the daytime, also difficult for taking Rebecca to and from school), we bought a house in Cambridge on Roseford Road which was to be our base for the next twenty years. I now concluded that my trans-Atlantic commuting would continue and that I would get back to Cambridge whenever I could for longer periods of time. I left Anna there and returned to Toronto, soon to attend another conference—with a bizarre sequel—in the United States, this time at the University of Tennessee at Memphis, where I had been asked to speak on advances in the study of Stoicism since the Second World War.

I had written a number of papers and a book on the Stoics, so was in a position to summarize what had been achieved since the days of Max Pohlenz, the acknowledged dean of Stoic studies in the interwar period and author of *Antikes Führertum* ("ancient leadership")—formally a study of the political theories of Cicero and conveniently published just after the "Night of the Long Knives." Pohlenz argues that the genuine leader—like Hitler, who had just rid himself of the undisciplined (and homosexual-led) thugs of the SA (the "Brownshirts")—would, according to Cicero, be no revolutionary: this to allay the fears of Krupp, Thyssen, and their fellow industrialists about the new leadership of the Reich.

Pohlenz's more general work on Stoicism, though at times distorted by a claim that the school was infected by "Semitic fatalism" (he excepted Posidonius who, as coming from the Macedonian military colony of Apamea in Syria and so being an Aryan, was more or less free of it), had been state of the art in its time. It had now been considerably improved on, so that I was able to outline not only how much we had advanced since Pohlenz's day but also that there were a number of themes which might repay further attention. Some of my predictions have proved correct. My account can be read in the *Southern Journal of Philosophy*.[1]

But I was increasingly interested in what might be called the philosophy of culture, and now as a Catholic, especially in its religious aspects. I had long been fascinated by radical religious groups, having taught a few ex-Mennonites who, I noticed, were unable to rid themselves of the guilt derived from their leaving the sect. I also was once long ago a "guest" at a "Shaker" community (now probably extinct) in western Kentucky. (Anna had encouraged this interest by giving me a Valentine purporting to record "Amish pick-up lines": my favorite was "Yoder" asking "Why don't we slip into something less comfortable?") So what I wanted most of Memphis was a visit to Graceland, shrine of the cultural icon Elvis Presley. Most members of the conference and of the local Department of Philosophy professed no interest whatever in his cult, even seeming unwilling to explain how I could get to the shrine. However, one of them, rather shamefacedly, admitted to knowing the way and even volunteered to drive me.

Nor did Graceland fail to impress. Viewing various letters from prominent politicians and businessmen, I particularly appreciated one from President Nixon actually congratulating Presley on fighting the drug culture among the youth! I descended to his "den" where three huge armchairs were arranged so he could sprawl in front of any of three huge television screens (one for each of the main networks) to watch himself playing the crowds. And pistol in hand he could—we were assured with awe—shoot out a screen displaying anything that displeased him. Thus I was hardly surprised when, emerging from the "den," a devotee dismounting from a tour bus told me this was his sixth visit to Graceland and that he was sure that Presley's resurrection would not long be delayed.

The scenario reminded me of Lucian's description of an ancient conman who had made a fortune (and married off his daughter to a senator) at Abonoteichos, a small town in Asia Minor, by establishing a cult, complete with a talking snake and a herald who at dawn would forbid entry to enemies of society with

---

[1] "Stoicism: Some Reflections on the State of the Art," *Southern Journal of Philosophy* 23 (supplement, 1985).

"Epicureans out, Christians out." Lucian alleged he had exposed this fraud at great personal risk. But I was not prepared to cast doubt on the sanctified Elvis.

After the Elvis experience I would run into another less localized source of disinformation. I have already recalled how astonished I was on returning from Iraq to recognize how news of the Suez affair was being seriously distorted. Now in Canada I saw something along the same lines. The CBC were running a series about old age, in which various "experts" were called on to talk about how the old were treated in different countries and cultures. I was aware, however, from the time I was first approached to talk about the treatment of old age in Classical antiquity, that the producers had an agenda: they were pushing the line that everywhere else the old were treated well but in our society they were treated badly.

I was aware that in the ancient world the old were often respected, so thus far the "agenda" was on the right track, but there is also much evidence of a very different view of the elderly — as useless and contemptible — so in my presentation I tried to give a balanced account. Unfortunately, I had to leave Toronto for a few days and did not insist on hearing my interview before it was broadcast. Nevertheless, I was astonished, when I returned and switched on to the relevant program, that my remarks had been completely distorted and my efforts at balance subverted, with every remark I had made about the old being mistreated or despised omitted from the broadcast version.

⸻※⸻

I spent the academic year 1986–1987 in Cambridge with the family, having been elected a Visiting Fellow at Saint Edmund's, still nominally a Catholic college, but which like many others (not least in North America, as we have seen) now found it more fashionable to limit its Catholicism to a minimum. Yet it remained a good-natured enough place and enabled me to make progress in the University Library on a study of Aristotle — to be the only book of mine rejected by the Cambridge University Press which breached its own rules in asking for only one referee's report — and that from a man whose views on a number of important questions I had rejected. Eventually my book was published by the University of Toronto. It was a detailed attempt to plot Aristotle's philosophical development and, although largely ignored in the Anglosphere, it became quite known on the continent of Europe. Its cover provoked a more local interest; it showed a bust of Aristotle. A certain Slovenian pupil of Father Krasovic (of whom more anon), pronounced that this Aristotle looked so like me that I was surely a reincarnation.

My stay at Saint Edmund's had a curious sequel in that some years later I was reminded once again that the spirit of Schicklgruber (see chapter one) was still alive, indeed that it had now come to Cambridge. Invited to lunch at High Table, Anna and I were able to renew our acquaintance with Professor Ernst Bammel. I was aware that in the archives of the Divinity Faculty there are records of Nazi Christianity: as of a distinguished biblical scholar in the 1930s lecturing in Cambridge in full Nazi regalia with swastika armband. But I was still unprepared for this lunch with Bammel, who had forgotten who I was, hence asked me my name and what I did.

To my reply that the name was Rist and that I did philosophy, Bammel commented, "Ah, Rist: good German name" (it is found in Germany but more probably derives from Estonia where, as already noted, it means cross). He continued, "Very zuitable for a philosopher!" Though no fan of German Idealism, I swallowed this, but knowledge of the first meeting of Herr Bammel with the distinguished Reformation historian Eamon Duffy might have prepared me better for what was to come. Duffy, then new to Cambridge and listening to Bammel lecturing, had asked his neighbor, "Who is this crazy Kraut?," to receive the reply, "It's my husband."

For no obvious reason our conversation at Saint Edmund's gave the "crazy Kraut" his chance to pronounce on the Holocaust: "It is absolute nonsense to say that Hitler killed six million Jews. It was only five and a half million." I later learned that Bammel was holding two full-time positions at the same time: one in Cambridge and another in Germany. That news got out and he lost both. His British wife, a distinguished Patristics scholar, died young. Recording these events in later tranquility, however, I can now juxtapose our Bammel experience with a no less informative pair of "German" incidents, both at conferences in the United States and both involving a man with whom I was on good terms.

The first time I met Dean Ritter, I asked him what his initials, which were A. M., stood for. He replied, "My father was a Lutheran pastor. A stands for Adolf (Hitler) and M for Martin (Luther)," both being famously antisemitic. Many years later I met him leading a seminar on John Chrysostom. It was not very good and the chairman let the question period get out of hand, so that members of the audience started addressing questions to Robert Wilken in the audience who clearly knew Chrysostom a good deal better. Ritter got more and more irritated at this, eventually bursting out with "I am giving this seminar!" Realizing his mistake, he added, "I'm sorry; I thought I was in Germany." Old habits die hard; in my case it is an almost visceral wariness of Germans!

❦

When I returned to Toronto in 1983, I completed the book on Aristotle's development, the last I then intended to write purely as an exposition of the thought of earlier philosophers, this time on the man who — after Plato and Plotinus — had most affected my own thinking. I hoped then to write philosophically in my own name on the foundations of ethics — until I realized I needed to know a lot more about Augustine. What I eventually came to write would include much more comment on what by then I recognized as mental compartmentalization — and this I would also need to view as a feature of my changing "self."

I had kept largely out of Augustine's way for about twenty years, but turning back to him I discovered first that he would indeed be very helpful for a book on the foundations of ethics, but second that modern discussion of his work seemed largely anachronistic, people writing about him through thirteenth-century or sixteenth-century eyes, very few in terms of his own age: thus putting to him not the questions that he was asking but questions which they wished to answer themselves. Of course, Augustine might be helpful for these, but would have to be approached more indirectly.

Thus was the die cast: I delayed the foundations of ethics and decided to write the overview of Augustine's philosophical stance — or rather stances — that would be published in 1994. But why had I hesitated for so long after that 1968 article, and what would "the die being cast" actually mean? The answer seems part happenstance but is also religious. When I began to work on Plotinus I had received much help from Professor A. H. Armstrong, an authority in the field and soon to edit Plotinus's text with an English translation for the Loeb Classical library. But for Armstrong, sympathy with Plotinus was accompanied by a "liberal" Catholic hostility to Augustine, regarded as source of problems he saw besetting the Church.

There was also a deeper problem which I now began to recognize: Christian scholars of Neoplatonism are known to wonder whether they are really Neoplatonists and not Christians at all: crudely put, they want the transcendental metaphysics without the demanding morality and earthy historicity of the Christian religion at least as originally preached. Armstrong's friendship cooled when he realized that I was moving from Plotinus to look at Augustine's corrections of his Neoplatonic master. Indeed he more or less succumbed to the Neoplatonic non-Christian version of metaphysics. He had begun as an Anglican, converted to a Neoplatonized Catholicism, gave up Catholicism after *Humanae Vitae* (the "Encyclical Letter of Paul VI on the regulation of birth") became the liberals' "last straw," and wrote an essay on the advantages of polytheism.

When Armstrong set his house on fire by falling asleep while smoking in bed, he almost miraculously survived, but even with this *memento mori* his Catholicism never returned. His trajectory back to a (diminished) Anglicanism had been eased by the death of his staunchly Catholic wife Deborah, daughter of a steel-baron. One of my last memories of him was at another Parisian conference engaging at the bar in a furious argument about *Humanae Vitae* with his now to become ex-friend Jean (later Cardinal) Daniélou, whom he accused of selling out on the "spirit of Vatican II." Daniélou would later become notorious for arguing that the "spirit of Vatican II" (rather than Vatican II itself) was destroying the religious orders, including his own Society of Jesus, and the Church more generally.

Many themes in Augustine I found important for a writer on ethics and political philosophy. Chief among them—apart from the Platonic transcendentalism which he understood (as did most thinking Christians in the patristic age) to be essential for any Christian metaphysics and indeed of any metaphysical basis for serious theological writing—was his emphasis on the individual differences between humans beings (as in its being pointless to emphasize courage to a brave man, whereas to a coward it is essential). Another prominent theme was the importance of an honest appraisal of man's wickedness after the Fall—not in the sense of a Calvinist total depravity, rather an awareness that support from God will always be necessary if one is to live adequately as a Christian. Augustine regularly affirms that the greatest saints, as Peter and Paul (he is silent about Mary in this connection), are weakened by "original sin" and must seek "perseverance to the end." For him that weakness can take two affective forms: one may, for example, be an alcoholic, *unable* to resist alcohol without medical help, or alternatively a person who has a *weakness* for alcohol and so must be watchful not to imbibe too much.

Then there is the matter of regret. As Augustine knew, the Platonists and other philosophers recognized that one needed to convert to the good life, but tended to see that conversion in intellectual terms (as Plato had put it in the *Republic*, of turning the head in the right direction). Augustine, while agreeing, would emphasize that one has not merely to change but to regret one's past performance though not dwelling on past errors to the point of being paralyzed for the present.

Augustine is also aware that in this life we will find ourselves in situations we wish we were not: where whatever we do we must do with regret, but where doing nothing is no honest option, that being part of "this darkness of social life" after the Fall. Hence, for example, although all wars are bad, it may be necessary to fight in a just war. Nor does he fall for the "modern" account of freedom; for him—as for most of the ancients—one is free not when one has uninhibited choice but when one wants only to choose the good: thus God does not debate whether or not to do something bad and then decide against it! Such Augustinian views helped me recognize that Christianity, properly understood, would correct the non-religious humanism I had looked to in my earlier days.

I had also come to realize that much of what I had learned from Augustine can be summed up as a critique of any system (including a deformed Thomism) which suggests that we can find a set of rules and sub-rules to tell us how to behave in every situation. For Augustine (to put it in modern terms) this would lead to a manualist, rule-bound account of morality as mere obedience, unfit for men created capable of choosing freely in circumstances where, through no fault of their own, no casuistry can offer an infallible answer—which is not of course to say that one cannot formulate rules which should be obeyed absolutely (as against the deliberate killing of the innocent). With all that on board, I finally felt I could write on ethics and philosophical psychology. The eventual result would be *Real Ethics*[2]—cast as a Platonic rather than an Augustinian book, since I wanted to emphasize that—as Augustine himself had realized—the transcendentalism of Plato must provide the foundation for any serious ethical theorizing.

Indeed, after *Real Ethics*, I determined to show in more detail that Plato must be credited (though he rarely has been adequately and explicitly) with being the first to see not only that ethical theories depend on a transcendental metaphysic, but that the basic choice in life and in an account of life is between the accepting or rejecting of that metaphysic. All other apparent choices are in reality fudges; any compromise with Platonic transcendentalism will, if pursued to its logical conclusion, lead to nihilism—or at least offer no way of avoiding a nihilistic conclusion even if one is afraid to enact it in life. The choice is between "the intelligible world" (in Augustine's version the God of the Christians) or Nothing: i.e., that if we live in a value-free universe, there is no reason (apart from fear and a delusory self-interest) why we should not follow a "Thrasymachean" view of the world whereby the "strong" (those who accept what it means to live in a value-free universe) can manipulate the "idiots" who believe in "morality."

In fact after *Real Ethics* I would have not one but three further projects in mind: first to write the book on Plato; then to try to explain why after Augustine so many of his would-be followers had got his views wrong on a number of key issues (this pointing toward first Protestant, then secular mis-adaptations of his ideas, especially about the "Will"); finally to advocate what seemed to me common sense about a number of historical-theological themes often ignorantly and foolishly misinterpreted by Catholic writers, especially about sexuality and the early history of the "See" of Rome. Eventually this would appear as *What is Truth?*.[3]

---

[2] John M. Rist, *Real Ethics: Reconsidering the Foundations of Morality* (Cambridge: University of Cambridge Press, 2001).
[3] John M. Rist, *What is Truth?: From the Academy to the Vatican* (Cambridge: Cambridge University Press, 2008).

⸺⸻⸺

When after Saint Edmund's I returned to Toronto, the strain began to tell on a by now middle-aged Anna, who made the mistake of mentioning to a doctor whom she trusted that suicide had presented itself to her (though with no intention of committing it), and then found herself sectioned in Fulbourn hospital, with Rebecca left to the temporary care of "evangelical" neighbors who made a point of expecting to be paid for it. It would transpire that Anna had been prescribed some sleeping pills that were withdrawn as causing depression. All this left me with a terrible dilemma: whether to ask permission to return for some time to the United Kingdom or whether to trust for a while at least that Anna would recover. I knew of a case where the man in question was given release time — and in the years of financial restraint at Toronto was not allowed to return. So I delayed any request and, thank God, Anna got up her courage to appeal, and before that could happen, being now clear of those particular pills — though still depressed — she was released on certain conditions. Rebecca had been very frightened and had sleep-walked. It was very painful and still haunts me.

⸺⸻⸺

During these years I was becoming aware that marriage and family were being threatened not only by the old-fashioned libertinism of the 1960s in new guise, but by the growing cult of homosexuality, as already promoted on campuses. A lifeline for what would later be called the LGBT movement was handed down in a court case in Denver, Colorado: Romer vs. Evans (1996). There existed in that state various laws penalizing homosexuals, and these were challenged by members of the burgeoning "gay" culture on the grounds that they offended against the separation of Church and State. Those opposed to the gay political agenda attempted to defuse the Church-State objection by arguing that homosexuality could be condemned without recourse to religious beliefs and had been condemned in pre-Christian societies.

In the end the arguments came to turn on the condemnation of homosexual penetration by Plato in *Phaedrus* and *Laws*, where Plato's position is developed without any appeal to religion. Pro-homosexuality defenders denied this in claims which they must have known were false. The principal offender was the public intellectual Martha Nussbaum (we have met her before) already known to me as a perverse interpreter of Aristotle's ethics—and who in Toronto would tell female graduate students of philosophy how lucky they were to be able to study their subject at an advanced level, the reason being that they could get abortions. Challenged by one of the students who asked her for a good argument in favor of abortion as a moral option, she could only reply by flying into a blind rage.

As an eminent Classicist and testifying as an expert witness in the Colorado case, Nussbaum pronounced what not only was false but also grossly misleading, being able to play on the ignorance of her hearers. Of this the most egregious example concerned the sense of *tolmema*, a word in Plato's *Laws* whose basic meaning "boldness" has a transgressive flavor: however, in the first edition of Liddell and Scott's standard Greek lexicon this sense is unmentioned, and Nussbaum would cite this first edition as authoritative, though by now no scholar would use it, the eighth or ninth having supervened and become normal. That the lexicon, after the first edition, had supplemented its information consistently in all later editions should have been damning of Nussbaum's use of it.

Aided by some of her opponents—as John Finnis in seeming to claim that Plato's views on homosexuality were similar to those of Pope John Paul II—the gay party won the court battle. Nor did the absurdities stop there, for Nussbaum published her contention in an over-140-page article in the *Virginia Law Review*. Noticing this, I sent the *Review* a rejection of her account of Plato running to a mere fifteen pages—but was told by the editors that there was insufficient space to print my "interesting" article. I later learned that a similar reply was given to Princeton's Professor Robert George, who had attempted to refute other parts of Nussbaum's tract. Thus what we now call "cancel-culture"—conspicuously in the service of anti-life groups—was underway. At about the same time, and with the advent of Mary Beard as the replacement for Pat Easterling at Newnham, Anna's old College, she lost her small teaching job, notably after revealing that she supported the Society for the Protection of Unborn Children. As for my essay on Nussbaum's Plato, eventually published in a *Festschrift* for John Whittaker, it could hardly attract the attention of readers concerned with the original Colorado court case.

⋄∞∗∞⋄

Meanwhile, our family had achieved a few milestones. 1990 brought Peter's marriage to Breton Dominique, first (civilly) in Paris, then (religiously) in Brest. We attended the latter of these occasions, which enabled us to look at various prehistoric monuments in Brittany, not least at Carnac, and also to enjoy a cheerful wedding with dancing from which we retired about 2:00 AM — only to be kept awake by activity downstairs. Descending, we found most of Dominique's family — having already enjoyed refreshments of which I think the number of courses ran to nine — consuming onion soup. On our declining their offer of this as having already had so excellent a supper, we were told that Bretons can consume onion soup at any hour of the day or night.

After the wedding we returned to Cambridge where, courtesy of Nicholas Lash ("Old Nick," as he was known), I had secured another Visiting Fellowship, for 1990–1991, this time at Clare Hall. Lash, more often an ecclesial enemy, had taken up an appointment there after creditably resigning from Saint Edmund's in protest against its now minimized Catholicism. Unhappily in this same year Anna's work for the *Canadian Catholic Review* came to an end when the Basilian Fathers, apparently unconcerned about Father Callam's donation of many years and much inherited money to building the journal up, decided that it was becoming too controversial, which is to say conservative, and that he must go, after which it predictably faded away: both he and it victims of clerical highhandedness and stupidity.

Soon after the wedding I was invited by a group of young scholars at the University of Riga to come and give a series of lectures on the relationship between Christianity and Philosophy, and a more technical discussion of certain themes in Plotinus. The group having named themselves, "Ad Fontes," had inaugurated an ambitious project to bring Latvia, after decades of Nazi and Soviet tyranny, back into the Western fold not only politically but also culturally. The Berlin Wall had recently fallen, and hopes were high, perhaps best summarized by their aim to produce a Greek-Latvian lexicon. It helped politically and financially that one of them was the daughter of the former president of the country. Almost all of them had studied with an old lady with a pre-war doctorate from Saint Petersburg who had welcomed them into her apartment after eleven in the Communist evenings to be taught Greek and Latin for free.

The opportunity was too good to miss and, I hope, helpful to the Latvians. I was put up in a comfortable hotel, being told that its makeover was one of the many contributions of Latvian-Americans now investing lavishly in the old country. The lecture course, in English—by now I had forgotten most of my Russian and in any case, although many Russian-speakers live in Latvia, their status (and language) is widely regarded as inferior—was attended every day by more than three hundred people. I could not but wonder how much they could understand, but they applauded vigorously when the sessions came to an end and rushed me off to a lavish reception where I met the "old lady" who had set the group off on their ambitious project.

No sooner had I arrived in the goody-packed room than she came racing over, despite her ninety-plus years, grabbed me by the hand, and loudly declared "How wonderful it is to meet someone who actually *knows* something." I could only reply that I hope I had transmitted some of my "knowledge" before being whisked off again, this time to the Presidential yacht. There I was greeted by a parrot the ex-president had received from "the people of Chile." As I appeared, it began to call out "Pieces of Eight."

And now further light was shining, this time from Israel. Through Denis O'Brien I had long ago been introduced to Guy Stroumsa, a true "wandering Jew" as he seemed not to have a country of origin, having been born in Thessaloniki, brought up in France, and moved to Israel in his teens, his name Guy being rendered as Gedalyahu: the man from Gedalya. Now a prominent scholar in the field of Comparative Religion, and assisted by Shmuel Scolnicov of the Philosophy Department of the Hebrew University of Jerusalem, Guy persuaded the head of that department—Marcel Dubois, a remarkable French Dominican turned prominent Israeli—to invite me to give a couple of lectures at the Hebrew University.

That would lead to my holding a Lady Davis Fellowship which enabled me to teach in both departments from February to June 1995, at which time Rebecca, having got into Corpus Christi College in Oxford, was spending a "gap" year doing archaeological work in Israel. And here I cannot pass over that in 1993 we were presented by Semproniano's Pro-loco organization with an award for "La Famiglia Rist" for "20 anni di Amicizia con Noi": a rare honor. The plaque rests on my desk as I write some thirty years later.

◦◦◦❋◦◦◦

I had since 1990 given up on Saint Michael's College and "gravitated" to the University Department of Philosophy in Toronto. I had been growing increasingly irritated with Saint Michael's for some time—despite the warm welcome I had received from members of its department of philosophy—since the aim of those Basilians who largely ran it seemed to be to reduce it to a cluster of residences plus a Newman Club.

Though my disillusion with its supposedly Catholic character was by now long established, what pushed me to leave the College was financial irregularity. Trouble in the College had begun in the aftermath of Vatican II, some of the effects of which I have outlined in treating of the revolutionary spirit of the late 1960s. What I have not mentioned is the moral and spiritual collapse of the Basilian Order, in which I could later recognize a phenomenon occurring throughout latter day Catholicism in the New World and wherever Catholicism had been substantially Irish-based.

It seems to have been the specifically sexual aspects of the 1960s which caused most of the trouble. In Toronto several dozen Basilians gave up on their Order or its chastity, some after visiting a sex-therapist who conveniently appeared on Avenue Road, others in more absurd circumstances: thus a distinguished scholar of thirteenth-century Trinitarian theology was banished to South America on few hours' notice after he had seduced the wife of a colleague on a pilgrimage to the Holy Land—the Basilians being told by the cuckolded husband that unless the culprit was out of Toronto immediately the story would be in the newspapers. Nor were male religious the only apostates: numerous nuns disappeared. It all led to the cohort being dubbed "late bloomers." One could not help wondering how their religious education—not to speak of their religious vows—seemed so ineffective against the changed climate.

Then Saint Michael's decided to sell a valuable piece of land near Saint Basil's Church to Tridel, a development company of which a friend in finance remarked that "Everyone on the Street (i.e., Bay Street, Toronto's financial center) knows they are Mafia."

Tridel was run by three brothers Delzotto, one of whom was not only a director of the company but a member of Saint Michael's financial advisory committee. When the sum the College agreed to accept from Tridel was very substantially less than what the property was worth, a number of us pointed to the conflict of interest—to no avail. That final disillusioning led to my leaving the College. Perhaps the saddest part of the whole sorry affair was that honest members of the Basilian Fathers were aware that much had gone wrong both religiously and financially but were inhibited by their membership in the Order from speaking out: this psychological contradiction was to have sad effects on Father Charles's health in the coming years, resulting in his increasingly severe attacks of migraine. And the clash, engendering "bad faith," between sordid reality and a publicly presented piety among "religious" was soon to become visible far beyond Saint Basil's.

While the College was thus striving to be a hardly Catholic institution, its offshoot, the Pontifical Institute of Mediaeval Studies, was in decline, for which the reasons were manifold, but first was financial chaos: at one point a new bursar told me that there were no "books" when he took over and the next day he realized that the Institute owed three million dollars—so it could not pay its lay staff. These it now needed additionally since the number of clergy who provided the Institute with "donated services" was declining.

Indeed the Institute had for years—when money was still available—declined to replace its increasingly aging professoriate who would appear to have considered no one good enough to replace themselves. The situation was made worse by hostility between the Institute and the College. President Kelly had objected strongly to the grossly unjust treatment meted out by the Institute to one of its graduate students who failed his doctorate after his thesis was attacked by its own supervisor who previously had not read it: whereupon the College appointed the unhappy candidate to a regular position, doctorate or no doctorate!

Matters were made even more unpleasant when unknown persons alleged (falsely) that the collapse of the Institute as a degree-granting body was the result of hostile scheming by the University of Toronto. In fact the University did what it could to relieve the Institute's self-inflicted troubles. By the time I left Toronto, in 1996, the situation had become dire. Many years later

I would advise the head of another Catholic Institute that if he wanted to see what not to do, he should study the later history of the Pontifical Institute of Mediaeval Studies in Toronto.

⸺◦◦◦✦◦◦◦⸺

But things were far from all bad in these last years of my "Toronto experience." Rebecca was planning to read Mods and Greats at Oxford, lured by their fourth year, for otherwise she thought of History, so in the summer of 1993 we took her to Greece, which we now visited for the first time since our student days. To Athens, Delphi, and Mycenae we added something new for ourselves: Sparta (where I sat on the wrong side of an Orthodox service and was urged to remain there though the congregation was supposed to be segregated by sex) and the near-intact Byzantine town of Mystra, where we were startled to be asked by an Australian cyclist passing outside a thirteenth-century church, "Was this place built before or after the time of Pericles?" Finally there was Santorini, where unfortunately Rebecca was hampered by a stomach bug. We attended an Easter Mass in the Roman rite translated into Greek, then, finding that on Santorini Easter is on the same day for Catholics and Orthodox, visited the Orthodox Cathedral where with occasional intrusion by a lay-person to light a candle and retreat, a four-hour service was in progress. Returning to our hotel we found decorated eggs in our room.

That same year, as I have mentioned in the Introduction, I contributed to a collection of essays, compiled by Kelly Clark of Calvin College, by philosophers who had either become Christian or returned to Christianity in later life, and who related this to their philosophical professions. I never knew why I had been selected and replied to Clark that I was not yet senile enough to write spiritual autobiography. In reply Clark wrote that he was regularly teaching students from Christian backgrounds who, arriving in "college," became convinced that philosophers had to be atheists or at least agnostics; he wanted to show that this need not be the case.

Being thus won over, what I then chiefly tried to do was to remember (and where possible check) views I had held as a student, but which I would now disclaim, then to examine the arguments by which I had once supported them but which I now found unconvincing. Revealed was a perfect example of the relevance of Newman's dictum (see the Introduction), "Ten years later I found myself in another place." Believing that, I tried (with limited success) to explain how the imperceptible changes had come about. However, I failed to recognize that the journey was far from finished, let alone that my Catholicism was to face an unexpected challenge not from philosophical and cultural enemies but from its supposed theological friends, not least the cronies of an apostate Bishop of Rome.

I was aware of what was happening in that Anglican communion against which I had rebelled as a boy, which awareness was confirmed by an incident in Toronto. When I was walking across the campus with a retired Anglican bishop who was also a Patristics scholar, he expressed surprise that the current Anglican bishop of Durham was widely thought to have unchristian views. "Well," I replied, "I have myself heard him say things which seem incompatible with all mainline Christian traditions." The bishop asked rather impatiently what I meant, to which on my questioning whether his colleague in Durham believed in the resurrection of the body, I received the reply, "Well of course he doesn't."

Sometime later I had a similar experience at one of the regular Patristics conferences in Oxford where at one point in the proceedings there is an "ecumenical" service and homily. I did not attend, although the homilist was a well-known Anglican theologian, but as I walked along nearby I saw approaching a Presbyterian scholar whom I had got to know in Aberdeen. He looked angry and I guessed why, so when we met I asked, "Good sermon, eh?," to receive the reply in broad Scots, "He should be prosecuted under the Trades Descriptions Act." A few decades on I would begin to wonder whether the Catholic Church was not setting out on a similarly slippery path.

More academic absurdities followed in late 1994 in the form of a conference in Naples, the result of an invitation by Professor Giovanni Reale of Milan to join in commemorating the 500th anniversary of Marsilio Ficino's translation of Plotinus into Latin, and to comment, with Professor Werner Beierwaltes of Munich and two others, on a newly published bilingual Greek-Italian text of Plotinus. The surprises began as soon as Anna and I checked into the chosen hotel, to find ourselves in the poshest such place in which we had ever been accommodated, with views over the Bay of Naples and to Vesuvius.

Once settled in I realized that although I had written my paper (comparing Ancient and Renaissance Neoplatonism) I had not yet seen the bilingual text I was to discuss next day. So I found the person deputed to look after us and asked him to get me a copy. He looked a bit sheepish but soon returned with the book, then remarking that he was "fra il martello e l'incude" (between the hammer and the anvil), Reale having realized late in the day that the new text was worthless did not want me to get a close look at it. The unhappy messenger adding, "If you condemn the book — as you are perfectly entitled to do — I will never get a job in Italy," I had to assure him that I would fix it. This I did by speaking (in the little time to remain for me) about Italian scholarship on Plotinus without mentioning the offending text.

My promise having won the messenger over, he further indicated that when I entered the hall the next day I would find it packed with schoolchildren, assembled so that viewers on RAI 3 state-television would get the impression that there was a revival of Neoplatonic studies in Italy. He added that in the front row there would be a group of young people, the males in Hell's Angels regalia with Mohawk haircuts, the girls in miniskirts "up to the navel." When I enquired as to who these would be, the reply was "Reale's graduate students dressed up."

Years later I recounted all this to a Neapolitan scholar-priest who asked me who paid for it, and when I replied "The Istituto Benincasa," began to laugh: "Don't imagine that has anything to do with Catherine of Siena" (her family name being Benincasa). "Then who has it to do with?" "Don Raffaele Cutolo" (the recently jailed Camorra boss). As an epilogue to the original tale, I should add that after we had enjoyed the lavish food and drink the Camorra had provided, we made a trip back to Pompeii on the Circumvesuviana railway. On the return journey Anna was carrying a pair of sandals inside a bag. When we reached Naples we found that these had disappeared. We remembered the old saying, "In Naples they can take off your socks without removing your shoes."

Thinking years later about the conference, it occurred to me that although I had given dozens of lectures myself and heard hundreds given by others (sometimes good, sometimes dreadful, but generally Laodicean), in the early nineties I had heard three which were particularly informative, though for different reasons. The first—I think on epistemology with special reference to Descartes—was given by a man whose speech indicated that he originated from well below the Mason-Dixon Line. It was satisfactory enough, and no one expected the ferocity of the attack launched against the speaker by an outraged feminist who posed the first "question" and whose tirade lasted a good five minutes during which the speaker sat motionless with a slight smile on his face. Then rising slowly he drawled, "Well, honeybunch! That's a mighty long list of questions there, but if you care to write them down for me on the back of a postcard, I'll sure give you a reply." Then he sat down to applause.

The second lecture was by Richard Rorty of whom I had heard in Australia that he had offended his hosts by being more interested in going bird-watching than in talking philosophy. Rorty offered something like "From Heidegger to Wittgenstein and Back." Being a characteristically "deconstructive" effort, it evoked questioning comment, especially from a woman who got up to say, "I gather, Professor Rorty, that you don't like metaphysical propositions." Rorty merely shrugged, so she told him she would give him one. "Supposing I said there is a difference between substance and quality, would you try to refute me?" "Not at all," came the reply, "If you want to believe things like that, it's up to you." This answer did not please the audience, and as I walked away from the meeting I overheard the comments of two graduate students, the first being: "This guy is an absolute fool." To which the other replied, "No he's not; no one would hand *you* a thousand bucks to give a lecture like that."

The third lecture was by the near-legendary Catholic philosopher Elizabeth Anscombe—about whom most of the urban myths are more or less true. Her paper was titled "What is the soul?," and she sketched a number of answers, concluding that Aristotle's was the best we had heard so far. She was now quite old and it was far from Anscombe at her best, but that came through when a very hostile question from Ian Hacking woke her up and there followed a devastating crushing, starting with "Your question does not make sense; probably what you wanted to say was.... But that does not add up either." This lasted for something like a quarter of an hour and when she eventually sat down she was given a standing ovation: the only time I have known that occur at a philosophical session.

During the course of the dinner that followed I asked Anscombe whether she would write her autobiography, to be told that one of her daughters had "threatened" to write a biography, of which the title was to be *Thinking Damages the Mind*. It was clear, however, that far from her mind being damaged, she had, in dealing with Hacking, offered a paradigm for handling fashionable claptrap and anti-Christian prejudice dressed up as argument.

◦○○✼○○◦

And so it was (in the words which conclude the Jewish seder) "Next year in Jerusalem!" There Rebecca had already been settled on a gap year doing archaeology first at Beit Sha'an (ancient Scythopolis), then at the Museum of the Hebrew University and eventually at Masada, where she was treated as an honorary male when invited with more senior archaeologists to a traditional dinner in a Bedouin tent. After my earlier lectures in Jerusalem (and still regretting that when I was in Iraq an opportunity to visit Israel and Jordan had lapsed—see page 53), I was delighted when Stroumsa and Scolnicov (the latter now Chairman of the Department of Philosophy) invited me to spend a whole semester at the Hebrew University, teaching a graduate course on Aristotle for the philosophers and another on Augustine in the Center for Comparative Religion.

A feature of Israel seemed to be that something unexpected would happen every day. When I reached the University the first thing that struck me was that there were not one but two departments of philosophy: that Department of Philosophy in which I was a visitor, and the Department of Jewish Philosophy. A further feature of Israel, as we were soon to comprehend, was that disagreements are taken very seriously, not rarely verging on hatred: thus the members of the Philosophy Department were almost unwilling to admit that members of the Jewish Philosophy Department were philosophers at all, while the members of the Jewish Philosophy Department would hardly recognize their more "analytic" colleagues as Jews. Many years later, at a dinner in Rome in honor of Lord Sachs, chief rabbi of the Commonwealth, I would be seated next to the Israeli ambassador to the Holy See, and on my enquiring of him how he found working with Catholics and what differences he noticed, his response was, "Well, *we* don't believe in forgiveness."

Teaching in the two Jerusalem departments offered other surprises. Among those to whom I was supposed to be expounding Augustine (a very self-selecting group), I found ignorance of the basic principles of Christianity so deeply rooted that the course almost morphed into "Introduction to Christianity." As for the philosophers (again self-selecting because philosophy and especially ancient philosophy is widely suspect in Israel as a "stalking-horse" for Christianity), they were perhaps the most able class I have ever taught, but rapidly divided into religious and seculars, fighting it out on every possible opportunity during the course on Aristotle's ethics, so that my role at times seemed like that of a referee at a boxing match. But being older, and having all done military service and thus knowing some unpleasant realities, they satisfied Aristotle's demand of students of ethics—as I had begun to satisfy it after my tour of duty in Iraq—that it is useless to teach ethics to those with no experience of the moral ambiguities of life.

That class also offered us a lesson of a different, though not unrelated kind. One of the "religious" students, originally from Chicago and having a very orthodox Dutch wife, invited us to dinner at their home at Shiloh in the Occupied Territories. We consulted various friends and even a couple of priests, all of whom advised us to go for the experience. So we were driven up to Shiloh, noticing at the edge of the settlement a number of half-built houses where work had been stopped when Prime Minister Rabin forbade further construction in the Settlements. At the student's home we were received by his wife who wore a rather elegant hat but said little before or during the excellent meal she provided. Looking however through the window toward an Arab village on a distant hill, I asked our host what he would do if they were attacked. To which he replied, "I would leave if more than two attacks were mounted by people wearing the uniform of the Palestine Authority police." His wife intervened to say: "I would fight."

Since it was late and we did not wish to put our host to the trouble of driving back to Jerusalem and out again, we were put on an Egged bus to return home. There were rather few people on board and no trouble until a few miles short of Ramallah there came a blinding flash as something hit and cracked the windscreen. The driver swerved the bus to and fro to avoid further attack, and Anna, sitting beside me, said, "That looks like a Molotov," as of course it was. And now an apparent passenger produced a radio and was speaking into it while the driver swung the bus from side to side at increasing speed—perhaps putting his skills as a tank driver to good effect—and a shower of rocks hit the back of the bus. The Molotov, having bounced into roadside shrub, started a small fire.

We reached Ramallah safely, to be met by tanks, ambulances, fire-engines, and a large number of armed soldiers, one of whom saw us off the bus and onto another, cheerily remarking, "You get two rides for the price of one." Indeed the incident had occurred at a quiet time and surprised my colleagues at the University. We found it briefly mentioned in the *Jerusalem Post*, it seemed because the driver was claiming compensation for a cut to his hand from the broken windscreen.

That was unexpected and seemed unique at the time, though when visiting Hebron with Father Krasovec to see the burial site of the patriarchs—now divided into a mosque and a synagogue—we noted a Jewish fanatic wandering around the building with a rifle, presumably intending to intimidate Muslims. In Hebron these, indeed, had reason to fear such people, for a few years later one of them gunned down more than thirty Arabs.

In light of such activity, combined with the fact that there is no civil marriage in Israel—couples who want one have to go to Cyprus—we were the less surprised when, visiting the home of Avery (Anna's friend from schooldays) and her Canadian husband Joe Rezek in Haifa, we also met their "sabra" son-in-law Leor. We had just returned from Jerusalem, after attending a conference at Bar Ilan University, and being taken by one of the participants—an American—to what he described as the most "liberal" of Israel's synagogues—"liberal" meaning that the sexes were separated only partly and by a see-through curtain. Leor asked what we had been doing, and I replied that we had just visited a synagogue, which was met with, "What the hell did you do that for?" Uncertain how to reply, I muttered something about it being interesting to see what went on, whereupon our interlocutor, digesting this, delivered himself of, "I hate religious people," before relapsing into a near-silence for the rest of the evening.

Further light on religious Israel was to be shed on the morning of a guided visit to Mia Shea'rim, center of ultra-Orthodox

Jerusalem. As we approached it, we noticed our bus driver inclined to get as near as possible to some of the bearded and black-robed "religious" without actually hitting them. We had noticed this before and been told that the ultra-Orthodox were disliked by a substantial part of the general public because they could evade military service while still enjoying the protection of the State's military—and though some of them did not even recognize the State! Reaching Mia Shea'rim, we immediately noticed a group of little huts, each apparently associated with a different sect, and almost all with lengthy notices pinned to their doors. When I enquired what these were intended to tell us, Scolnicov, our guide, said that most would be attacks on the rabbi next door.

Inevitably, as we wandered on, conversation turned on Judaism's tendency to splinter. I recalled the line "Two Jews, three synagogues." Scolnicov was a "secular," though well-versed in Jewish lore and history, and at one point he observed that "As you know, for Jews, the Torah, the five books of Moses, is what matters." I knew this but had always found it somewhat puzzling. Now Scolnicov observed, "We tend to leave the Prophets to you Christians."

My reaction to that was to think—though not to say—that the Prophets might seem to point too inescapably to Christianity. That said, for those who combined the religious right with the Nationalist right, it was easy to see why some of the earlier heroes were found encouraging. Scolnicov drew attention to texts papered on buildings near the Wailing Wall; often they referred to Samson smiting the Philistines—for Philistines one could understand Palestinians.

The enigma of the State of Israel was becoming clearer, and a visit to the Dead Sea would open our eyes in a more secular way. Father Krasovic, from Slovenia, was an old Israeli hand, having earned a doctorate on the Old Testament at the Hebrew University. More immediately relevant was that he shared a birthday—April 20—significantly for one who had grown up under Nazi occupation—not only with Anna but with Hitler. He told us how during the war they had been forced to celebrate the Führer's birthday with parties on decorated streets. We decided that this time it should be celebrated in a more appropriate way: we would take a trip to Sodom—now the spa Ain Boqqeq—on the Dead Sea.

We all bobbed about in the waters, mostly accompanied by new immigrants from the Soviet Union until Father Krasovic began to feel unwell. While he disappeared into the posh hotel to meet an old acquaintance, we found in a less salubrious area perhaps the only stall in Israel selling bacon sandwiches—though we had at Easter sampled the wares of "Chaimy the non-kosher butcher" who in Jerusalem made good money selling to the country's élites. Or as Joe Rezek put it wryly when he ordered a steak for Rebecca, "It's non-kosher. It must be good."

Thus far I have said little about "Christian Israel," not least perhaps because many Israelis seemed to act as though it did not exist, while benefitting from the tourism and pilgrimage that Christianity brought them. Perhaps the theme can be developed further by looking at part of a tour given by the Rezeks when, toward evening, we reached the village of Cana. "Is there not something about Cana in the New Testament?" asked Avery. Anna recounted the story, emphasizing the importance that Jesus, as a Jew, placed on marriage. Avery commented: "Yes, marriage is important; a pity he wasn't married himself." Anna feeling for the moment unable to respond, Avery, perhaps thinking of the Caliphate, added: "Though that could have produced problems about the succession!" To which again Anna felt unable to respond.

Nor was Cana the only Christian site we visited with or without the Rezeks. Joe also took us on a tour of the Golan—in Rabin's fateful words "not God's country but tank country"—where we could view the hulk of the Soviet-built Syrian tank that had advanced furthest in the Yom Kippur War—and from there to the Jordan where Jesus was baptized—where Joe noted that the bridge had been strengthened to bear the weight of a tank, while Avery insisted we take some Jordan water home for baptisms. (It reposes on the top of a cupboard still.) We would later visit Herodium and ascend Masada, holy site where new recruits to the Israeli Defense Force would be encouraged to imitate the heroism of its defenders—then move on to Qumran and the caves where the Dead Sea Scrolls were discovered and where we bought a small can containing "Air from the Holy Land," which one was advised not to pierce!

We were also able to visit Ein Karem, where John the Baptist was reputedly born, majestically located just west of Jerusalem, and to take the road—still said to be dangerous—from Jerusalem to Jericho. There were no thieves, but outside Jericho, high up on a hillside, we noted the "Temptation Restaurant": we did not risk it! Then the visit at Pesach/Easter of Cardinal Lustiger—"Jewish boy" converted to Christianity—provided an occasion to see the two religions both converging and diverging when his arrival, at the invitation of Tel Aviv University—though "at Jerusalem they study, at Haifa they work, and at Tel Aviv they dance"—split the two chief rabbis, one denouncing the archbishop and those who had invited him, the other more welcoming.

We heard Lustiger's homily at a Mass at the Maison Saint-Isaïe, home of Marcel Dubois of the Philosophy Department. The language was French, with translation into Hebrew which at one point Lustiger stopped to correct. Being asked by a journalist whether he might become pope, he replied with the one word: meshuga ("Are you mad?"). He told us that he had visited Yad Vashem, the World Holocaust Remembrance Center, and was still seated in a chair, deep in prayer, after the building officially closed, when a custodian approached, tapped him on the shoulder and being unaware of the name and vocation of the man he was addressing, told him, "Go home and say kaddish."

We would be lucky enough to get the chance—not always available—of a coach tour to the other side of the Jordan where further Christian and non-Christian sites awaited us. We had developed the habit of listening to Radio Jordan in English where the king's efforts to improve the lot of women in his kingdom were plainly discernable. Not, of course, that all was sweetness and light: on one occasion we heard Saddam Hussein's son Uday lambasting the late Egyptian President Nasser: "What a fool that man was; he talked about driving the Israelis into the sea; why, some of them might escape by swimming."

Our high hopes of Jordan were not to be disappointed. On entering the country, after a long delay—those Israelis who were travelling on Israeli passports were delayed even longer—being presented with a family tree of the Jordanian Royal Family by the guide, one could not but notice that the apparent heir had been passed over for the succession. Someone enquiring about this, we were told primly that His Royal Highness Crown Prince Abdullah has his own life-style—on hearing which a Cockney voice called out, "So you can draw your own conclusions!" (In fact after marrying a Palestinian, Abdullah was reinstated and still reigns, showing indeed much dexterity in the complex situation in which he has found himself.)

So we drove first to Petra, the "rose-red city half as old as time" (on a coach which being winged by a Bedouin car, the driver simply accepted since in Jordan Bedouins lack both driving licenses and insurance). Then back to Roman Jerash via Madaba—Moabite or Ruth country with a sixth-century map showing Jerusalem in exactly the right direction—and Mount Nebo from where Moses, it is said, was able to see the land of milk and honey which he was not to enter. Finally to Amman, where from the summit of ancient Philadelphia we could hardly fail to notice an enormous new mosque, of which we enquired of our guide, to be told, "He who built it very bad man, drink much alcohol."

Not only did we reach Jordan but the frontier at Sinai being open we crossed from Israel into Egypt, noting a Swiss-German tourist telling the driver that they had been crazy to give such a beautiful place back. We could see his point when, having spent the previous night in a large and comfortable tent, we reached Saint Catherine's monastery before the crowds came. I remember especially a fresco of the Transfiguration. Later we climbed Mount Sinai in running shoes, descending with some difficulty as darkness fell.

No need to chronicle all the other Christian sites in Israel itself: Nazareth, Bethlehem (with Jerome's reputed cave), and marvelous walks with the Rezeks around the Galilee: Capernaum, Montfort, Tiberias. At Caesarea we spent an idyllic few days on a nearby kibbutz and met Gisèle Littman, also known as Bat Ye'or (the name means daughter of the Nile), chronicler of the *dhimmi* conditions of "infidels" under Islamic rule. Especially moving was a drive up Mount Tabor, on the top of which we were able to reflect on the Transfiguration almost alone.

All this from our base in a Jewish quarter of Jerusalem, outside the Old City but within reach of it via the Jaffa Gate, where we could regularly enjoy coffee with cardamom. At the edge of the Muslim quarter, facing Palestinian East Jerusalem, we could resort to The Bethlehem Star, a fine restaurant full of memorabilia of the Mandate. I hope it still survives, but I fear it does not. By the time we left Jerusalem I felt I could have done a better job than many of the official guides whose sentimentalized and romanticized versions of history were—as at Masada—repudiated by more knowledgeable people in the University.

Among the many attractions for pilgrims in the Old City and nearby, I cannot pass up mentioning the Easter Vigil on the roof of the Zion Convent, as the moon lit up the sky and an African group danced in ruins supposed to house the pillar at which Jesus had been scourged. Still, for me the *pièce de resistance* was the Church of the Holy Sepulchre itself, an utterly chaotic building both architecturally and religiously with the various Christian groups vying for whatever proximity they could get to the site of the crucifixion and burial; the Ethiopians have to be satisfied with a space on the roof. We heard Mass there several times, once on our Easter Day having difficulty getting away as the Orthodox — whose Palm Sunday it was — were seething to get in. Aware that disputes among the Christian groups had led to riots and killings at the holy site, this was symbolic of too-human attempts to live a Christian life.

On our last visit to the Sepulchre we stopped at an Arab stall to consider buying a woolen scarf as a gift for Rebecca, but agreed to visit the church first and then make our decision. On our returning the Arab asked whether we had been to the Holy Sepulchre. When we said we had, he told us that he went there every day. He was assuredly a Muslim, so was it fear or habit which prevented him from changing his religious allegiance? At the Carmel in Haifa we had watched Muslim women invoking the Virgin by placing infants on her altar, and the same thought had occurred to me — even though such devotion could claim Qur'anic authorization.

Our wholly unpredictable experience of Israel was drawing to a close, and we were finally to celebrate it with Fakhri, an Arab who was working at Beit She'an while Rebecca was there and had taken a fatherly interest in her. Fakhri invited us to his house in a township north of Haifa near the Lebanese border, the Rezeks to accompany us, and we visitors were splendidly fed, although it was Ramadan and too early for the family to break the fast — except for a lone dissident who had studied at the University of Manchester and made a point of showing that such "superstition" was not for him. Fakhri proudly showed us photographs of his life, including one of himself riding to his wedding on a horse. He and Israeli Joe had at first seemed a bit wary of one another but shook hands as we left and agreed that they needed to understand each other better. Anna's schoolfriend

Avery, a doctor, was used to Arab patients and pointed out a little charm Fakhri's granddaughter was wearing.

We were to leave the country soon after, but first would learn of one more feature of the Israeli enigma. I was told repeatedly at the University that there was a danger of Premier Rabin's being assassinated: an outcome deemed unthinkable outside Israel—until it occurred and the murderer was a Jew. It was not unthinkable to Israelis, one of whom had told me that Rabin may have signed his own death-warrant when he remarked (see above), "The Golan is not God's country but tank country": a challenge for those intent on a Davidic kingdom stretching as far as "the Great River." It is said that the ultra-Orthodox have saved Jewish identity, which may be true, though they could also bring about the destruction of the State of Israel. In light of the behavior of the ultras in Netanyahu's government—one of whom had hung in his office a portrait of the murderer of the thirty Arabs in Hebron—that risk might seem nearer in 2025 than when we were there.

Yet the enigma of Israel is more serious even than the fate of that country in that it raises the question: why, when many states continue to act far less morally than Israel, the Israelis are the regular target of a condemnation rarely directed at worse offenders. A theological explanation is possible (as Marcel Dubois seems to suggest): if Israel (as Christians as well as religious Jews believe) is the "Chosen People," then precisely as chosen, it is the likely target for enemies of God and for those who would deny his existence. Unjust attacks on Israel, and Jews more generally, can be explained as an attempt, if futile, to attack God himself.

As we waited in line for security procedures to be completed at Tel Aviv airport, a delay arose because a man seemingly a Filipino bishop, had aroused suspicion, it being not uncommon for terrorists to dress up as "religious." Anna murmured to me as we stood waiting, "If they could see him from where I see him, they would know that he really is a bishop; no one dressing up as a bishop would be wearing a pair of running shoes!"

⋘✻⋙

So back to Toronto where, in 1996, the University, in serious financial trouble, offered senior (and therefore expensive) professors early retirement on attractive terms. Having long found transatlantic commuting depressing (despite the two Cambridge Fellowships and the extended visit to Israel) — and harder for Anna — I took up this offer, not knowing what I would do next, but that I would need to do something more than wait to die in Cambridge. Anna returned for my last lecture, and as we crossed the campus before it was to begin we met Father Jeanneau whose family home in Normandy we had visited but whom Anna had not seen for some years. At first he failed to recognize her, and when he did, he observed that he had supposed her to be "John's 'petite maitresse.'" At that, she told him he had spoken like a "true Frenchman."

The lecture itself Anna thought a bit on the lewd side — though she defended it when it was criticized for this. It was on Plutarch's *Amatorius*, the only ancient text in which the pros and cons of homosexual and heterosexual love are debated philosophically, so in light of the coming decades — not to speak of the Denver law case — the topic was certainly "relevant." The paper would be published in the *Classical Quarterly*.

CHAPTER 8

Across the Tiber and Along the Potomac

Più vicino a Roma, più lontano dal Cielo.
— Traditional

Roma veduta, fede perduta.
— A more modern saying

Only God knows how much money the Franciscans have.
Only God knows what the Augustinians are for.
— Heard in Rome

You have to watch your back in this city.
— Anytus to Socrates in Plato's *Meno*

1997 was a quiet year, but after our usual drive through France to Semproniano, a message reached us from Rome. It came from Eric Osborn, an Australian Patristics scholar (for some reason known to our children as "Tortoise") whom I had met in Sydney during my visit "down under" a few years earlier and with an unusual history. Born in the Australian outback inland from Melbourne, he had served as a paratrooper in the Second World War, survived some years of capture by the Japanese, and having become a Methodist minister arrived in Cambridge to do a doctorate in Patristics with Henry Chadwick. He was teaching a year at the Patristic Institute in Rome, thanks to his friendship with its current head, Father Angelo di Berardino, OSA, who had relatives in Australia.

At some stage I had intimated that I would not pass up the chance to teach in Rome. Now the letter suggested that if I wrote to Di Berardino I might be able to replace Eric himself who needed to resume work in Melbourne. I wrote, and somewhat to my surprise my proposal was snapped up; all I had to do was to ensure that Anna and I could live in the Collegio Internazionale Santa Monica, the house for non-Italian, mostly Third World Augustinians studying in Rome — though only few at the Patristic Institute next door. I was to teach one graduate course, and supervise doctoral theses as required, from October to December each year, and could choose whatever I wanted in the area of Greek and Roman philosophical material influential on early Christian theologians. This normally meant Platonist and Stoic texts, and especially Plotinus: I avoided Augustine — though constantly alluding to him — whom the Augustinians claimed to handle well themselves; this was true of exegetical material but hardly with much philosophical.

Starting in 1998 I taught unproblematically in the fall semester every year till 2019 — except that in 2014, noting a swelling in my leg, I appealed to the College's doctor, who immediately put me in the hospital: I had a thrombosis. In Italy, however, there are two medical systems, private and public, and I was put into the private hospital, Salvator Mundi, on the Janiculum, where we soon realized that the fees were to me — unlike such previous patients as Princess Diana or even Mother Teresa — out of reach. Anna had to get me out fast (which apparently required some legal tampering), and I was dispatched to San Filippo Neri in a hired ambulance staffed by a Coptic doctor with whom I discussed whether Christ had two natures.

The arrangement with Di Berardino enabled me to live part of the week in Rome and the rest in Capalbio, where Anna's cousin Adrian and I had purchased an apartment within easy reach of the Rome–Pisa railway. I taught dozens of priests — plus a few nuns and laypeople — many of whom came from Latin America (and knew English better than the Italian in which they were expected to study). Santa Monica being located just outside the colonnade of Saint Peter's on a street once called Via del Sant' Uffizio, now Via Paolo VI, I was also able to observe close up the "religious" life both of the Augustinian Order and of Rome more widely. The successor of the Holy Office — until recently called the Congregation for the Doctrine of the Faith — was located in a square just around the corner.

Before taking up my new post in Rome and while we were in Semproniano very sad news arrived from Catania. We knew my old friend and travelling companion Henry Blumenthal had been suffering from depression, and we had invited him to visit us at Pian Rocchetto. After giving a fine and final lecture, then phoning his daughter, he had thrown himself from a high window in his Catania hotel, thus following his mother in death by suicide: one more death to be ascribed to the Nazis, for, as I have noted, five of his father's brothers had died in Auschwitz. It seems that as Henry grew older this horrendous past came to haunt a man who, when I first knew him, seemed to want to have nothing to do with his Jewish roots: yet some version of "Jewish guilt" for being a survivor had caught up with him.

Not that he was alone nor the last of my Trinity contemporaries in committing suicide; it was becoming ever more prevalent in an increasingly secular world which seemed on the edge of collapsing — so I was coming to think — into nihilism. Nor was the suicide-increase limited to the United Kingdom: before leaving Toronto I met a colleague whom I had not seen for a couple of years who told me that he had been teaching at Santa Barbara. "Did you enjoy it?" "In a way, yes; the trouble was that my colleagues kept committing suicide." "Why was that?" "I suppose it was the American dream — 'Go west, young man.' But California was the most westerly point you could reach, except by walking into the sea. Which some did."

◦◦◦✶◦◦◦

What I saw from the viewpoint of Santa Monica confirmed my impression that the higher reaches of the Roman Church were adopting ever more of the claimed "values" of an increasingly nihilist secular society: demonstrating how in most coteries and organizations there is financial and sexual corruption that many good people have to put up with. I had seen the effect of such psychological pressure on our friend Father Charles; in Rome I was to see it on a much magnified scale. The question arising in such circumstances, if the community is Christian, is whether Christianity can corrupt, or whether, as Augustine put it, the Church is a *corpus mixtum*, the evil being bound together with the good, as in Christ's parable of the wheat and the weeds growing together until the Last Judgment.

Experience of this wisdom was provided by the case of my first doctoral student in Rome, Sister Benedetta, OSB (as she then was) whose revised thesis was eventually published in 2007 under the title *Desiderio della Bellezza*: that is, from Plato to Gregory of Nyssa. Benedetta was one of the most able students I have taught: well-trained before I met her in Greek, Latin, and

Hebrew and with capacity to assimilate ideas at breakneck speed: thus, she was no ordinary nun and had lived all over the world, her father having been an airline pilot and she having been a champion water-polo player. She once remarked enigmatically that to be a nun in the modern age you had to be able to swim!

Benedetta had done most of her work at the master's level with Dom Basil Studer, a distinguished scholar who hoped she would become his Doctoral student, but though appreciating what she had learned from Studer, she was not happy to continue with him for the Doctorate, as she wanted freedom to express her views in what would typically be an Anglo-American rather than an (old-style) German thesis: hence she asked me to be her supervisor.

For a while things went well; she completed the majority of the required courses easily. Then she was informed by her abbess that she must not spend so much time in Rome. This put her in an impossible situation since she could not finish the required course-work elsewhere. At this point I asked Di Berardino if she could be excused further course-work (which she certainly did not need) and simply write her thesis, most of which she could do in her convent. Di Berardino agreed that she needed no further course work, but decided against this on the grounds that it would set a precedent. That looked like her having to give up graduate work, but happily the American Dean of Theology at Sant' Anselmo agreed that she needed no further courses, and that if she transferred she would only have to write the thesis, adding that it was fine for me to continue as her supervisor. And that is what happened, Benedetta completing a large thesis in a remarkably short time and then being offered a temporary teaching position at Sant' Anselmo.

That worked well, though it was only temporary, but she was then lucky enough to secure further appointments, one being at the Lateran University where she was to teach "Christian spirituality," the other at the diocesan seminary in Ancona, where her abbess no longer objected to her being away from the convent; she was after all bringing in money! Then things began to go wrong. At the Lateran she was popular among the students and well thought of by the faculty. Then without being consulted, the Dean received a letter from the office of the Vatican Secretary of State saying that she was to be "let go": no reason given.

The Dean, supported by the abbess, appealed to the Congregation for Catholic Education, but got nowhere; apparently rulings of the Secretary of State are incontrovertible, so Benedetta lost her job at the Lateran. But worse was to come; her convent closed down with most of the nuns either returning to their own countries (often Romania) or giving up the religious life. Benedetta transferred to another religious house; rumors (in Italian "*voci*") began to circulate that she held heretical views about the Immaculate Conception: rumors entirely false, but in the "Infernal City" that cannot matter, as I was beginning to understand.

At the outset she was defended by her bishop who pointed out that if other bishops who were sending their students to his seminary wanted to believe charges about Benedetta they had better believe them about himself, since he was employing her regularly to write his pastoral letters. For a while that settled the matter until eventually Benedetta lost her position in the seminary — and at this point I more or less lost touch with her, but discovered that she had been left with little option but to give up the religious life and had set up as some sort of therapist. I feared that the squashing of her interest in a more "feminist" vision of the religious life had made a secular "New Age" spirituality attractive. It was not the first or the last example in my experience of the Church driving away and indeed abusing a most promising and able individual who could have given excellent service, even if some who, like Di Berardino, thought her too "uppity" were probably happy enough with the outcome. Anna intuited that her attachment to me (to whom she would always refer as "My Prof.") was found excessive. However, her problems with authority arose chiefly after she had left Sant' Anselmo, and by that time I had little to do with her.

By this time we had learned much about life in our part of Tuscany, and now, through my teaching in the Patristic Institute, we were learning about odd happenings at the higher levels of the Catholic Church. Some of this was financial and resulted from the Vatican being in a country where financial corruption is rife, especially in the southern half of the peninsula, which we knew so far only as tourists. Now, thanks to Benito Maio, we were able to see at least a part of the "South" in its actuality.

We had been introduced to Benito in Cambridge by Joyce Reynolds, Anna's Director of Studies in Classics at Newnham;

he had worked for Joyce as a gardener. When he appeared at our door, he greeted us with, "I am Benito. You remember Mussolini, you remember me!" We imagined his parents saying of their newborn boy, "We must call him after the dear Duce." By now he had been in England for many years and was accumulating money, much of which was sent back to his village, Gioia Sannitica ("Joy of the Samnites"), located between Monte Cassino and Benevento, where he was constructing a palazzo, floor by floor. Gioia Sannitica was his birthplace — or at least near it, for once when Benito was working on a tree in our garden and Tom said "You know a lot about trees, Benito," he replied that he had been born under a tree. He had, however, failed to learn to read, not least because as a boy he spent the months between April and the end of October looking after the family sheep high up in the mountains, food being brought to him by truck once a week.

We got on well with Benito, and he invited us to visit him at Gioia Sannitica where his status (following that of his wife) was quite different from that in England; out there he was almost regal. Reaching him via the highway leading to Naples was wearing, with the rules of the road seemingly often in abeyance, but we eventually managed to meet him at a local hostelry, where first he offered us wine (declined as we were driving). From there he led the way to his palazzo having, it appeared, consumed a fair quantity of wine himself before getting behind the wheel. As we passed through the gates in a high fence leading to his courtyard, he remarked, "I have discussed the matter with the Carabinieri and they tell me that if my fence is over three meters high, then, if anyone tries to climb over it, I can shoot them!"

No idle threat, as we discovered when he took us to various palazzi in the valley where other members of the Maio clan were feasting — insisting that we sample something in each place. At one place we learned that some weeks earlier one of the girls of the family had gone to her room, only to find someone trying to break in. She gave the alarm, whereon the would-be burglar had to run for his life as family and guests blazed at him with shot-guns though failing to hit their target, owing perhaps to their feasting.

We proceeded to the other palazzi and at the last one encountered a scene somewhat different, the lady owner seeming more educated and aware of the world beyond Gioia Sannitica. Just as we were leaving, her younger daughter arrived: all dolled up, having just auditioned for a role in the new Italian version of the reality show Big Brother, *Grande Fratello*. So not the old-style Gioia Sannitica, but perhaps no less ominous, for both mother and daughter seemed delighted by the prospect the reality-show might offer. That said, I treasure a piece of Gioia wisdom which Benito uttered in his less than literate Italian: "*L'occhio del padrono ingrassa il cavallo*" ("The eye of the boss fattens the horse"): a maxim to take seriously in Italy.

If, that is, Gioia Sannitica is to be regarded as really Italy; many northerners seem to assume that it is not: and not only Gioia Sannitica, but everywhere south of Rome, Sicily especially. That was made clear to us on a plane to Libya (to visit Leptis Magna and Sabratha). As Anna leaned past him to look down on a Sicily burnt by the sun, a Milanese businessman muttered the one word, "*Africa*." Anna replied in her best Italian, "*Non è Africa, è Sicilia*," which elicited, "*Sicilia è Africa*." Later we would read that when the Naples soccer team arrived to play Roma, they were greeted with "*Benvenuti in Italia*" ("Welcome to Italy").

Plane-trips sometimes provide ecclesiastical as well social information. Flying from Rome to Cagliari in Sardinia we were rather surprised to notice that a good section of the passengers were clerics. When we reached our rather expensive hotel we found to our surprise that they too had arrived there and were Franciscan "Conventuals" (sometimes styled *Eventuali*—"possibles"—by Romans). I could not help remembering that when the earthquake at Assisi destroyed many homes, the prioress of the Poor Clares found it her duty to castigate her Franciscan brethren for stuffing themselves in posh restaurants while their flocks went hungry. As we would hear it said in Rome, "Only God knows how much money the Franciscans have got."

◦∞◦✳◦∞◦

1999 was another eventful year: Tom, now equipped with a PhD, got a job in Tampere in Finland on the basis of a telephone interview and set off for that logging town, established in the nineteenth century by a philanthropic Scot. Luckily he was expected to teach in English! In this same year Alice was married to Thomas Pavey on a blazingly hot September 11 in Saint Laurence's Church in Cambridge. Before the wedding the hairdresser and heat reduced her to a near faint while I sweltered in too tight a collar waiting for all to be ready. Eventually—we arrived twenty minutes late—I drove off with the bride. Anna followed in the second car—her vision impeded by the brim of a large hat—with Peter next to her. In the back seat were Peter's father- and mother-in-law—just arrived in England and exclaiming in French at everything they saw. Then, "Watch out, Mum," exclaimed Peter, as Anna just missed clipping a cyclist as she entered the church parking lot.

Meanwhile poor Tom Pavey, kept waiting at the altar for the proceedings to start, told us later that he felt some anxiety lest his Northern Irish relations, some of whom had never been in a Catholic Church before, might make for the exit. But in the end all was well. A former member of the Royal Ulster Constabulary took to the floor with Anna in a passable waltz at the reception in Newnham College, where in my speech I managed to get in a few swipes at Henry Sidgwick, whose portrait faced us and who, good for women's education as he certainly was, was also a forerunner of contemporary utilitarian dishonesty, being more concerned about the social effects if the common man should become aware that he could not reconcile duty and happiness, than for the necessity for philosophers to seek and tell the truth.

Aimée, Peter's mother-in-law, had never before been outside France and persistently compared the sights of Cambridge with what was available in Brest, as well as being especially determined to tell her friends that despite all the myths English food was good. She spent a large part of the next day writing postcards to this effect and expressing annoyance (*"Auguste, tu m'ennuies"*) when her husband interrupted her. Auguste had been a cook in the French army in a number of war zones and was anxious to eat something typically English, so we took them all to the Eagle pub and ordered sausages and mash: however, I made the mistake of referring to the sausage with the pig French "*C'est du chien chaud ça*," which called forth from Auguste in broken English, "Ah, dog! We had that every day in Vietnam." All in all it was a good wedding, made especially enjoyable by the dancing.

Thence to the millennium, which both Anna and I had in our childhood wondered whether—at the advanced age of sixty-four—we would reach. We saw in the New Year quietly at the Mulino, a restaurant in Semproniano at that time run by Pina, a marvelous Roman cook. She and her husband had made a lot of money at a restaurant in the smart Parioli district of Rome, but advised that stress perhaps contributed to their having no children, had decided to move to peaceful Semproniano. On the drive up from Rome they had stopped at the village of San Martino sul Fiora and entering the church Pina had prayed for a child and if it was a son it would be named Martino. According to the local tale, Martino was born some nine months later, being followed by a daughter Margherita. Eventually, her husband, son of a member of a papal orchestra, was "done" for pushing drugs, after which *disgrazia* Pina sadly moved on, though to a good position as chef in a very expensive hotel in Castiglione della Pescaia on the coast. Drugs in Italy were often signaled by roadside graffiti reading *Dio c'è*, which puzzled us as apparently meaning "God exists" but in fact stood for *Droga in offerta* (drugs available).

Tom's being in Tampere gave us the excuse to visit him. We reached Helsinki which, to our astonishment, was littered with beer bottles broken, we gathered, to celebrate the end of the academic year—and all swept away by next morning. Invited to visit Tom's head of department, we were bitten savagely by mosquitoes at a Finnish lake and declined the invitation to the sauna—which Tom accepted, later observing that it was not done to decline. Fortunately our host was English and his wife overlooked it. We then took Tom with us on a Finnish boat from Helsinki along the Baltic, passing Kronstadt, home of the Russian Baltic fleet and scene of carnage after the 1917 Revolution, to Saint Petersburg, where our Russian guide told us how lucky we were to be Finnish (though the majority of us were American).

Saint Petersburg was magnificent: the icon-strewn, onion-domed cathedrals, the Nevsky Prospekt, the Peter and Paul Fortress—grim "home" for centuries for innumerable political enemies of Russia's variegated totalitarian régimes—and especially the Hermitage where, because Joyce Reynolds knew the wife of its Deputy Director, we were able to spend an afternoon in a private tour of its treasures, often accompanied by the strumming of baroque lutes. Finally, before returning to Helsinki, we reached the Tsar's summer palace—Tsarskoye Selo—outside the city with its curated landscape stretching down to the sea.

The next year we were back in Finland, this time to attend Tom's wedding to Anna-Maija Koivisto in the Lutheran Cathedral of Kuopio, with the actual wedding conducted by a Catholic priest from Poland, and the preaching by the Lutheran pastor in Finnish, thus ensuring that we did not understand a word he said. Typically, we had arrived by an unorthodox route, being driven in Anna's cousin Adrian's big German car across the lands and ferried over the seas from Harwich to Helsinki, passing through Denmark (glimpsing Copenhagen with its underwhelming royal palace, its waterways — one had to lie flat to avoid having our heads knocked off under the low bridges — and its Mermaid), then Stockholm where, in the pouring rain we were overawed by the recovered seventeenth-century warship Gustav Vasa.

After the cathedral came all sorts of wedding rituals, including the "kidnapping" of the bride, the putting the married couple to the task of sawing through a vast log with a rusty saw, masses of food and especially drink to accompany the eating and dancing — and finally, for those young enough to continue into the night, an "international" sauna where, after each singing his or her national anthem, all leaped into the lake to cool off: not for us oldies, though overall a clearly joyful occasion. And to sanctify it — despite the Lutheran cathedral (merely described in the relevant document as "the cathedral") — Father George Lawless, OSA, a good friend from Santa Monica, acquired for the couple a papal blessing. Our final joy in Finland was a visit to the Castle of Savonlinna where in summer operas — in this case *Rigoletto* — are regularly performed in a perfect setting. Driving back to Kuopio after midnight, we were still able to catch sight of an elk lurking at the edge of one of the endless forests. Finally we returned by roughly the same route, though held up for a day by a ferry-strike in Denmark.

―○○○✻○○○―

George Lawless (mentioned above and author of a standard work on Augustine's rule), an excellent influence on what could be the fractured house of Santa Monica, and also often good of an evening for what he styled a "snort" — though of whisky, not of cocaine — came along to welcome an honor which, quite surprisingly, I was to receive when back in Rome in that same year 2002 at the University of the Holy Cross, an Opus Dei institution: an honorary degree in Philosophy.

The idea of an honorary degree had never occurred to me, let alone one from Opus Dei, an organization of which I had been suspicious. I had consulted a number of people as to whether to accept and opinion seemed to be divided. In the end I asked Father Kurt Pritzl, OP, then Dean of Philosophy at the Catholic University of America, who had himself earned a PhD from the University of Toronto and with whom, though no pupil of mine, I had become acquainted. Pritzl's advice was that if I thought that the University of the Holy Cross was a genuine academic institution rather than a propaganda center, I should accept. From what I knew of it—and my judgment has since been confirmed—it was genuinely academic, so I followed Pritzl's advice, Anna warning me that "If you accept, you will never be offered another honorary degree."

The ceremony unfolded with lots of display, with singing by a large choir and other excellent music. The University was in the habit of offering three honorary degrees a year, one (this time for me) in Philosophy, a second in Theology (this time given to Cardinal Tettamanzi, Archbishop of Milan) and a third in Canon Law (this went to a Spaniard who, however, was too ill to attend). So it was just Tettamanzi and me, each of us dressed in the ritual kit and expected to give a fifteen minute *"lectio"* which in my case was on fundamentalism and seemed acceptable. Tettamanzi's, however, I found unintelligible, even though I thought I could follow the Italian. We had previously been asked for my head-size for presentation of an academic (European-style) hat, but lacking a tape-measure, Anna advised "Just tell them the largest size." The result being larger than expected, the hat kept falling over my eyes as I gave my *"lectio."*

Sister Benedetta had turned up in support and I asked her what she thought of Tettamanzi's effort: "Beautiful Italian, no content" was her judgment, confirming my own. Perhaps relevantly, I had shaken hands with Tettamanzi after the ceremony and felt a flabby lifelessness in his "grip" such as I had once felt when, in Trinity years before, I had shaken hands with tired old R. A. Butler: which grasp I had been warned would express a weariness to be compared with that of a punch-drunk boxer (and in Butler's case of the moral guardian of the youthful Prince Charles, then an undergraduate at the College). Anna later informed me that one does not "shake" the hand of a Cardinal (or bishop) but merely "kiss" it by bending one's head.

Present for my honorary degree were not only Father George and Sister Benedetta, but—astonishingly—my old Brentwood

Classics teacher Michael Benson, his unexpected presence welcome indeed: not that he was a Catholic, rather an Evangelical in and out of Anglicanism. I made sure that he was invited to the somewhat uncomfortable but well-stocked supper laid on after the ceremony. I was now in possession of a BA (earned), an MA (bought) and a PhD (honorary). I reflected that Socrates, not having a degree at all, presumably would not get an appointment in a modern philosophy department.

◦◦◦✻◦◦◦

Two years later and back in Cambridge, in virtue of my new role as defender of the faith, I was called on to lay into one of its opponents, in the form of the Oxford Dominican Father Gareth Moore: another case — after that of Benedetta (or rather overlapping with it) — of threats to the Church deriving from its stultifying authoritarianism combined with a lust to follow many of the worst moral features of the secular West, and thus protect itself — for a while — from standing out. In this case the call came from Father David Sanders, OP, editor of *Priests and People*, who told me that Moore — almost elected Dominican Prior in Oxford, as I later heard, then gaining a similar post in Belgium and now deceased — had written (published posthumously) a lengthy and sophisticated biblical and philosophical defense of homosexuality.

The English Dominican Provincial had banned any review of Moore's book from appearing in a Dominican journal, but Sanders, as editor of a non-Dominican journal, asked me to review it. My surprised reply was that I would if what I wrote was not censored, to which Sanders said there would be no censorship and that I could have as much space as I liked. So I wrote a review-article, which (not to my surprise) finished off the journal (it was later continued under a different name and with a new editor) and put Sanders "on leave" for the next few months. And copies were immediately withdrawn, seemingly world-wide: some years later a moral theologian from the Beda who had also been asked to review the book tried to find a copy of my review in Rome, but failed to do so. I would have liked to have added to my entry in *Who's Who* under hobbies (in addition to "Preventing Principals from getting knighthoods," see page 168) a further allusion to closing down Catholic journals.

The next few years were comparatively peaceful, as I continued teaching each fall at the Augustinianum, a task made the more congenial when an American Augustinian, Robert Dodaro, took over as President. Dodaro, who had studied for a doctorate in Oxford with Henry Chadwick, was not a popular appointment among his Italian colleagues, primarily because he was not Italian, but there was no one else of the right age and qualifications to do the job. And he had a vision for the Institute: he hoped that, with the decline of Christianity in Europe and the traditional centers of patristic scholarship—Paris and Oxford—on the wane, the Augustinianum would be able to fill the vacuum created. Thus he wanted to internationalize the Institute: not to the delight of his Italian colleagues but for me a good reason to continue teaching there.

Living there on and off for about three months in the fall each year meant that we made many new friends, especially among the Nigerians (of whom there were many) and more immediately a Polish pupil of George Lawless, Father Wieslaw Dawidowski, and a Maltese, Father Caruana. Before long Caruana invited us to Valletta where I was to give the annual Augustine lecture, an event on the island apparently not only academic but part of the social calendar, both the Archbishop and the President of the country being expected to appear. In my case, however—seemingly a surprise to Caruana—the president arrived but the archbishop's chair remained empty. No matter; it was a happy occasion in a beautiful city with very hospitable inhabitants. We were astonished by the Caravaggios in the pro-cathedral and the day after my lecture a lady who owned a tourist shop greeted us on the street and almost ordered Anna to take her pick from its contents for free. Anna chose one of the more modest of the artificial pearl necklaces. That was followed by lengthy tours of the archaeological sites of the island, and a visit to the old capital and religious center of Medina.

In another year Wieslaw, now returned to Poland and having become Provincial of the Augustinians there, invited us to Krakow, home of Anna's Jewish (though unknown to her) grandfather. Krakow proved full of vast Gothic churches, one of which—in what was once the largely Jewish quarter of Kazimierz (though there was no ghetto until Nazi times)—belonged to the Augustinians and provided us with a base. It was still perhaps the most

Catholic city we had visited and, as headquarters of the German Governor-General Hans Frank, was hardly damaged during the Nazi occupation. We were especially impressed by the restored altarpiece by Veit Stoss: after being shipped off by the Nazis and recovered from Nuremberg Castle, it had now returned to its home in Saint Mary's Basilica. And we could climb up to the old Wawel palace and cathedral overlooking the Vistula, dating from days when Krakow was the capital of Poland.

But we had a further aim: to investigate any Voglers—Anna's father's family—who might survive in the city. In the 1920s, as we saw from city censuses we obtained, there were about twenty Vogler families living there; now there appeared to be only one, represented by an old but distinguished poet who had written a terrifying book about his experience in various concentration camps during the war. Since he was by now extremely old, we contacted his wife and learned that their relatives had gone to France, where they might well not have survived. We also looked for Vogler graves in what survived of the Jewish cemeteries, at least where we could read the names of the dead, those in Hebrew being closed to us. The rest were commemorated in German or Polish, these "Gentile" languages perhaps at times indicating a less than "Orthodox" religious affiliation. We visited the three remaining synagogues, one still in use, another transformed into a museum. We noted many Israeli visitors and that those who were Cohens (*Kohanim*, or the priestly descendants of Aaron who must maintain ritual purity) were advised as to which streets covered older Jewish burials and which they must therefore avoid.

Krakow proved a beautiful city, its buildings marking humanity's achievements, but not far away is Auschwitz, a stark reminder of a very different side of human nature. Despite Anna's anxiety about visiting it, we knew we could not evade going there, and did so on a private tour—I recalling the remarks of Martha Gellhorn as she entered another camp with the liberating American army: "What we saw defies the liberal imagination; only a long abandoned theory of human mass depravity could begin to explain it": that "theory" that is, so powerfully expounded by Augustine! Yet while over Auschwitz the entrance sign ARBEIT MACHT FREI remained in position, to us the impact was of a dead place, reminding us of the remark of Hannah Arendt about the banality of evil.

Despite inflicting massive misery for as long as they could, the Nazis had failed to wipe out the Chosen People. Others have hoped to imitate them, I thought — remembering the words of Uday Hussein that I have recorded earlier. If nihilism is ultimately the only logical alternative to Christianity, we should ignore the self-serving and self-flattering observations of "liberals" who tell us that it could not happen again — or that it was a peculiarly German phenomenon: more than half of the members of the Waffen-SS were of non-German origin. Already as I write, there are thousands of pro-Hamas demonstrators in London, some with posters and slogans implying that Hitler was right.

If Auschwitz is a warning, we found another in Istanbul. I have indicated that I had been there before, and we now accepted the kind invitation of Denis O'Brien's brother-in-law, a Turkish professor of ophthalmology, to return. Güngor had been Honorary President of the Ataturk Youth League and was a strong opponent of fundamentalism — indeed of theocracy in general. Still, the spear-headed minarets, the damage inflicted on Hagia Sophia, and the dreadful history of the Janissaries and of bowstring-strangled sultans, all reminded us that Nazism and Communism are not the only threats to our foundering Western culture.

We roamed around Istanbul's usual sites, I impressed again by the underground cisterns which one can tour by boat — but noting that even churches supposed to be open were normally closed — then dining at Güngor's club, which turned out to be one of the old Ottoman palaces on the Bosphorus converted for more contemporary use. Güngor brought his cousin with him — a wine producer with considerable estates near Izmir — and the conversation turned to Islamist extremism and how to handle it. If Güngor was fierce, the cousin was more direct, exclaiming "Hang the lot." In view of more recent history one could see his point!

Rain pouring down on the penultimate day of our visit to Istanbul, Anna decided to stay at our lodging in the University, whereas I wanted to buy a carpet. I found in the area near the Blue Mosque a likely place to haggle for one, so simultaneously seeing another face of Islam. The negotiations lasted some six hours as cups of mint tea were downed until we were both satisfied with the price — which was about a third of what the vendor had originally asked. In the course of reaching this conclusion, we discussed the situation of Turkey in the modern world; of this he had more knowledge than I would have expected until he told me that he had learned his English while working with an uncle who sold women's underwear in the East End of London. He also had a girlfriend who was an Algerian journalist unable to return to her country for fear of assassination and was therefore living in Egypt.

I asked him whether he was a Muslim, and he allowed that he was, so I enquired whether he ever went to a mosque. He said that he didn't—and on my asking why not, explained that he could not be an active Muslim because (a) he liked to drink alcohol, (b) he liked the company of young women and (c) that if he had stayed in his home town in the south of the country (where the carpet in question came from) he would have been expected to marry by the age of fifteen. Finally we shook hands and I lugged off the carpet to grace our front room in Cambridge.

Returning home and preparing to go back to Italy, I found a surprising message in my computer's inbox; it was from John McCarthy, Dean of the Faculty of Philosophy at the Catholic University of America in Washington, asking whether I would be willing to become the first holder of a new chair in his Department to be named for Kurt Pritzl, the former Dean whose advice about Opus Dei I had recently followed. He had died prematurely of cancer in his late fifties—a great loss for the department. It seems that before his death, knowing that a new Chair would be established in his honor, he had expressed a wish that it be offered to me.

The offer was for a full time position, but that would have been too much, and further, I was still committed to teaching the fall semester in Rome, so I suggested that I would come on a half-time basis in January. To my surprise that was accepted and I began a four year stretch teaching in Washington, thus combining one job at the center of the Catholic Church with another at the center of the political world. And I recognized a curious similarity between Rome and Washington quite apart from Washington's "Roman" architecture. Both lie between North and South—the South in Italy being the world of which Gioia Sannitica was part—while in the United States, Washington (where more than forty-two percent of the residents are of African descent) was where escaping slaves might first have found a safe haven. Thus it was a mixture of North and South, or in the ironic words of John Kennedy, of

"Northern hospitality and Southern efficiency." In the first year, I came to Washington on my own, living in various religious houses — of which more anon. After that Anna joined me and we were able to live on campus and eat in Caldwell Hall, home to a number of priests engaged in teaching or in administrative work.

I enjoyed Catholic U from the start, finding my colleagues exceptionally friendly and able, and while the undergraduates were ignorant and often poorly motivated, the graduate students were serious and hardworking, many showing considerable philosophical acumen. Unlike the rest of the University, the Philosophy faculty were — almost to a man or woman — serious Catholics. (I was to learn over the years that, generally speaking, philosophy departments in Catholic universities in the United States are orthodox, while their theology departments, particularly in the richer institutions — and especially if Jesuit-run — are not.)

That said, my first year lodging in one Irish-American religious house was informative in an unexpected and unpleasing way. When the Saint Patrick's Day celebrations began, drinking was heavy and accompanied by the singing of IRA songs:

> On the twentieth day of November
> Outside of the town of Muldoon,
> The Tans in their big yellow tender
> Came hurtling along to their doom,
> 'Cause the lads from the section were waiting
> With gunpowder primed on the spot
> And the Irish Republican Army
> Made shit of the whole fuckin' lot.

Looking back on this IRA experience, I hope it was not fear which prevented me from protesting, but rather a paralyzing astonishment at the sheer effrontery of it. I was reminded of an occasion in Aberdeen when, debating with a fellow professor on a local radio station what seemed to be infanticide, I referred to an illegal experiment on human subjects in which I had reason to know he had participated — and was taken aback when, looking me straight in the eye, he brazenly retorted that of course he would never get involved in that kind of thing.

The "IRA show" concluded with the drinking of "Car bombs": large doses of whiskey topped up with large doses of Guinness, to be drunk in one gulp. Nor at that time had I yet understood the significance of the fact that among the Irish clerical diaspora—and not only in the United States—homosexuality and the abuse of minors had become fashionable. Not unjustly did the magazine *Private Eye* satirize a certain Father P.D. O'Phile.

That the political and moral perversities were not disconnected became apparent when Sinn Fein, the political wing of the IRA—"our boys," as an Irish archbishop denoted them and whose leaders always grasped the opportunity to be photographed receiving Holy Communion—became a force for abortion and LGBT ideology in Ireland and beyond. Thus in New York, under the financially-concerned gaze of Cardinal Dolan, LGBT flags fluttered over many of the floats in the Saint Patrick's Day parade. In Washington I was beginning to learn—though its full implications were as yet unclear—the nature of that "tribal Catholicism" that was the religion of large sections of both Catholic clergy and laity in America. I remembered that years ago in Toronto IRA bagmen would often come fundraising at the Catholic College. I have discussed this tribalism in the preface to a book by Don Tullio Rotondo.

Somewhere about this time, while Benedict XVI was still pope, I took part in a conference in Rome on Augustine's *City of God*. This was followed by a visit to the pope's summer residence at Castel Gandolfo to hear an orchestra and choir from Würzburg perform an opera which their choirmaster had written about the early life of Augustine. The composer had predictably emphasized Augustine's relationship with a North African woman who appeared among the *dramatis personae* bearing the implausible name "Stella." (Indeed, it has become a bit of an academic parlor-game to propose often anachronistic names for her.) The Bishop of Würzburg had funded the conference and apparently as part of the payoff was able to dedicate the first performance of the opera to Pope Benedict, who attended in person. Those of us at the conference had been invited to hear it.

It was an incomplete success: the music was tolerable (though hardly such that Benedict would appreciate), but the lyrics sentimental and cliché-ridden. At its ending we were taken by coach to a *trattoria* in one of the other Castelli where the food was good and a man entered playing his accordion, which displeased several clerics, who asked him to leave. This displeased several of the rest of us, so I told him to continue his serenade. When he asked me what he should play, remembering the good old days in Semproniano I suggested *Romagna Mia*, which he could more or less handle, thereby winning a good tip. At its conclusion he asked me whether I came from the Romagna, which was also pleasing in that it seemed to imply that I spoke a competent Italian. Thus we put the day to bed on a more melodious note.

⋄⊙⊙✶⊙⊙⋄

In 2014 a further pleasing surprise awaited me. As the American Catholic Philosophical Association met in Washington, I found myself that year's recipient of its Aquinas Medal, named for the "Angelic Doctor." John McCarthy introduced me, remarking that it might seem odd that since I was neither angelic nor a Doctor (or only an honorary one) I was thus rewarded. If I found the award more flattering than I should have, it did give me the opportunity to discourse on "Sophists then and now." I argued that there were philosophy departments awarding doctorates in sophistry rather than philosophy, recalling that Elizabeth Anscombe, asked in a BBC interview what most of her colleagues at Oxford were doing, famously replied that "I suppose most of them are corrupting the youth." In 2023 I would be told that a philosophy professor at Oxford had said that his job was to eliminate religious belief among his pupils.

Invitations to foreign campuses continued, among them to Leuven—where on receiving a receipt in triplicate from my taxi-driver and remarking that I had never received such before, he replied (in English), "Sir, this is Belgium." To observe that I now understood why Brussels is the heart of the European Union would have been only appropriate. I would meet the European Union again on a visit to its "college" outside Warsaw where youthful would-be bureaucrats—the supposed pick of our continent's élites—were being initiated into its rituals. There I lectured on the Roman Emperor Marcus Aurelius's world-weary attitude toward government, but have no idea if to any effect. I would comment more generally on the bureaucratic and undemocratic European Union in 2021 in a volume of essays in honor of Rémi Brague.

Far more interesting were three other very different visits: to Iceland, to Siberia, and in 2017 to Nigeria. For me Iceland had always been a travel target and the presence there of Father Edward Booth, OP, who was passing his declining years as chaplain to a small group of nuns at Stykkishólmur, provided the chance. Apart from the astonishing raw rock, volcanoes, massive waterfalls, and that cleft between tectonic plates where early Icelandic parliaments met and transgressors were thrown to their doom, we were introduced to another phase in the history of Christianity under the guidance of a young Icelander recently converted to Catholicism.

In the mid-sixteenth century the King of Denmark, at that time ruler of Iceland, decided, Henrician-style, that the country must go Lutheran. There being considerable objection, the last two Catholic bishops needed to be dispatched. One of them, bishop of the southern part of the country, was a learned humanist who had translated Latin and other texts into Icelandic and was so popular that the king found it impossible to find anyone to cut off his head. So spirits were poured down the throat of an adolescent cretin, to enable him, after some failed attempts, to effect the decapitation.

Olafur took us to the place of execution where a new church had been built; we had initially supposed it to be Catholic from its having, *inter alia*, a Lady Chapel, but it turned out to be Lutheran. On leaving, we met a female German pastor at the door and Anna, somewhat mischievously, told her that we had supposed the church to be Catholic, whereupon she asked whether any of us were Catholic—turning her eyes especially at the Icelander. When Anna told her that we were all Catholics, she enquired, "But what about that dreadful pope (i.e., her compatriot Benedict)?" I retorted "Best pope for three hundred years" as we emerged.

As we walked on, Anna remarked that the bishop surely should have been canonized and Olafur replied that he had children, one of them a priest who was killed with him; the Gregorian Reform had hardly reached the shores of distant Iceland. But the unfolding of our friend's story was sad, if again informative. Having decided that he might have a vocation, he was sent by the then ex-pat bishop of Iceland to the English College in Rome, where things did not go well. At a meeting with Pope Benedict, Olafur was made much of—Icelandic Catholics being rare—but he would leave after a few months, disillusioned on finding homosexuality rampant. He returned to Iceland where acquaintances he had not seen for some time asked what he had been doing and he told them that he had tried to be a seminarian. This would elicit the question, "What's the matter with you, pedophile or something?"

Such was the effect of clergy abuse and a "lavender" culture on non-believers!

My next expedition would be to Siberian Novosibirsk, which I reached by air via Moscow, then waited inside the terminal building while an official taxi was booked: unofficial ones I had been warned to avoid as there was the possibility of being forced to pay excessively at gun- or knife-point. I had been invited — somewhat similarly to what had occurred earlier in Riga — by a local group based in what had been a secret military institution, Akademgorodok, a few miles from industrial Novosibirsk. Astonishingly, I was to give a series of lectures on Plotinus to an audience not only of locals, but of Russians from especially Moscow, Ukrainians from Odessa, Georgians, and even the odd Kazakh.

The Institute, once significant and secretive, only the well-vetted being allowed access, had given up on astrophysics when under Brezhnev the money ran out. The staff who remained were able to turn Akademgorodok into some sort of research center for the humanities, while a few of the older scientists stayed on, some of whom entertained science-fiction views about the paradise that science would soon bring to humanity. I would come to realize — or rather to recall from my service days — that an effect of the ignorance of the outside world which was a legacy of Communism, was that almost anything could be believed: I would be told that one of the best-selling "History" books to be found on Russian campuses argued that the ancient world had never existed, being a self-serving invention of Renaissance scholars. That said, the ex-scientists had apparently decided that the humanities were worthwhile, and over recent years had invited a number of Western scholars, particularly those who, like me, who were interested in ancient philosophy.

During my visit, it being February, the temperature was twenty-seven degrees below zero Celsius, so that it seemed almost warm when it rose to twenty-three. All was covered in deep snow and the Institute was surrounded by dense forest stretching perhaps thousands of miles in several directions. At night I could hear wolves howling, and in the daytime, the season being appropriate, I was able to watch endless footage on television of the 1942 battle of Stalingrad. I knew that the Institute was near the River Ob — in the hotel lobby there were pictures of men and women sunbathing on its banks in some past July — so I asked to be taken to see it.

Accompanied by a guide, I set out across the snow. Coming into what seemed open country, I asked when we would reach the river which I knew to be very wide at this point. Came the reply, "we have been walking on it for some few hundred meters."

The lectures were well attended, questions constant and sharp and in the evenings the food was good. On the final night there was a banquet in honor of my visit, which was unexpectedly noisy, a similar, much more uninhibited banquet being given in the same room for the employees — mostly French — of some oil company. After the meal we walked up to the local opera house for a splendid recital by a local boy who had recently won the Odessa piano competition; he received fifteen encores.

I was, of course, interested to hear as much about politics and religion as I could, and no one was inhibited from talking. All, whatever their religious beliefs or lack of them, were agreed that most Orthodox bishops were KGB: I was told that you could tell how high they were in that organization by the size of the car they drove, or in which they were driven. All also enjoyed telling "Brezhnev jokes" (as of his visit to Lenin's mausoleum and onlookers being unable to tell who had come out). When I asked how Putin, an ex-colonel in the KGB, had managed to become autocrat (they often used the word "Tsar"), they replied that the oligarchs had supposed him to be their puppet, but that the reverse had turned out to be the case.

After Iceland and Russia came Nigeria, where a better side of Catholicism was in clear view. In Rome we had come to know Nigerian priests from different parts of that vast and varied country. Alex was a novelty: a psychologist born in a largely Muslim Kaduna where he said that as a boy he had experienced no tension between the religious groups ("We used to play football and go drinking together"), but with the arrival of Saudi money for mosque-building all that changed and groups of young men living in and around the mosque would emerge only to burn down a church or a Christian home.

Then there was Augustine, always known as "Babs," who once expressed surprise that I did not seem at all racist. He was the son of a Yoruba king and "lucky" not to be king himself, having entered the religious life before the death of his elder brother. Finally there was John Abubakar, son of a Muslim who had studied accountancy in Italy and who — when we first met him — was himself studying at the Biblicum. He told us that he had no difficulty with Hebrew because he was a Hausa and his language was Semitic.

Prematurely, Father John found himself elected Provincial (partly because though a Northerner, and many Northerners wanted a separate province, he was for a unified Augustinian presence in Nigeria as a whole). And Father John invited us to come out to Nigeria; there I would give a few lectures to seminarians and Anna was to address a vast hall of schoolchildren. Besides knowing that we liked travelling, I think John wanted to show us the work he was doing in his Province, where it seemed that every other month he was presiding over the building of a new school, for both boys and girls and many of them Muslim.

Our plan was to go first to South Africa where my mother had been born. The family of her brother Jack lived in Johannesburg in a gated community, the center of Johannesburg being by then virtually a no-go area for whites — indeed for many blacks too, being largely controlled by criminal gangs at war with one another. But it was a great visit and we managed not only to take in Soweto — seeing the church which had acted as a place of refuge for African protesters under apartheid and still showing the police bullets on its walls — but also going north to a game park abutting the Kruger National Park and part-owned by Alan, the successful businessman of the family. It was a truly idyllic spot where we managed to see four of the "big five" (lion, elephant, rhino, and hippo, but no leopard) and to end the day with the traditional Safari cocktail hour — "sundowners," as they say in South Africa — while watching the sun set over the northern end of the Drakensberg mountain chain.

From Johannesburg we flew to Nigeria, via the utter chaos of Lagos airport. There we were eventually found by some of Father John's priests and whisked off to the local Augustinian house and church where some ten thousand attended Masses the next day, the preaching being decidedly "hell-fire" — and Father John told us later that the congregation would be markedly smaller without such preaching. It seemed that some of the children had never seen a white person (unless on television) when on that first day in Lagos one little boy kept running up to me to get a closer look. When I turned, he would back off until, finally emboldened, he touched my leg to satisfy himself that I was a real human being.

Thence to other parts of Nigeria, by car or plane: Abuja, Jos, and most strangely Makurdi, which turned out to be the worst city we visited in the country for humidity and mosquitoes (even though, we were told, fewer than usual), but it was also the scene of a remarkable honor bestowed on us. Father John had told us that there would be a "reception," though that was not quite the right word: I was to be appointed an honorary chief and Father of the Tiv tribe of Benue state, with Anna a Mother of the tribe. To achieve this, we had to process across an open space—followed by a group of drummers and teenage girls doing a "cat dance"—from the church to where the Paramount Chief and his Council waited to present us with the insignia of our new office, mostly clothing and headgear, but also a spear. When Anna noted that British Airways would scarcely allow the spear on the aircraft, we were assured that it was only for the occasion. We were to keep the clothing which, being black and white, symbolized that the people were black and also peaceful Christians.

Especially when compared with some of their neighbors; this we realized when we were told that we must start early the next day to drive the few hundred kilometers to Jos in order to get through a Muslim village before Friday prayers began: otherwise, the road would be blocked and there might be violence. As we were driving, we passed several army checkpoints, Father John explaining that these were originally intended to control the thugs of Boko Haram (which means "no books"). In fact Boko Haram had been driven from the area some time before, but the roadblocks remained, with the army extorting payment from passing drivers.

When we were not stopped, I enquired why. Father John offered possible explanations: first that our car was comparatively large, so we might be diplomats; second that priests—John was wearing his "collar"—were respected; third and related, "Were there interference with a priest, the One 'up there' (Father John pointed to the sky) might be displeased." We had no trouble, but it was clear that Nigeria was not an easy place for Europeans, and we were more than once asked why we had risked coming. To this we replied that we wanted to see what life was like in this large, religiously divided country south of the Sahara. When we enquired why the question had been asked, we would be told that there were three good reason for Europeans to stay away from Nigeria: the malarial mosquitoes, the humidity, and Boko Haram.

Despite that, we would never regret our visit, nor cease to be astonished at the good work the Augustinians were doing in Nigeria, ranging from the blessing of a shop selling local costumes and perfumes to the building of schools and working for religious harmony. That "only God knows what the Augustinians are for" might be only too true of the Order in Rome but was untrue in Nigeria — even though most of the Augustinians there had only a limited idea of who Augustine was.

So we left Abuja by air — running again at the airport into instances of petty bureaucracy designed to extract extra cash from uninformed travelers — to fly back over the astonishing Sahara, with air so clear that even at thirty thousand feet we could see the aridity of sand and rock spreading for miles in every direction under the blazing sun.

⸻❋⸻

Nor in these fascinating years did we fail to take advantage of our presence in Washington to visit or revisit parts of the United States which especially attracted us; we celebrated the fiftieth anniversary of our youthful trip to Las Vegas and the Grand Canyon by a return to the same area, this time managing both to live for a few days in a comfortable "family hotel" in the far-from-family-oriented city of Las Vegas where most of the students in the University were studying Hospitality and Gaming. We then descended to the torrid bottom of the Canyon by helicopter for a brief trip along the river. Then on to Albuquerque and Santa Fe, the latter once the northern end of the royal road to Mexico City, both with their Spanish and Franciscan past distinct from the homogenized commercialism of most northern American cities.

Elsewhere we broke new ground south of the Mason-Dixon Line, flying to Charleston where we could visit Fort Sumter (scene of the first shots in the Civil War) and the old slave-market where we learned of the extraordinary career of Olaudah Equiano, a former enslaved Nigerian who when eventually freed came to England, married in Soham, Cambridgeshire and became a prominent abolitionist in late eighteenth-century London. We also had dinner with Leslie Kaufmann, publisher of Anna's first collection of poems. Next was beautiful Savannah, a one-time military fort built in squares with parks at their intersections and intended to keep an eye on anything Spanish coming from further south.

Finally there were places nearer to "home": Virginia's Williamsburg, Yorktown, scene of the final American victory in the Revolutionary War, and Harpers Ferry at the confluence of the Potomac and the Shenandoah, famed for the ambiguous exploits of John Brown before his soul went marching on.

<hr />

Our visit to Nigeria was in 2017 and there at least the Catholic Church seemed in reasonably good shape—far from the case in Europe and North America, which were now ambiguously governed by the Argentinian Jorge Bergoglio, elected as Pope Francis: Argentinian, indeed, as a master of that country's political tactics as exhibited by Juan Perón, the earlier twentieth-century dictator. Teaching in Rome, and with some awareness of the distorted ways the Vatican works, I was suspicious of the new pope even before the publication of his apostolic exhortation *Amoris Laetitia* showed my fears to be justified.

I had watched the rigging of the two Synods on the family so well documented by Edward Pentin and the distress of Robert Dodaro, still in charge at the Augustinianum when he was summoned by the General of his Order and told that the pope was furious with him for editing—at the instigation of Cardinal Burke—the collection of essays (to which I contributed) in refutation of the views on marriage and divorce held by Cardinal Walter Kasper—then rumored to be the pope's favorite theologian: which views the synods were rigged to show as widely accepted.

Dodaro was notified by the General that he would shortly be summoned by the pope and told to get out of Rome. Remembering his shocked demeanor, I can testify that the whole business brought about his imminent collapse. His expulsion did not happen at once and a few days later the General explained that it was not the pope who was furious—his mood-swings we would later learn were an effect of his being bi-polar and on medication for it—but those around him: an economy with the truth common to autocratic régimes. But the "writing was on the wall" for Bob and for the internationalizing project he had been developing at the Patristic Institute.

Amoris Laetitia aroused much concern among a number of senior members of the church hierarchy and four Cardinals sent questions (*dubia*) to the Congregation for the Doctrine of the Faith, intended to clarify that the apostolic exhortation had no unorthodox intent.

Silence followed; clearly Francis's policy was to ignore all criticism, or even questions, operating on the principle later stated to Cardinal Müller that "I am the pope and I do not have to give reasons for my actions." The Cardinals sought an audience; again there was no reply. They then went public, bringing the problematic of the present papacy to the attention of a wider audience of Catholics.

Unfortunately, the Cardinals failed to follow up their action with a "Filial Correction," though others tried that. All were ignored while the pope pushed brazenly on with his policy (given a "theological" basis by Kasper) of *Sola Misericordia* ("mercy alone") — over emphasizing, that is — as had Luther — one aspect of Christ's teaching at the expense of others: in this case Christ's injunction to the woman "taken in adultery" not just to "go" but also to "sin no more." Further attacks on Catholic tradition followed, especially the encouragement of homosexual acts, coupled with complicit silence about the abuse of minors by clergy and cover-ups by bishops — as displayed by the following:

Doggerel in consolation for a seminarian

The time has come to decide
to confess without signaling Pride
that the rector's been up my backside.
And though his rent-boys are well paid,
some finish up getting AIDS.

Well:
Too often these rectors are bent.
Corrupting 'em young's the intent.
No chance this guy will relent
(nor — God forbid — repent).
The dog-collared sods live in hope
to be absolved by Saint Francis our pope.

So:
Lest fruit-flavored Death come for you,
get a good lawyer and sue.

As the scandal — to my mind of worse than Arian proportions (indeed itself implying a hidden Arianism or, more plausibly, an odd mixture of Adoptionism and pantheism) — went on without effective challenge, I was drawn into the fray, agreeing to add my name to an Open Letter asking the bishops to enquire into the apparent heresies of the pope — aware, as we were, that heresy disqualifies a pope, whether or not validly elected. As a result, although papal courtiers and lower level cronies were unable to harm me as seriously as they could clergy, they were to do their mean-spirited best.

The first indication of such malice took me completely by surprise. With Rebecca and Anna's cousin Adrian I was driving back from Capalbio and reached the gates of the Augustinianum, to be told I could not leave my car in its parking lot, nor even enter the premises: this despite the fact that nominally I was still on the staff of the Institute and had one remaining PhD candidate working under my supervision.

Naturally I tried to find out why I could not enter. Indeed the ban on entry (which I eventually heard extended to all pontifical campuses in Rome) also covered my companions, Adrian being refused entry even to use the toilet. At my insistence, the gatekeeper agreed to find out why he had been told to deny me entry and contacted the General, at that time in Spain, to be told simply that I was not to be admitted: no further questions. Rebecca persisted in trying to find an explanation and eventually gathered from the new President of the Institute that it was because I had signed the letter to the bishops and Cardinals. There was nothing in writing; to this day the order against me has only (so far as I know) been transmitted by word of mouth.

And mouths were opening well beyond Rome. A few weeks later I received a message from Barry David, a former pupil who was editing a *Festschrift* in my honor and had secured an agreement to publish from the Catholic University of America Press. Barry told me that the Press had now decided not to publish "because of the letter" — though I am happy to record that those members of the Press Committee who belonged to the Faculty of Philosophy all maintained that publication should proceed as originally agreed. That did not happen, leaving Barry to find another publisher. This he managed with the help of Ed Halper, another long-ago student of mine in Toronto, now Chairman of the Philosophy Department at the University of Georgia in Athens. And the Academia Verlag doing an excellent and speedy job, malign intent was overcome.

The fate of Dodaro was much worse. Having finished his three terms as President of the Institute, he had a nervous breakdown, which gave his enemies the chance to mistreat him. He was shipped off to Saint Luke's hospital outside Washington, a facility where pedophile priests and other transgressors were enclosed, and there dosed up with lithium: a treatment by then normally discarded by more humane medical institutions. Anna and I visited him — though after great difficulty in getting permission to do so — and found him in distressing condition.

I drew Cardinal Burke's attention to the way Dodaro had been treated, to find he had already grasped the truth of the matter — but apparently nothing could be done. Eventually Bob made a partial recovery and was sent to an Augustinian house outside Toronto, but since for months he no longer replied to my emails and apparently contributed little to Burke's second book (*The Faith Once for All Delivered*), of which he was supposed to be co-editor, I assumed he had relapsed again. Though he has now partially recovered once more, he will probably never return to his old ebullient self. Nor did he receive much acknowledgement, let alone thanks, for the years he devoted to the Patristic Institute.

After the car incident, I never received any acknowledgement from the Augustinians in Rome for the years of service I gave them — nor for the useful collection of books I donated to their library. The letter to the Cardinals and its aftermath finally made clear to me in a personal way that something was radically wrong in the Church: something far wider than the abuse of authority and heresies of a pope. On a couple of occasions I was able to indicate something of this at Saint Edmund's in Cambridge, where in successive years appeared Cardinal Cupich, one of Bergoglio's closest cronies, and the Basilian Father Thomas Rosica, deputed to interpret papal doings to the English-speaking world. In the question periods following their performances I was able to inform Cupich that there seemed to be a disconnect between Pope Francis's apparent friendliness to "one and all" and his savage and sometimes foul-mouthed abuse of more traditional Catholics. As for Rosica, my questioning would lead indirectly to his exposure as a serial plagiarist.

In 2019 I published perhaps my most ambitious book, an account of the development and deconstruction of the concept of the person: a project begun in antiquity and developed to its fullest extent through the influence of Christianity. I argued that we are not serial selves and should not allow ourselves to be "mentally compartmentalized" — even if complete decompartmentalization is impossible in the present life, our tendency being always to shut off inconvenient demands of conscience if fear, lust, or greed overcome us: at times indeed it is more than a tendency and we consciously do not want to know what our conscience is clearly saying. For an abortionist, on the day before birth a child is still not a person — while if duly born, he is!

Anna and I followed up "*What is a Person?*" in 2022 with a related book entitled *Confusion in the West* in which we tried to analyze this moral and spiritual confusion and identify some of its philosophical sources. Our basic theme was that Westerners now try to combine ideas deriving from an original Graeco-Roman base in Christianized form with others deriving from non-Christian, indeed often anti-Christian, sources, being too often also contradictory to one another. Far from this producing a coherent view of man's nature and location in the world, it points either to self-deception about the coherence of our moral universe or toward nihilism. For without a coherent foundation moral ideas, however individually satisfactory, can never cohere with one another; when their "owners" are enough pushed, they are seen as indefensible. Thus the future of Western man can seem all too open to submission to totalitarian controllers — who may just provide him with "bread and circuses" to compensate for his loss of freedom and dignity.

In the course of helping to write *Confusion* I realized more fully the problem of compartmentalization to which I had already paid some attention, if rather too casually. Now I realized that it was a more serious problem than any implausible thesis about serial selves and that compartmentalization is a temptation and threat to anyone who, to avoid facing reality, shuts off unpleasant personal aspects of his experience of Augustine's "darkness of social life," and thus avoids responsibility.

That is a threat not only to the individual but also to the wider society which my long experience of Italy has enabled me — with regret — to recognize more clearly. For many Italians, at least those of the educated or semi-educated classes, will combine a graciousness (when convenient) at the personal level with a persistent imperviousness to the need for honest and corruption-free civic government. They now face a demographic crisis which threatens to produce a radical change in their culture, yet when challenged on such questions they are inclined to dismiss them with an uncritical shrug: compartmentalization being justified by fatalism when they say that soon there won't be any Italians left.

∞∞❋∞∞

In 2019 the COVID pandemic—thought to originate in a Chinese laboratory—confirmed the confusion of the Western world it infected. There was a rush to conform to authoritarian measures, followed by an occasional libertinism when the state-pressure relaxed; then, when the virus and the emotional contagion had calmed there followed an insistence that everyone other than oneself was responsible for mishandling the situation. A doggerel sonnet I composed at the time will give a taste of the mindless and irresponsible mood which was society's response to the threats faced. Hence:

On Bournemouth Beach

> Come one and all to Bournemouth beach,
> though open sea you'll never reach
> nor loos unlocked for nature's call.
> So foul the beach where children crawl.
>
> Come one and all to Bournemouth town.
> Pollute the streets by throwing down
> not only condoms, also masks:
> (but keep a few 'case some cop asks).
>
> Come one and all to Bournemouth's malls:
> first loot a store, and if that palls,
> pull out a knife—show might makes right—
> stab the owner, win the fight.
>
> Speed one and all back home again.
> Ten lagers gulped can ease the strain.

∞∞❋∞∞

After writing (with Anna) an analysis of the confused secular society of the West, I thought again about the recent situation in the Church, both in light of the absurdities inflicted not only on myself, and more seriously on others—not least on Dodaro and another friend, Father Aidan Nichols, OP—but on reality itself; I started work on a further project and *Infallibility, Integrity and Obedience: The Papacy and the Roman Catholic Church, 1848–2023*, was published in 2023. In this book I attempt to show how, in a Church replete with servile bishops and an ignorant laity, an irrational, indeed anti-Christian attitude to the papacy has arisen over the last two hundred years. It had taken me more than forty years to recognize the truth of the basic teachings of the Roman Catholic Church; in the next forty I came to understand what Augustine meant when he denoted it a *corpus mixtum*: an organism normally functioning more or less along the right lines and enjoying the services of many good people, but always in need of repair and radical purification. Now the Church was facing an existential crisis worse than that caused by those in the fourth century who denied the full divinity of Christ, her leaders often looking to the secular world for ways to deny transcendence and transform the Church into a spiritually-flavored NGO, packed with ranked office-holders so compartmentalized that they continue to perform their duties (saying Mass, performing baptisms, marriages, and funerals) while—whether by negligence or by deliberation—shutting their eyes to manifest heresies taught by the pope and his disciples. In a mystique of the papacy growing since Vatican I they had discovered a new pretext for avoiding their apostolic responsibilities.

I have recalled that as a student who had as yet seen little of the world, I would pontificate that the only thing Christians had got right was the doctrine of Original Sin—for it was not hard even then to understand that my life, and that of millions of others, was overshadowed by the actions of wicked men and enemies of God, Hitler in particular, followed by Stalin. Now in my years as a Catholic I have seen the Church I had come to view as bulwark of love and truth threatened from within: more fundamentally by a near-universal servility toward the pope, more immediately—from the throne of Saint Peter itself—by a misguided and ambitious occupant who took advantage of that servility to the point of treating observant Catholics with contempt. Among his more recent insults to his flock were the appointment of a pornographer as president of what was once called the "Holy Office" and his enthusiasm for Church blessings of homosexual couples. As comment on the servility of those bishops who have allowed such a bizarre situation to develop, I here republish a revised version of an old anonymous ballad. Hence:

The Bishop of Bray

In good pope John's exciting days
when breath blew through the casement
a zealous update-priest was I
and so I got preferment.
And to my flock I boldly preached
the Church's new directions,
for cursed be he who dared resist
or challenge Küng's projections.

*And this is law I shall maintain
until my dying day, Sir,
That whatsoever pope shall reign
I'll be the bishop of Bray, Sir.*

To end the chaos, calm the strife
I called for Paul Montini
And hooting down the Latin tongue
embraced hit-man Bugnini.
Pelagian collects I adored,
I urged Old Mass cessation
and had become a Modernist
but for the Pill's damnation.

*And this is law I shall maintain
until my dying day, Sir
That whatsoever pope shall reign
I'll be the bishop of Bray, Sir.*

When John Paul Two from Krakow came
to mend the barque that's Peter's
I hailed the papa boys each day
and ruled out female preachers.
All heretics I did detest;
I stood for truth and duty
And every day would pray that God
restore the Church's beauty.

*And this is law I shall maintain
until my dying day, Sir,
That whatsoever pope shall reign
I'll be the bishop of Bray, Sir.*

When Cormac's boys failed to subvert
the Ratzinger election,
I praised our learned tower of faith
and moral truth's protection.
The Legionnaires I helped expose,
the Marxists called in question
and offered heartfelt thanks to hear
of clergy sods' rejection.

And this is law I shall maintain
until my dying day, Sir,
That whatsoever pope shall reign
I'll be the bishop of Bray, Sir.

When foul-mouthed Frank grasped Peter's Keys,
our pantheistic charmer,
I switched my holy stance once more
and bowed to Pachamama.
I came to see that Chairman Xi
is Xisus' true Defender
and prayed to serve a new Pope Joan
when Frankie changed his gender.

And this is law I shall maintain
until my dying day, Sir,
That whatsoever pope shall reign
I'll be the bishop of Bray, Sir.

The porno star from Buenos-Aires
and Sodomite succession,
to them allegiance I do swear,
while they can keep possession.
For in my faith and loyalty
I never more will falter.
My lawful pope shall Jorge be
until the times do alter.

And this is law I shall maintain
until my dying day, Sir,
That whatsoever pope shall reign
I'll be the bishop of Bray, Sir.

Almost whistling in the wind, I became one of a small group — all laymen but one — calling for Bergoglio's deposition, since as a blatant heresiarch he had disqualified himself from holding the office to which he had been elected, though we realized that as yet no mechanism exists in Canon Law to secure that needed result. Meanwhile I was completing my book on the papacy in the hope of explaining how a heretical pope was only to be expected in view of a mentality developing since Vatican I whereby Catholics accept arbitrary autocracy at the top and servility among the "lower ranks." My primary aim was to target not Bergoglio but the mentality which had generated his election to Saint Peter's Chair and the inability of the "flock" to recognize his manifest unorthodoxy. The book was reviewed by Archbishop Chaput, former Archbishop of Philadelphia, whose position on it, as assessed by my publisher, was that "he grudgingly agreed with you but was determined not to say so." It was neglected by the leading Catholic papers in the United Kingdom, the *Tablet* and the *Catholic Herald*, the review editor of the latter telling me — absurdly enough — that he could not find anyone to review it.

On April 21, 2025, Bergoglio died, but the doctrinal harm he has inflicted on the Church remains his legacy. We now have Robert Prevost, OSA, who as Leo XIV seems to have been elected to calm the waters (and whom I met on one occasion when teaching in Rome); only time will tell whether he will succeed in his apparently allotted task and hence what kind of further verse I should add to "The Bishop of Bray." But the omens are not good as Bergoglio has never been called to account for his manifest delinquencies — which means they could be repeated at some not too distant point — while his moral ambiguities are already hailed as modish greatness in the secular media and the task of cleaning up the Augean stables at the Vatican might seem too much even for a Hercules.

As for the present ecclesial situation more widely, Catholics divide into three groups, generally, if crudely, identifiable as liberals, conservatives, and tribalists. Liberals if successful will destroy the institution they want to liberalize; conservatives, though often divided among themselves, attempt to remain in the "faith of our fathers," but contain a fair group of madmen who believe that there has been no pope since John XXIII, Paul VI and those who followed him having all promoted the revised form of the Mass.

These often apocalyptic fanatics have given "conservatives" a bad name. I myself was recently honored to be targeted by several of them when in a "Q and A" with Edward Pentin I made the "mistake" of pointing out that Bergoglio had been elected legitimately as Pope Francis. That produced a social frenzy of which the following ignorant rant is worth recording:

> The devil, the purveyor of diabolical distinctions, manages often to give targeted Catholic leadership and academics (like Prof. Rist) a perception quite different from reality, and yet the person so diabolically disoriented is convinced that what he says is the truth when it is a lie (e.g., Bergoglio is pope). Sadly, Prof. Rist appears to be affected by the same diabolical disorientation which has afflicted millions of nominal Catholics throughout the world. It is precisely the same affliction that Saint Lucy of Fatima warned us about in writing over 50 years ago.

My third group of Catholics is made up of those "tribal" Catholics who have scarcely asked themselves why they are Catholic, and so solve the "problem" of secularism by compartmentalizing their beliefs. In the world of today such unthinking behavior cannot survive, and later generations — unless they come to accept Catholicism in the way a convert has to — will cease to be Christian at all. I note the decline of "tribal" Anglicans — one of whom I was designated to be — who it seems will soon be reduced to a historic remnant like the "Assyrians" I met in Iraq.

⋄∞∞✳∞∞⋄

Nor is it only in the Church but also in academia that in 2025 the 1960s are back. Whereas Church truth has been compromised by an apostate pope, so in academia an ideological denial of truth, denoted "cancel culture," has been widely tolerated by government and promoted in the universities themselves — and increasingly so since many university entrants derive an apparent knowledge of the world from such social media as can in a few seconds spread a lie believed by thousands. Such disinformation makes it easier for lazy or ideological students to resist being taught what they don't want to know, such resistance appearing again — in that revealing metaphor of the 1960s themselves — as virtuous objection to "having one's mind fucked": the gross language of which should give it away.

To the confused academic mix has been added a further disturbing reality: to a far greater degree than in the 1960s a substantial portion of younger faculty, being transformed into "useful idiots," suppose that their new-minted (and, at least in the humanities, often "trivial") doctorates have made them wise. Hence ideological zealots—in reality *de facto* moral anarchists—gain opportunities of which in the 1960s they could only have dreamt, all this being symptomatic of how Western civilization—and much of Western Christianity—has since the 1960s lost belief in itself. As then occurred, senior university administrators again betray the institutions they are supposed to guide, judging that subscribing to "woke" culture will give them a more peaceful life along with media-adulation. Those in lower ranks (as bureaucrats more generally) find it convenient to follow suit, obedient to the dictum of John Dean of Watergate fame that: "If you want to go up, go along."

⊸∞∞✺∞∞⊸

So in academia in 2025 as in the Church, prospects are not encouraging. Though still alive—and still "kicking"—but now largely out of active service, I am left to reflect on the strange outcomes and changing fortunes of some I have met. Among academics is one who told me that the best thing in the world is entry into the body of a woman and finished up as a respectable family man and first-class public servant. Another, who averred that the most important thing in the world is "to get an argument right" ended as an internationally famed groper. So I am left to ponder on my unexpected delights and ephemeral successes and am aware of such spiritual incompleteness as only a god could cure, while anxious how Anna will fare if I die first.

CHAPTER 9

On Chance and Providence

> The Unexamined life is subhuman.
> —Socrates in Plato's *Apology*

> And Nicholas was branded on the bum
> and the Lord bring us all to kingdom come.
> —concluding lines of Chaucer's
> *Miller's Tale* (modernized version)

> All the world's a stage,
> And all the men and women merely players;
> They have their exits and their entrances,
> And one man in his time plays many parts,
> His acts being seven ages. At first, the infant,
> Mewling and puking in the nurse's arms.
> Then the whining schoolboy, with his satchel
> And shining morning face, creeping like snail
> Unwillingly to school. And then the lover,
> Sighing like furnace, with a woeful ballad
> Made to his mistress' eyebrow. Then a soldier,
> Full of strange oaths and bearded like the pard,
> Jealous in honor, sudden and quick in quarrel,
> Seeking the bubble reputation
> Even in the cannon's mouth. And then the justice,
> In fair round belly with good capon lined,
> With eyes severe and beard of formal cut,
> Full of wise saws and modern instances;
> And so he plays his part. The sixth age shifts
> Into the lean and slippered pantaloon,
> With spectacles on nose and pouch on side;
> His youthful hose, well saved, a world too wide
> For his shrunk shank, and his big manly voice,
> Turning again toward childish treble, pipes
> And whistles in his sound. Last scene of all,
> That ends this strange eventful history,
> Is second childishness and mere oblivion,
> Sans teeth, sans eyes, sans taste, sans everything.
> —Jaques, in Shakespeare's *As you Like It*, 2.7.139–166

As I look back on my life, questions that arise in my mind are, "Did all this happen to *me*?" and "How is it that overall, though often apparently the result of chance events and arbitrary decisions, my account seems to suggest a roughly coherent picture of a life?" In what then does that coherence consist? I hope it is that I have, however erratically, tried to see through sham, hypocrisy, and falsehood (deliberate or not), and thereby come a little nearer to truth, though it seems that the more truth one sees the more there is to see. And in the course of living, am I right to see some sort of guidance? It was in hope of shedding light on these questions that I decided to write this memoir. First then "serial selves."

The idea that we are serial selves was already current in the ancient world, but Hobbes reintroduced it in early modern times. In Hobbes's version the question asked concerns a "ship of Athens" which on a number of occasions undergoes repairs leading to the eventual result that none of its original timbers remain. Then is it still the same ship? Not that this model can simplistically be applied to men, since the "ship of Athens" is not a self-mover; that is, it is not alive.

Nonetheless, in a mechanistic universe (Newtonian or other) Hobbes's model was applied to living beings, including men, viewed less as machines than as members of a material set given an abstract description. Thus Hume thought that we resemble a club, the members of which change over time while the name remains the same and the club performs the same functions. This model has attracted interest in that it denies responsibility for "our" past acts: only in a restricted (perhaps legally established) sense are the members of a club responsible for the actions of their predecessors.

The discovery of our DNA's identity from conception to death is a strong argument against such theories; there is at least something physical which continues throughout our lives — and even beyond. But DNA is not conscious, nor does talk of the "selfish gene" solve our dilemma. Our conclusion must be that our genetic structure remains the same while the question is still open whether or how "we" are the same, "I" not being identical with my genetic structure, even though partially determined by it.

Newman, as I have noticed, observed that "Ten years later I find myself in another place." What he seems to imply (though with knowledge of DNA he might now express it more clearly) is that something—i.e., our genetic structure—remains in the same "place" while other features of our being change imperceptibly. The question then is, How do they change? Or, to what degree and to what end do they change? Perhaps, genetics apart, we are best described not as serial selves but as the mere product of casual circumstances.

Yet "circumstances" are of two sorts: there are things which simply happen to us. I have been threatened by a Mi'kmaq Indian with a knife and previously the hook of a crane crashed down in front of me as I approached the Great Gate of my college in Cambridge. Nor are such unexpected happenings always potentially lethal; many can bring huge advantages: thus Anna's coming to be auditioned for a play in 1957 led to over sixty years (and still counting) of a magnificent marriage-partnership which among other benefits has given me four children and helped me understand Catholicism. On lesser but still significant occasions have life-changing messages reached me: that from Professor Woodbury led to my initial appointment for one year in Toronto; then a letter from Eric Osborn helped me secure a part-time teaching post in Rome; then a message from John McCarthy invited me to be the first holder of the Pritzl Chair of Philosophy at the Catholic University of America; finally—non-academic but culturally and spiritually significant—a letter from Emmet Robbins suggested we might be interested in buying a *casa colonica* in southern Tuscany.

There are also things that happen not by apparent chance but as the result of my own decisions. These decisions too must be subdivided into those taken with some clear aim in mind and a reasonable awareness of the likely consequences, direct or indirect, and those which are "plumped for" when I am unable to give much consideration to the effects they will have on my later life: such was my decision to study Greek rather than German at school: had I decided otherwise, my life, as is clear by hindsight, would have been different, perhaps less coherent. Such "plumpings"—along with more immediately plausible decisions—are part of my present project, of which the aim is to see whether they form a pattern and thus help to explain why (as in the case of Newman) "ten years" (or whenever) "later" I find *myself* in another and a *particular* place.

What interests me is how a combination of the effects of random events, along with both "plumpings" and reflective choices, will be recognizable as the changing "I" which yet remains the same "I" in some more "metaphysical" sense than the continuity of my genetic structure and its persistence even as my body changes. Also whether the "deliberate" and the "casual," as well as those happenings outside my control, seem to presuppose anything other than mere chance. To approach that question I shall need to look at the *kind of* "I" that I have become, thus: How have I become it? Might what I have become have been more coherent?

To rule out one answer to these question, turn to Shakespeare's Jaques and his "seven ages of man." In comparing man to an actor, Jaques observes that the same man "plays many parts." Yet the comparison is inexact, for the actor is performing acts for which he is not ordinarily responsible. Obviously he is responsible in that he must play the role as well as he can, but there is no question as to whether, if, say, on stage he is a murderer, he could be charged with murder. It is possible to "play-act" in life, yet "play-acting" in life is very different from play-acting in a "play."

Thus while the actor plays his many roles, he remains free of responsibility for the "actions" of his "roles"—that whether or not he later forgets the words he pronounced on the stage, or even that he played any particular role. Yet in real life, even if you forget that you (say) stole your Rolex watch, you still can be legitimately prosecuted (barring statutes of limitation) if it is discovered that you stole the watch you are wearing. Such differences between the actor and the "self," serial or otherwise, might seem irrelevant—except that they point to something deeper than does Jaques's "man," for to pass through the stages of life we all pass through if we live long enough tells us nothing about the *kind* of life we live and have lived. At the least Jaques's comments are superficial: no mention, for example, of whether the soldier murders the innocent or tortures captives, or refrains from so doing. And no suggestion of religion or the after-life: it all ends in "oblivion"—this written at a time when atheism was beginning to take hold of Western man. In sum, Jaques's man is an incomplete specimen. (Perhaps there is a pun on his name, if pronounced "Jakes" like the archaic slang for privy: maybe Shakespeare is suggesting that his views are horse manure!)

Shakespeare has presented a character for the stage who gives the impression of wisdom, but offers only a limited account of human life and comments on it from a skeptical (even cynical) standpoint. Of course, there is nothing wrong in Shakespeare's presenting a skeptic any more than if he had presented a tyrant or a wise man; it is we, not Shakespeare, who are at fault if we make more of "Jaques" than Shakespeare intends. What does matter is whether each of us is wise or a tyrant — or can merely be *reduced* to Jaques's description.

So what has Jaques left out? First, the pleasant fails to appear alongside the unpleasant for, besides "mewling and puking," infants smile and gurgle. More significantly, as we have noticed, there is no suggestion that we may be morally pleasant or unpleasant: that is, honest or dishonest. Jaques but brushes the surface of such questions when he alludes to the oaths of the soldier or the "saws" of the "justice." Nor does he pay attention to what the man makes of his life as a whole; he gives the impression that all that can be said is that he passes through the stages he enumerates. And he does not even frame the question whether in the one life each of us leads we might make more or less of it, might as we age live by a more coherent moral standard, might just possibly see the point — not merely the actualities — of the changes of life we undergo and the possibilities they offer. No room in Jaques's schema to ask whether we made fools of ourselves when young, or fail to learn from experience. Jaques suggests that life, whatever its character, is essentially meaningless and summed up in "oblivion."

This listing of the stages of life will hardly satisfy us if we are enquiring — as I am now — whether a combination of chance events with deliberated or "plumped-for" choices might seem to push us, even against our intent at any particular time, in a particular direction. No room to ask whether we might learn from our developing life by hindsight. A richer account is required than Jaques's skepticism provides.

That said, Jaques does provide a framework within which the events and decisions of my life can be conveniently considered. Thus I can begin with the pre-school and early school years: the years before the age of much satchel-wearing and beginning with those when I no doubt "mewled" and "puked." Most of the roughly first four years of my life are uncharted territory; although I was aware of what happened to me, I took no deliberated decisions, merely reacting to external or bodily stimuli, even if more permanently affected by them.

Nevertheless, although these years saw no decisions by me, and few happenings of which I at some point became more clearly aware — though very early I will have learned that the world is differentiated, that there are other people than myself who are not mere "extensions" of myself — as I would learn later that my mother disliked the idea of childbearing, often saying that when she experienced it, she just wanted to be "put out" while the process was carried to its conclusion. She did not, it seems, want to risk the experience again, saying that the only good thing about it was that I was a boy rather than a girl, which sounded as though she found her own femininity inferior. Hence when the likelihood of becoming a parent myself arose, I needed either to accept or reject such significant conclusions. I have even wondered whether before I was born I was aware of my mother's ambiguous feelings about my approaching arrival, and whether that helped generate the wariness I had as a boy of the intentions of others.

Plainly, since I was born in 1936 my mother's attitudes were greatly affected by the threat of the Nazis. Because of them, and even before Dunkirk, I would experience the care of a famous and distinguished (as was believed) headmistress of a kindergarten where, as I have recorded, my mouth was taped up because I was alleged to have bitten another boy: an offence which (at least as my memory goes) I denied from the start. So did I learn to fear that in the world (and not only as regarded Germans) there were bad guys and good guys and one needed to be wary as to which was which. As for Germans, I have recorded how from the early years of my life I experience a reactive suspicion of them. But how could a serial self feel such suspicion?

My memory of the distinguished kindergarten head is of dislike and disgust: she and the Nazis both were the enemy, with the Nazis a less immediate source of resentment. Indeed, throughout my early childhood I feared the threat that if I did not behave better I would be sent to a boarding school — which in my mind suggested my kindergarten experience. That fear would diminish in my high-school years, when I was presumably less of a nuisance, but what I saw of the boarding life at my school certainly assorted with the image which Mrs. Hourihane had conjured up, nor did it eliminate my continuing anger — and then my reflection on that anger — that I had ever been sent away to her establishment.

Certainly I was as yet unaware that the problem of unfairness — and of my being unfairly punished — was no merely local problem; even less was I able to ask why things *should not be* "unfair" or to recognize the implications if they are or are not, or should be, or should not be, unfair. Somehow I intuited that fairness is part of justice, though even as a child I would not have accepted that justice "simply is fairness" — for in that case I would treat everyone "fairly" if I treated them (and expected to be treated myself) equally badly.

At this point I lacked distinctions: there were Nazis and Germans, though my parents (and so I) scarcely distinguished the two — hence my suspicion of Germans has never entirely waned. Even the tendency in Germany to atone vicariously for wartime guilt can seem to me hypocrisy and virtue-signaling. In my early childhood the thought crossed my mind that the kindergarten head might be "German," or at least a German sympathizer. Nor was my general view of "Johnny foreigner" enthusiastic: we knew about the French "betrayal" at Dunkirk, heard of the Italian use of poison gas in Abyssinia — and feared it might be used against us: hence in the early days of the war we carried gas-masks. It was only by education that I was able to see that not all foreigners were alike — not that education erased all my earlier view of "Johnny foreigner."

Nor did I think any better of the Japanese, their atrocities against prisoners of war being frequently related by our elders. Other foreigners struck me as nasty too. The Irish (especially their leaders) seemed largely pro-Nazi and we had few illusions about the Russian Communists: I became early aware of people selling the Moscow line in the *Daily Worker*. My parents saw through that kind of servility and (as did I as I understood more) regarded the alliance with Stalin with reference to Churchill's declaration that he would make an alliance with the devil to get rid of Hitler. Other people too, outside (even inside) our circle, seemed suspect and undesirable.

Nor in those years did I have many friends, apart from "lower class" Clive — and I was overawed (even frightened) by some of my relatives, especially Josephine ("Brentwood Nan": distinct, that is from "Littlebury Nan," of whom I was very fond and whose kindness I have never forgotten). I conclude that in my early years I learned who to hate, who to be suspicious of, and that there were only a few people who would like me or whom I would be able to like. It was good, if crude, training for Augustine's view of the world's members, whether in groups or individually, as subject to outbursts of depravity (though not wholly depraved!).

⋘✴⋙

So we come to the satchel-wearing schoolboy at Sir Anthony Browne's School, already wary of likely dangers but interested in learning about them. From my earliest years I wanted to read and study, and to learn not least why there were a few good people and so many bad, not only among historical brutes or "Johnny Foreigners" — though perhaps "the wogs" (in the pithy English saying) did "begin at Calais" — but among those whom I came to know better and frequently found hostile. Like Mrs. O'Brien next-door who was not only Irish (and so Catholic, though that meant little to me at the time) but who also (as had Mrs. Hourihane) accused Clive and me of a crime we did not commit: this time breaking her man-hole cover.

To this already engrained wariness Sir Anthony Browne's establishment would add a further acquaintance with snobbery, about which my mother seemed especially ambiguous: it might be fine so long as we could do the looking down rather than being looked down on! I have recalled my dislike of conventional sports-admirers at school, often from snobbish families and patronized by my Housemaster; hence I tended to look elsewhere and was attracted not only to study in general (being especially fond of History) but later by the chance to "visit" in imagination an ancient world in which I could "travel" to strange and foreign lands. I wanted to live in a less conventional world and, I now realize, to understand the relationship of others, past and present, to myself.

⋘✴⋙

My wariness of "Johnny foreigner" would diminish, though any over-romantic view of foreign parts and foreign mores would be countered by the brothel-haunting young gents of the Venetian high-school. I was aware of "variable" sexuality at school, but inclined to think that "perversion" (not that I would have used that word since the phenomenon seemed common) was more found abroad than at home: as I would come to see, a judgment based on an inadequate awareness of the hypocrisy characterizing

British society at least since the eighteenth century (identified—indeed applauded as "social glue"—by Bernard Mandeville).

At Brentwood I also became aware of the adolescent homosexuality (better perhaps experimental sexuality) of my schoolmates and watched it develop into a not always more heterosexual pattern. I had comparatively little interest in experimenting myself, being more impressed, as I have noted, with the pedophile inclinations of several masters. Hence I began to develop largely unconscious beliefs about proper and improper sexuality, though its overall significance escaped me and I had little idea of how important sexual attitudes and behavior can be among adults; Freud claimed that most males (but of what age?) think about sex about every two minutes. Nor of how sexual vices can induce worse vices, as on occasion proceeding from lust to murder.

I also failed to notice that my choice of Greek, which would lead to such opportunities to study the ancient world, was the result of an ill-thought-out but fortunate decision which would steer my entire life. The first leg of the journey was toward a non-religious humanism quite foreign to my relatively uneducated family and acquaintances. Having few friends and immediate interests (apart from chess and the hill-walking which I came to love), I developed an intellectualist cosmopolitanism which abjured patriotism as mere nationalism and over-estimated the worth of cosmopolitan organizations, above all of the United Nations whose original aims seemed worthier than they would become.

Thus I was gradually becoming a traveler in abstract time and space, with all the discomforts of rootlessness. The old certainties—patriotism, the Church of England, the easy way of life which seemed the goal of most of my contemporaries and their parents, the mythology of English "Whig" history (though I did not as yet know the term) to which my attention had been drawn so sharply by that History-master's opening question: "Give me five reasons for the Tudor despotism"—all these certainties began to fade. Was "Good" Queen Bess a despot? But as yet I had little understanding of that despotism's roots in Tudor (and more generally national enforced) religion. My limited understanding of such matters could be summed up by that Irish citation of "the bollocks of Henry VIII" as sole cause of the Reformation in England.

Nor was learning Greek the only unpredictable experience of those years. Of three other factors two were positive and one negative. The first positive relates specifically to what Greek I was asked to read in those early days, since a text that would dominate my thinking in later life was set for Ordinary Level: namely the first book of Plato's *Republic*. Apart from opening my eyes to Plato himself, who has imparted real continuity to my career, in the *Republic* I also read what I would later identify as the radical choice between a metaphysically transcendent foundation for morality or no intellectually respectable morality. This was no religious understanding—indeed it might have seemed anti-religious, but it paved the way for religion by being compatible with it.

Which brings me to the negative factor, namely my decision to abandon not only the Church of England but Christianity itself, being now made suspicious about its origins. Not that I ever thought of it as a crude fraud but I wondered whether it might be a product of emotional contagion, hysterical visions being found among the religious. Beyond that, if the Church of England was a sixteenth-century stitch-up, other Protestant sects found in England would seem little more than spin-offs from a fraudulent starting-point—only inferior in their frequent hostility to love of beauty. I at this stage knew nothing of Roman Catholicism, while what little I knew (always at second-hand) of Orthodoxy suggested it to be a "Henrician," nationalist religion where politics would ultimately dictate theological stance.

The second positive factor again arose largely by chance. Before Sixth Form I had been in Italy twice and had begun to love the country, primarily for its reminders of the ancient world—but not only. Florence would confirm that wider interest when I managed to get there on leave from the RAF and Signora Riddiford guided me into Italian literature of two very different kinds, the *Inferno* of Dante (which impressed me more then than perhaps now) and the racier tales of Don Camillo. It seemed that something of ancient Rome survived in literary form in contemporary Italy; I suspected I would not find the same in the case of Greece. Yet despite Dante I failed to notice the enduring role of the Catholicism of Medieval and even modern Italy. Nor did I recognize the weaknesses, as well as the beauties, of Italian culture and life, let alone of the broader "humanism" as commonly understood.

For when I left Brentwood I intended to be a cosmopolitan humanist: hostile to religion, wary of the world in which I lived, little interested in sexuality, or of being, as MacIntyre was to put it, a "dependent rational *animal*." Nor did I—and nor did my contemporaries—dream of thinking, as I later came to think, that marriage is more than a deal between two individuals, but has huge implications for the wider society. Still, certain impressions had been made on me about sexuality and marriage which, when fitted into a larger picture, were to become part of my changing self—or perhaps I should say soul, albeit having then little idea of what a "soul" might be.

Jaques misses out the higher education which I—and perhaps at Houghton Hall in Lancashire Shakespeare himself—acquired, and puts the "lover" before the swearing soldier: in my case the wrong order. Yet moving from school into the military and then to Cambridge changed me in two ways which were to turn out to be complementary, though still allowing my older "humanism" to survive only mildly transmuted. The military years—apart from encouraging me to swear, if with more conventional oaths than Shakespeare's soldier and taking me outside a European world—suggested that abstract thinking was not enough. Trinity College Cambridge would show me why it was not enough and that truth must be more earth-bound: not that the intellectual life should be rejected but it should be interpreted in its historical and cultural contexts. Nor did this make me a relativist about truth or "values"; I never fell for that convenient option.

When I reported to RAF Cardington, I had little idea what to expect; most of the boys I met there (and later at Hednesford) were less educated and from a much rougher home background than I—especially if they were from inner London or the North of England. They swore regularly, smoked far too many cigarettes, fornicated when they got the chance, but generally seemed pleasant enough and, surprising as it seemed, I fitted in easily. Of course, the choice of military service was not mine, though having been a cadet at school gave me a small say in being able to enter the RAF rather than the army. Nor did I expect to be sent to learn Russian; for this I volunteered, partly because I wanted to learn the language—and something about Russians generally—and partly because it seemed less of a waste of time than other options. Nor did I as yet recognize that my half-educated fellow "airmen" might be profiting from not having moral and aesthetic assumptions "educated" out of them by "liberal humanists."

The only choice which was entirely mine during my National Service was to decline the possibility of a commission. Here anti-snobbism played only a minor part in a decision which most of my schoolmasters would have deplored, for by doing so I secured the chance to go to Iraq: a learning experience which again was to have a permanent effect on my later life. Not that I did not realize that I profited from learning Russian, which was interesting in itself and introduced me to the semi-sophisticated, semi-barbarous "Russian soul." I never read any of the major Russian novels in their original language, but I learned much about them, later realizing how much could be understood about the contemporary world from the writings of Dostoevsky: a Christian for whom the ills of nineteenth- and by implication twentieth-century Europe must be attributed to "the loss of Christ, nothing else." That too would influence my moral and metaphysical journey, not least when I came to realize that though Dostoevsky and Nietzsche drew opposing conclusions from their analyses of nineteenth-century Europe, their diagnosis was in many ways strangely close.

Among other "earthy" effects, Iraq confirmed my awareness of how males of my age inclined to see almost anything through sexualized eyes. This I had begun to grasp at school and notably during the earlier parts of my military experience. It also suggested an imminent possibility of human savagery and began to show that "progressive" accounts of human nature were self-deluding. I had not hitherto met men who liked killing people, but I was beginning to become aware that one's character—as I would later realize was particularly well understood by Augustine—is formed by people and actions you love and hate. And in Iraq I could see humanity in the raw.

Before Iraq, and despite the Nazis, my expectation that men would *choose* wickedness if it suited them—or if they were afraid—was still largely "academic" in an odd but informative sense of that word. In Iraq I could also recognize the accuracy of what I later read near the outset of Aristotle's *Ethics*, namely that without experience of the more ambiguous aspects of life, one cannot "do" ethics since one does not know what one is talking about. Indeed I would read many a recent writer who seemed to have not the least grasp of how precariously moral—how conventionally "decent" — his life had become. A conspicuous example was the Bloomsbury group, guided by the ethics of G. E. Moore; he offered them a shallow version of consequentialism (despite some chatter about non-natural qualities and friendship) inferior even to that of Sidgwick.

At school it had been hard to imagine that one military defeat could cause death or enslavement — or in the words of Xenophon that after the defeat at Aegospotami "in Athens no man slept." Even Dunkirk had not really sunk in, what with my tender age and its not being followed up by the Nazi invasion which many feared. With an increasing suspicion that if skeptical humanism implied a facile portrait of human nature and behavior it would need to be corrected, I arrived at Trinity College Cambridge.

Not that I had not been deluded by some progressive beliefs of the day. Of colonialism I disapproved in principle, though recognizing that the spread of the English language and the educational opportunities made available to some at least of the inhabitants of the colonized territories were indeed beneficial. My stay in Iraq and tales of South Africa told by my grandfather had warned me off romanticism about the motives of colonists and carpetbaggers who benefitted from Empire. Yet I was seriously deluded, along with most of my "educated" contemporaries, in supposing that when (say) Africa was decolonized, ensuing "black" governments would prove efficient and honest — as would turn out to be far from the case. As I might have put it in theological terms, I assumed that Original Sin did not affect black (nor brown) humans — a part of the mind-set about human nature I would come to reject.

Thus had I accepted a bit of fashionable progressivism especially useful when castigating our ancestors for their faults (even their then unrecognized faults). Nor in my evaluation of colonialism did I pay enough attention to the differences between its manifestations: thus whereas a German commander was awarded honors for genocide in what is now Namibia, and atrocities were enacted daily in the Congo by the Belgians, the British had put an end to widow-burning and "thuggery" in India. It is dishonest of "progressives" (such as I then largely was) simply to tar all opponents with the same brush.

Thinking back to my attitude to colonialism, I can wonder what fashionable but ill-grounded beliefs I uphold to this day.

As I have understood, in trying to avoid the "unexamined life" one may reflect on past "swallowings" of too much contemporary fashion, while avoiding the even more common mistake of "compartmentalizing" one's mental outlook. But I came to recognize the pitfalls of compartmentalization only late in life, albeit early sensing in the life of Socrates, as passed down by Plato and others, a model of how to avoid it.

⸻※⸻

In the late 1950s the Church of England (and Protestant Christianity more generally) seemed, though damaged, still alive and active and I would never have imagined it would be so side-lined in the Britain of the present day. We were living before the cultural storm broke: a storm which could not but invite even the most conventional Christians and ex-Christians to re-evaluate their attitudes to religion (and even to metaphysics), the smarter sort then seeing more clearly what I had recognized in embryo at school when I read the first book of Plato's *Republic*, namely that men in the West were (logically) going to have to choose between God (or at least some transcendency) and nihilism (or rather nothingness); all intermediate positions were a fudge hardly supportable in hard times. This Plato again had prophesied, in whose *Phaedo* we read that those contented to live "decent" lives in a peaceful and fairly reasonable city will be reincarnated as such "social" insects as bees or ants.

Yet in my student days religion remained largely unexamined, though it was at Cambridge, both in Trinity College and in the bar of Fisher House, that I first came across intellectual Catholicism, in the first instance in Denis O'Brien. Denis became a regular sparring partner from whose example I learned that to suppose Catholic philosophy a contradiction in terms is false — even though it may apply in certain instances, all arts having good and bad practitioners. Denis, however, had no particular philosophical position. He believed in God and therefore in the transcendent, in his case not tied — as is more normal in Catholic circles — to a Thomist orientation. That he knew little about Thomism from my point of view was an advantage, since Thomists will often give the impression (contrary to Thomas himself) that the *Summa* contains all or almost all the answers, and this I would have regarded as pathetic.

Nor was Anna any conscious Thomist, though when I first met her she was returning to the Church in which she had been baptized if little reared. I do not think she had any particular philosophical orientation, just a general idea that God was much more likely to exist than not, and that given God, Catholic Christianity was best not merely emotionally but intellectually. But through Anna I first met an actual Thomist, albeit a very idiosyncratic one, in the person of Father Kenelm Foster, OP, University Reader in Italian, to whom Anna had been sent by Monsignor Gilbey for instruction. Kenelm was immediately congenial, being not dogmatic in any fundamentalist sense, though standing firmly on intellectually respectable religious foundations. It was to take another twenty or so years for me to convert, but Kenelm had finally laid to rest any assumption that Catholicism was disreputable intellectually and morally.

By then I did realize more clearly why Protestantism was intellectually inadequate, a Catholic response to many Protestant problems being readily available. Thus by the time I left Cambridge it seemed to me that I had to agree with Anna that if any religion was intellectually respectable, it was Catholic Christianity, as being able to answer the challenges of Protestantism, and—even in the unreflective outlook of most of its adherents—to face down the "problem of evil" in a way I by now realized to be impossible for "progressives" (including those calling themselves Christians).

I had been urged by my school mentors to apply to Trinity because they thought that it was both good for Classics and would offer a challenging vision of the subject: above all that because of its insistence on philological excellence it would provide what I have called "humanism" in its Renaissance sense. What I am sure they did not foresee was that I would appreciate the technical skills I would acquire at the College while becoming skeptical of skepticism itself and of the "humanism" which I would be offered and earlier would have welcomed—and that I would come gradually to judge "humanism" by the character of the humanists! Nor probably did those in the College realize that the requirement that we do National Service before "coming up" might produce this effect, with military experience thus preceding more formal thinking.

A further and most unexpected phenomenon I began to notice in those Cambridge days was that I seemed to lead a charmed life, and perhaps was meant for something or other. I had survived Nazi bombing. In Iraq I had survived a knife-wielder (and two others would later cross my path). I had come within a foot of death from the crane-hook outside Trinity. I seemed to be in remarkable "luck." Then at the end of my final year I experienced a piece of unexpected good fortune—the offer of a temporary position in Toronto. Among its entirely unpredictable effects it justified my decision—which seemed absurd to many contemporaries—to leave Cambridge when I might have stayed on. So why was I again "in luck"?

The offer and my decision came to seem of "metaphysical" import and I was to learn that the academic outlook from which I had profited—but eventually rejected—at Cambridge was not the only profile on offer. I leave to others to judge how good an academic I have become, but I am certain that had I stayed in Cambridge, I would have been emasculated, both academically and spiritually, Cambridge requiring submission to intellectual snobbery. In Toronto the academy was not only in many respects more humane, it was also less compartmentalized, more "freewheeling"—as had always been my style.

◦◦◦✵◦◦◦

To move from Cambridge to Toronto was to move from a sophisticated university culture in what was already a dying cultural world to a city—if suffering still the miseries of its Calvinist past—full of latent energy, with a University already distinguished and confident that it would do even better. When I arrived, though no premature version of Shakespeare's plump old pillar of society uttering wise "saws" (or as Irwin Edman put it, "casting false pearls before real swine"), I found that I had accumulated knowledge but had hardly begun to think it through, being as yet far from any "wisdom" (and in that at least resembling Jaques's magistrate, though as yet without his "fair round belly").

After I had been in Toronto a few years, Fritz Heichelheim, a Jewish refugee from the University of Giessen, had a serious heart-attack from which he would recover—for a time. His office was below mine, so when he returned to the department I went down to express my happiness at his survival. His reply was: "Ze angel of death has visited me but zimply left his card": a response that brought home to me that we have a time to live, and time past is never recovered. Thus I was gaining a clearer recognition of mortality, though little idea as yet of what in my time I might do in support of an institution which had given me the chance both to teach good students and to write what I liked—and that largely free of the pretentiousness and place-seeking encouraged by Oxbridge college rituals. As for Heichelheim, I am happy to record that before he died, Giessen, from which he had been expelled in the 1930s, awarded him an honorary doctorate which he was delighted to accept.

The first indication of how I might need to act—apart, that is, from my ordinary teaching and research—for the University of Toronto, was provided by the murder of John Kennedy. As I have recalled, I had been carried away by Kennedy's rhetoric and failed to detect his assemblage of a nominal Catholicism (retained in only some of its social justice aspects) with a fashionable progressivism which I had not yet learned to abjure. For, as was said in the aftermath of his murder, "Jack was not sanctified by a bullet."[1] Nor did I yet understand him as a prime example of mental compartmentalization: not as extreme as that which I was to observe when I visited the Mormon University in Salt Lake City but far more influential. But I would soon be introduced to compartmentalization as analyzed by Alasdair MacIntyre who shows how contemporary Westerners' heads are weighed down with ideas from incompatible sources, inducing incoherent beliefs and behaviors.

Justice movements—as often theological movements—are liable to advance beyond their original aims in a dynamic which carries their adherents along in a rush to challenge not only the bad but also even the good aspects of the culture they would pull apart if not overthrow. Kennedy—and later Pierre Trudeau—decided to play down his Catholicism to win votes and power; it paid off and was duly noted by Catholics across North America, not only in politics but on campus. At first (as in the Land O'Lakes

---

[1] Revilo P. Oliver, "Marxmanship in Dallas," *American Opinion*, Volume VII, No. 2, February 1964, 13–28. "Rational men will understand that, far from sobbing over the deceased or lying to placate his vengeful ghost, it behooves us to speak of him with complete candor and historical objectivity. Jack was not sanctified by a bullet."

Conference) this escaped my attention, but when in the late 1960s I was involved in the campaign to deny student radicals a determinative role in University government, I noticed that those most active in trying to undermine academic standards—and in tolerating those who wished to push the University in a more Marxist (or post-Marxist) direction—included prominent Catholics in Saint Michael's College.

All this was occurring as others calling themselves Catholics in Canada—as in the United States—were promoting abortion with virtually no contradiction from the nation's bishops who might seem, like Kennedy, to have compartmentalized their religion. As for the Catholics "in the pews," they seemed to evince little sense of when a push for reform becomes a push for the destruction of a religious or academic community—in the latter case to be reduced to an ideological institution where students would be taught only what they wanted to hear and would be given the power to suppress alternative thought.

This struck me—by now the father of a growing family—as a simple pursuit of injustice: students were not to be taught to think, let alone to acquire wisdom, only to parrot ideological claptrap. That to my mind was not liberation and nor did I recognize in my "conservative" position any of the "fascism" with which I and like-minded others would be regularly charged. Put bluntly, I got involved in University politics in Toronto because I did not want to be part of an institution where one would be attacked for thinking critically. However, though I was moving gradually on a path which with hindsight might seem foreordained to lead to Catholicism, and though I noticed the undesirable role some Catholics were playing in academic disputes, I did not yet link such academic turmoil with the battle in the Church between those who wanted to introduce the reforms of Vatican II and those who wanted to proceed beyond them in the direction of what they asserted to be the Council's "spirit."

Despite my "fascist" labelling, I did not think my beliefs about the nature of a university much changed. Nor did I realize that the skeptical humanism which I had begun to adopt at school, having begun to fray at the edges at Cambridge, was fraying further as I was forced to concede what the first principles of a true humanism must be. When, having signed up as a Roman Catholic, I left Toronto for Aberdeen, I had no idea that the problems about the subverting of truth that I met and struggled with during the late 1960s and early 1970s were going to occur in substantial form in what was now my Church: that despite the fact that before leaving Toronto I heard about abuse of minors by clergy—heralding later ecclesial troubles—from Father Dan Donovan, whose enquiry into it was archived by the American bishops who had commissioned it.

⸻

Despite the roller-coaster of my life between 1980 and 2008, moving first back to Toronto, then spending two years as a Visiting Fellow in Cambridge Colleges and a semester teaching in the Hebrew University in Jerusalem—then finally "retiring" at the end of 1996—it seemed that my intellectual-spiritual situation was by now more or less settled. But in 2008, while teaching in Rome at the Patristic Institute, I published *What is Truth?*—with its chapter on the early See of Rome. As I later came to realize, I had stumbled unwittingly into what was to turn out to be a major new challenge when in 2013 the Jesuit Jorge Bergoglio became Pope Francis.

For though in *What is Truth?* I had no idea of the character of that papacy to come, the chapter on the early See of Rome raised the question of truth among "tribal" Catholics. I had realized that the history of the Holy See, as presented for centuries, is untenable, even though in earlier days such historical ignorance was the more excusable. Yet such false beliefs about the past, apparently tolerated by church leaders, and by the clergy more widely, seemed not only in themselves offences against truth but to encourage false beliefs about the nature of the papacy and its developing authority in Western Christianity. The result seemed to be bad faith among those who knew better and a cult of popes, whether good or bad, among Catholics in the pews, itself encouraged by a servile attitude among bishops who seemed to envisage themselves as middle-managers to the pope as CEO rather than successors of the apostles.

I had also come to realize that Newman's work in *An Essay On The Development Of Christian Doctrine*, in some respects made the problem worse. For being primarily concerned with the development of Christian doctrine after the Council of Nicaea, and rightly assuming that in the fourth and fifth centuries the theology of the Trinity and of the Person of Christ was brought to a level beyond which we have advanced but little, he more incautiously inferred that in earlier centuries similar doctrines were held, failing to realize that the formulations produced by the great theologians of the fourth and fifth centuries could not have been explicit in earlier times.

Just as Nicaea was not a statement of what everyone "knew" earlier, so the papacy of Leo the Great was not the Church of Rome in AD 200, still less of AD 100. Just as understanding of basic Christian doctrine developed over time and was given something approaching final form at the Council of Nicaea (then later at Ephesus and Chalcedon), so, as the centuries passed, understanding of the role of the Roman See and the Roman bishop developed and was clarified from its necessarily inchoate beginnings—and is still incomplete and, in my view, has now been deformed.

Looking back on my reaction to the behavior of Bergoglio as pope, I notice that once again I became involved in controversy almost accidentally, this time because teaching in the Patristic Institute gave me the chance to observe Vatican doings at first hand—and to speak to some of those concerned about them. Eventually, this would lead to my attempt, in *Infallibility, Obedience and Integrity*, to analyze a corrupt mentality in the wider Catholic Church: the substantial cause more than effect of the election of Bergoglio. I also came to realize that the confusion in the Church, brought into the light by that election, was significantly parallel to the struggle in which I had been engaged during the 1960s and early 1970s against ideologists bent on destroying serious academic life in Western Universities: also of the fight in Aberdeen against a self-serving attempt by the Principal to curry favor with the Prime Minister by decimating the academic staff: "For a knighthood, George, for a knighthood!"

Both in the Church and in the academy what was at issue was truth and reality. Secular ideologists of the 1960s wanted to replace the search for truth in the academy with the imposition of some sub-Marxist ideology. More recently, supporters of a deviant pope—in the wake of those who wanted to work *not* with the Council's teachings but with some subjective "spirit of Vatican II"—want to replace truth as the reflection of objective reality with a theory which constructs "truth" from the fashions of each succeeding age. My continuing outlook on both these phenomena does seem to me to display coherence.

⸻✦⸻

When irresponsibly elected by Cardinals most of whom knew next to nothing about him, Bergoglio set out to change the Church into a spiritually flavored NGO: something like a Ministry of Religious Affairs of the United Nations, with a suggestion at times that Jesus is just but one prophet among many. That project was to require "modifications" — some of his disciples correctly spoke of "paradigm-shifts" — both in moral and dogmatic theology. In contemplating this new reality, I recognized that Bergoglio had made two fundamental mistakes. First, he held that by his own will as pope he could change basic tenets of Christianity and that, second, these basic tenets can properly and in principle be changed, because doctrine is now dependent on the varying relationship between earlier Catholic beliefs and the contemporary *zeitgeist*. This was the "spirit of Vatican II," sometimes explained as a variant on Hegel's theory of truth, though the pope and his collaborators had little serious interest in Hegel who had become philosophical point-man for those (especially Germans: them again) who felt the need to find one.

Teaching in Rome, I first realized what was happening in the Church by observing Bergoglio's two Synods on the family, both "rigged" in favor of the results the pope and his disciples wanted while excluding (or deforming) the views of dissenters. In that contempt for facticity I could recognize once again the destructive and libertine mentality of the 1960s, with now added the power of social media to diffuse falsehood among an ignorant public, not least in that promotion of homosexuality such as I had challenged both over Nussbaum's interventions in the Denver court case and in my review of Father Moore's "fruit-flavored" tract. Sexual deviations, and the contempt for marriage and its commitments which will accompany them, are corrosive of both the Church and the society where they flourish.

In the years after the Synods on the Family I taught in Washington in the Catholic University of America's Faculty of Philosophy, where I was able to recognize something approaching a model academic attitude toward Catholicism and its truth. At the same time in Rome I watched the initial success of the Patristic Institute gradually sink back into mediocrity, its brief opportunity to become a major center for the study of the early Church being casually abandoned with the discarding—and worse—of the man (significantly an American) who had striven to advance its standards. My teaching there, as I have recorded, would abruptly end in 2019 after I agreed, with a number of others world-wide, to sign a letter to the Cardinals and bishops of the Catholic Church urging them to call the pope to account.

We lost the battle but the war continued. As I have recalled, in early May 2024, with some sixteen others, I signed a statement detailing Bergoglio's crimes and heresies and calling for his resignation or removal. Although several clerics were involved in drawing up this detailed "bill of attainder," only one of them was not afraid to sign it: *oderint dum metuant*, as Caligula said. Of course we achieved nothing tangible, and Catholicism, under Bergoglio's leadership, seems to have set out on the same path which has led to the irrelevance and near extinction of the Church of England and other Christian denominations. Too many Catholics care little for doctrine and are satisfied (for a while) with viewing the Church (in the West) as a benevolent institution with a few continuing pieties but little dogmatic foundation, catering for a smallish group of *ben pensanti* if not yet merely "cultural Catholics," tending in that direction.

⸺◦◦◦✵◦◦◦⸺

I am approaching my ninetieth year and may, though becoming a bit mangy, even get beyond ninety. As I look back on a soon-to-be-forgotten life, I cannot but notice that a love of truth has sustained me just so far as I was able to be sustained by it. My present narrative treats as absurd any notion that I am not the same person as I was, say, during the war, and also suggests that in what I must call my search for truth, I seem to have been blown along in a particular direction: first recognizing the weaknesses of secular humanism, then turning to a Catholic humanism, thence to admitting that in the present age the Catholic Church has widely grown too close to secular mentality, allowing its relationship to truth to be compromised—or even among too many of its leaders abandoned altogether. Perhaps it takes advancing age to recognize such an unpalatable fact without recklessly concluding that the Church is a more or less coherent but ultimately seductive fantasy.

For I have come to conclude that, despite present discontents and that universal tendency to compartmentalize to which I too am inclined, my life, with its choices and unpredictable experiences, must somehow have been providentially disposed. That certainly did not make it easy, but it seems that my loves and hates have fallen into some coherent pattern. In the Comédie Humaine, however, coherence, while a necessary feature of truth, is not identical with it. Unless, that is, in its absolute form! And unless this conclusion indicates that I have now reached the stage of Jaques's "slippered pantaloon."

INDEX OF CONTEMPORARIES

Abubakar, John, OSA, 224–25
Allison, C. Ralph and Rita, 12, 18–22, 27, 34–35
Andronikos, Manolis, 168
Anscombe, G. E. M., 192–93, 221
Armstrong, A. H., 186
Arneson, Olafur, 222

Bagnani, Gilbert, 100–1, 128
Bammel, Ernst, 278
Bardot, Brigitte, 62, 150
Barmann, Bernard (aka Ps-Mühlenberg), 171–72
Barnes, Timothy, 128, 161
Barron, 'Spud', 25, 34
Baum, Gregory, OSA, 134
Benson, Michael, 27, 32, 34–35, 214
Bergoglio, Jorge (Pope Francis), 228, 237, 258, 260
Bianchi, Alberto and Valeria, 144, 156
Bissell, Claude, 130, 134–36, 139
Blumenthal, Henry, 62–64, 69–74, 78–88, 96, 134, 204–5
Burke, Cardinal Raymond Leo, 231

Callam, Daniel, CSB, 141, 184
Carlucci, Fernando, 143–44, 151
Carter, Cardinal Gerald Emmett, xvii, 126–27
Corbould, Edward, OSB, 174
Crouzel, Henri, SJ, 143–44

Dani, Albano and Isidoro, 144
Daniélou, Cardinal Jean, 143, 180
David, Barry, 230
Davidowski, W., OSA, 215
Di Berardino, Angelo, OSA, 203–6
Dihle, Albrecht, 172–73
Dobson, Bernard, 24

Dodaro, Robert, OSA, 215, 228, 230–31
Donovan, Rev. Daniel, 159–60, 258
Dubois, Marcel, OP, 186, 201

Elvin, Rev. J., 7, 12, 14, 17
Eschmann, Ignatius, OP, 106

Fairley, Barker, 133
Foster, Kenelm, OP, 92–93, 159, 173, 254

Gilbey, Mons. Alfred. N., 65, 92
Goold, George, 125
Gow, A. S. F., 60
Grant, John, 116
Graziani, René and Dorothy, 141–42

Hall, Phyllis, 23, 27
Halper, Edward, 230
Harper, Dr Jack, 114, 125, 141
Hawley, Adrian, 230
Heichelheim, Fritz, 101, 103, 255
Henrichs, Albert, 148
Hough, James (Jimmy), 12
Hume, Basil Cardinal, 168

Jeauneau, Canon Eduard, 106, 202

Kallmeyer, Jean and Bruce, 134, 156
Kelly, John CSB, 113, 188
Ker, Alan, 57, 188
Krasovec, Rev. Joze, 178, 196–97
Küng, Rev. Hans, 134

Landolt, C. Gwendolyn, 126–27
Lawless, George, OSA, 212, 215
Leland, Charles, CSB, 105, 120, 148, 159, 174, 205
Lustiger, Cardinal Jean-Marie, 198

Macfarlane, Leslie and Leila, 163, 168
Maio, Benito, 207–8
Malone, Sr Bernard, OSB, 145
Mansfield, Robert, 4, 5, 123
Mariotti, Merope and Menotto, 148
McCarthy, John, 218, 221, 242
McLeod, Jack, 102, 104
McNicol, George, 161, 166–68, 259
Meek, Theophilus J., 157
Moore, Gareth, OP, 214, 260
Morrison, John, 79, 94

Nelson, W.H., 99, 135
Nussbaum, Martha, 168, 184, 260

O'Brien, Denis, 65–66, 78, 90, 93, 159, 186, 217, 253
Osborn, Eric, 203, 242
Owens, Joseph, CSsR, 106, 134

Page Denys, 58, 75
Passey, M.L.S., 87
Pentin, Edward, 228, 237
Prevost, Robert (Pope Leo XIV), 237
Pritzl, Kurt, OP, 213, 218

Reynolds, Joyce, 207, 211
Rezek, Avery and Joe, 195–96, 200

Ritter, Adolf Martin, 179
Robbins, Emmet, 142, 242
Rorty, Richard, 192
Rosica, Thomas, CSB, 231
Rudd, Niall, 103

Sandbach, Harry, 90, 95, 142
Sanders, David, OP, 170, 214
Satiroglu Güngor, 217
Schiff, Stanley, 140
Scolnicov, Shmuel, 193, 195–96
Sheridan, Rev. James, 113, 133–34, 159
Stroumsa, Guy, 186, 193

Tebbitt, Norman, 27
Trudeau, Pierre-Eliot, 126–28, 256
Truman, Donald, 69, 92, 96
Tyrer, Jill, 76, 79, 192, 196

Vermeule, Emily, 168

Wallace, William, 103, 120
Woodbury, Leonard and Marjorie, 107, 115

Young, Brad, 141, 152
Younger, Clive, 9, 13, 19

Zorzi, M. Benedetta, OSB, 205–7, 213

ABOUT THE AUTHOR

JOHN RIST, an "Essex man" born in 1936 and educated at Brentwood School and Trinity College, Cambridge, has taught Classics and Philosophy at the University of Toronto, the University of Aberdeen, the Hebrew University of Jerusalem, the Istituto Patristico Augustinianum in Rome, and the Catholic University of America. He has published 20 books and more than 100 articles, mainly on Ancient Philosophy, Patristics, and Ethics, the most recent being *What is a Person?* and *Infallibility, Integrity and Obedience*. He has been married to Anna for 65 years and has four children. He became a Catholic in 1980.

www.ingramcontent.com/pod-product-compliance
Lightning Source LLC
Chambersburg PA
CBHW020326170426
43200CB00006B/285